S0-AUZ-754

In Search of Leadership

In Search of Leadership: West Bank Politics Since 1967

Emile Sahliyeh

THE BROOKINGS INSTITUTION
WASHINGTON, D.C.

Copyright © 1988 by
THE BROOKINGS INSTITUTION
1775 Massachusetts Avenue, NW, Washington, DC 20036

Library of Congress Cataloging-in-Publication Data

Sahliyeh, Emile.
  In search of leadership: West Bank politics / Emile Sahliyeh.
  p. cm.
  Includes index.
  ISBN 0-8157-7698-5 (alk. paper). ISBN 0-8157-7697-7
(pbk. : alk. paper).
  1. West Bank—Politics and government. 2. Palestinian Arabs—
West Bank—Politics and government. 3. Political parties—West Bank.
I. Title.
DS110.W47S24 1988
956.95'3—dc19   88-15083
                                                                      CIP

9 8 7 6 5 4 3 2 1

The paper used in this publication meets the minimum
requirements of the American National Standard for Information
Sciences—Permanence of Paper for Printer Library Materials, ANSI
Z39.48-1984.   ∞

Set in Linotron Baskerville with Trajanus display.
Composed by Monotype Composition, Baltimore, Md.
Printed by R.R. Donnelley and Sons, Co., Harrisonburg, Va.

₿ THE BROOKINGS INSTITUTION

The Brookings Institution is an independent organization devoted to nonpartisan research, education, and publication in economics, government, foreign policy, and the social sciences generally. Its principal purposes are to aid in the development of sound public policies and to promote public understanding of issues of national importance.

The Institution was founded on December 8, 1927, to merge the activities of the Institute for Government Research, founded in 1916, the Institute of Economics, founded in 1922, and the Robert Brookings Graduate School of Economics and Government, founded in 1924.

The Board of Trustees is responsible for the general administration of the Institution, while the immediate direction of the policies, program, and staff is vested in the President, assisted by an advisory committee of the officers and staff. The by-laws of the Institution state: "It is the function of the Trustees to make possible the conduct of scientific research, and publication, under the most favorable conditions, and to safeguard the independence of the research staff in the pursuit of their studies and in the publication of the results of such studies. It is not a part of their function to determine, control, or influence the conduct of particular investigations or the conclusions reached."

The President bears final responsibility for the decision to publish a manuscript as a Brookings book. In reaching his judgment on the competence, accuracy, and objectivity of each study, the President is advised by the director of the appropriate research program and weighs the views of a panel of expert outside readers who report to him in confidence on the quality of the work. Publication of a work signifies that it is deemed a competent treatment worthy of public consideration but does not imply endorsement of conclusions or recommendations.

The Institution maintains its position of neutrality on issues of public policy in order to safeguard the intellectual freedom of the staff. Hence interpretations or conclusions in Brookings publications should be understood to be solely those of the authors and should not be attributed to the Institution, to its trustees, officers, or other staff members, or to the organizations that support its research.

Board of Trustees

Louis W. Cabot
Chairman

Ralph S. Saul
Vice Chairman;
Chairman,
Executive Committee;
Chairman,
Development Committee

Samuel H. Armacost
J. David Barnes
Rex J. Bates
A. W. Clausen
William T. Coleman, Jr.
Richard G. Darman
Thomas R. Donahue
Charles W. Duncan, Jr.
Walter Y. Elisha
Robert F. Erburu
Roberto C. Goizueta
Robert D. Haas

Philip M. Hawley
Roy M. Huffington
B. R. Inman
Vernon E. Jordan, Jr.
James A. Joseph
James T. Lynn
Donald F. McHenry
Bruce K. MacLaury
Mary Patterson McPherson
Maconda B. O'Connor
Donald S. Perkins
J. Woodward Redmond
James D. Robinson III
Robert V. Roosa
B. Francis Saul II
Henry B. Schacht
Howard R. Swearer
Morris Tanenbaum
James D. Wolfensohn
Ezra K. Zilkha
Charles J. Zwick

Honorary Trustees

Vincent M. Barnett, Jr.
Barton M. Biggs
Eugene R. Black
Robert D. Calkins
Edward W. Carter
Frank T. Cary
Lloyd N. Cutler
Bruce B. Dayton
Douglas Dillon
Huntington Harris
Andrew Heiskell
Roger W. Heyns
John E. Lockwood
William McC. Martin, Jr.
Robert S. McNamara
Arjay Miller
Charles W. Robinson
H. Chapman Rose
Gerard C. Smith
Robert Brookings Smith
Sydney Stein, Jr.
Phyllis A. Wallace

To Amanda and Christine

Foreword

◧ ◧ ◧

THE WEST BANK and the Gaza Strip are central to any lasting solution of the Palestinian problem. Although far-reaching sociopolitical and demographic changes have taken place in these territories, occupied by Israel since the 1967 war, little attention has been given to the study of the social structure.

In this book Emile Sahliyeh, a native Palestinian, traces the evolution of political trends in the West Bank between 1967 and 1987. He analyzes the rise and decline of the pro-Jordanian traditional leadership and the coming to power of pro-PLO leaders in the 1970s. He investigates the emergence of a group of pragmatic politicians in the 1980s and discusses the factors affecting their ability to lead the Palestinians in the occupied territories. In addition, the author examines the rising political power of student groups, women's societies, labor unions, and other mass organizations and assesses the strength of the communist and Islamic political movements. This background helps to provide an understanding of the Palestinian uprising in the West Bank and Gaza that began in December 1987.

This study is based in part on the author's personal experience and observation when he taught at Bir Zeit University between 1978 and 1984. He interviewed a large number of West Bank leaders, student activists, and representatives of numerous organizations and political movements. For reasons of personal safety, many of those interviewed preferred to remain anonymous. He also relied on numerous leaflets, pamphlets, and statements issued by West Bank political groups, organizations, and institutions, as well as on more widely available books and journals in Arabic and English.

In the course of his work Emile Sahliyeh, who is currently associate professor of international relations and Middle East politics at the University of North Texas, was helped by many people. This study would not have been possible without the cooperation of his students at Bir Zeit University; many of them read and recorded material for the author and helped him in collecting data and conducting interviews. He is especially grateful to William B. Quandt, senior fellow at the Brookings Institution, for his continuous support and encouragement. Quandt read many drafts of the manuscript and provided invaluable comments and conceptual guidance. The author also thanks Moshe Maoz, Mark A. Tessler, and David Shipler, who reviewed the manuscript in draft, for their many useful and thoughtful comments. Helena Cobban, Thomas Ricks, and Harold H. Saunders read individual chapters and made many helpful suggestions.

Michael McLarjick, Margaret Siliciano, and Linda Strube provided research assistance. Alice M. Carroll edited the manuscript; Susanne Lane, Bernhard Walker, and Amy Waychoff verified its factual content; and Susan L. Woollen and Ann M. Ziegler assisted in preparing the many drafts.

Brookings gratefully acknowledges the financial support for this book provided by the John D. and Catherine T. MacArthur Foundation and the Rockefeller Foundation. Additional funding was provided directly to the author by the Ford Foundation and the Woodrow Wilson International Center for Scholars.

The views in this book are solely those of the author and should not be ascribed to the persons or foundations whose assistance is acknowledged above, or to the trustees, officers, and staff members of the Brookings Institution.

BRUCE K. MAC LAURY
President

May 1988
Washington, D.C.

Contents

🔲 🔲 🔲

1. The Palestinian Question 1
   West Bank Leadership 2
   The Focus on Ideology 5
   Dependence on Outside Forces 6

2. The West Bank under Jordan's Rule 10
   Jordan's Integration Politics 13
   West Bankers' Reasons for Maintaining Unity with Jordan 18

3. The Traditional Elite after the June 1967 War 21
   Leaders of Protest 22
   Loyalty to Jordan 24
   Dissenting Views 26
   The Disappearance of Old Illusions 33
   The 1972 Municipal Elections 36
   Waning Influence 40

4. The Ascendancy of the Pro-PLO Urban Elite 42
   The Demise of the Pro-Jordanian Elite 43
   A New Nationalist Elite 47
   The Palestine National Front 51
   Politicization of the Municipalities 63
   The National Guidance Committee 69
   Israel's Policy toward the New Elite 81

5. The Communists' Quest for Leadership 87
   Precursors of the Palestine Communist Party 88
   Breaking Away from the JCP 91
   The Communist-Nationalist Rivalry 98
   Communist Activities in the West Bank 102
   The Communists' Political Stance 108
   The Future of the Communists 112

6. The Radicalization of the Student Movement 115
   Early Student Organizations 116
   The Rise of Political Activism 120
   Political Blocs in the Student Movement 125
   The Future of the Student Movement 134

7. Islam as an Alternative   137

   Islamic Groups under Jordanian Rule   137
   The Rise of the Islamic Movement   139
   Signs of an Islamic Reawakening   144
   Political Positions of the Islamists   148
   Islam and the PLO   151
   Opposition to the Islamic Youth Movement   156
   Prospects of the Islamic Movement   158

8. The Crisis of Leadership in the West Bank   163

   The Ascendancy of the Moderates and Pragmatists, 1982–86   163
   The Future of the Pragmatic Elite   174
   Determinants of the Elite's Political Behavior   176
   The Future Struggle   186

   Bibliography   189
   Index   195

In Search of Leadership

CHAPTER ONE

The Palestinian Question

〽 〽 〽

SINCE JUNE 1967, Israel has occupied all of the territory commonly referred to as the West Bank and the Gaza Strip. With occupation has come Israeli responsibility for ruling approximately 1.3 million Palestinian Arabs who live in the West Bank and the Gaza Strip. While Palestinian claims against Israel go well beyond the status of the occupied territories, it has become increasingly apparent that any satisfactory resolution of the "Palestinian question" would hinge on resolving the future of the West Bank and the Gaza Strip and their inhabitants.

Over the years, the Palestinians have relied on Arab military and diplomatic efforts to redress their grievances against Israel. Yet, the various Arab-Israeli wars have left Israel in control of all of Palestine instead of redressing Palestinian national grievances. In addition, diplomatic efforts over two decades have failed to find an acceptable solution for the future of the West Bank.

Soon after the 1967 June war, Jordan, by virtue of its former control of the West Bank, renewed its claim to sovereignty over the region. United Nations Security Council Resolution 242 of November 22, 1967, envisaged, as part of an overall peace settlement, that Israeli military forces would withdraw "from territories occupied in the recent conflict."

Yet by the mid-1970s, a growing segment of Israel's body politic defined the West Bank—which some Israelis referred to by the biblical names Judea and Samaria—and the Gaza Strip as "liberated territories" and integral parts of the historic "Land of Israel." From this perspective, these two areas were not subject to any negotiations or territorial compromise. Indeed, the coming to power of the nationalistic Likud bloc in 1977, its intensification of settlement activities and expropriation of Arab land, and the rise of extremist Israeli religious and nationalist groups were all political translations of this line of thinking.

1

Jordan's quest for the reconstitution of its sovereignty over the West Bank was also challenged by the emergence of the Palestine Liberation Organization (PLO), with its claim of exclusive representation of Palestinian interests within and outside the occupied territories. The PLO's position was accorded to it by the Arab heads of state at their conference in Rabat in 1974. At that time the Palestinian nationalist community was beginning to recognize that the West Bank and Gaza Strip should form an independent state. The Palestine National Council (PNC)—the equivalent of a Palestinian parliament in exile—endorsed the idea of a "national authority" in 1974. During its meeting in Cairo in March 1977, the PNC called for the establishment of an independent Palestinian state, presumably in the West Bank and Gaza Strip.

Despite the acceptance of the PLO's legitimacy by Palestinians and Arabs, the PLO remained an unacceptable partner in the peace process. Both Israel and the United States refused to include it in peace negotiations because of the PLO's reluctance to recognize Israel and to renounce the use of violence. In the fall of 1978, new diplomatic efforts were initiated to deal with the future of the West Bank without giving an active role to the Palestinians. The Camp David Accords, signed by Egypt, Israel, and the United States, proposed autonomy instead of establishing an independent Palestinian state. The signatories of the accords, however, differed over the interpretation of autonomy as it related to the occupied territories.

Following the 1982 Lebanon war and the termination of the PLO's political and military presence in Lebanon, Jordan and the PLO embarked on a joint diplomatic venture, culminating in the signing of an agreement between King Hussein and PLO Chairman Yasir Arafat in February 1985. They endorsed the idea of a confederation of the West Bank–Gaza Palestinian state with Jordan as the basis for a political settlement. But a year later the agreement was suspended and Jordanian-PLO relations were ruptured.

West Bank Leadership

With the failure of diplomatic efforts to resolve the status of the West Bank and Gaza Strip, it seemed logical for West Bank Palestinians to take matters into their own hands. The diplomatic efforts to produce a solution to the Palestinian question pointed to the centrality of the West Bank and Gaza in the search for a lasting settlement of the Arab-Israeli conflict. Yet little attention has been given to political trends and the complex environment within which West Bank Palestinians have operated. Numerous questions can be raised about the ability and willingness of the West Bankers to attend to their own interests and concerns. Do they possess sophisticated political institutions and a recognized, legitimate leadership capable of making crucial decisions and implementing them? Or will they continue to be satisfied with being little more than spectators in the political arena in which their destiny and the future of their land are being addressed? Will West Bank Palestinians, living under conditions of military occupation and influenced by strong pan-Arab and Palestinian nationalist sentiments, continue to allow outside players to speak on their behalf, thereby diminishing the possibility of local initiatives?

Will they try to adapt to Israel's occupation by developing their own political institutions and leadership and demanding self-rule under a Jordanian umbrella? Or will they seek political rights within Israel, as many of their fellow Palestinians did after 1948?

The *intifadah*, or uprising, that began in early December 1987 provided partial answers to these questions concerning the ability of Palestinians in the occupied territories to organize themselves without outside intervention and leadership. Initially, the uprising came in reaction to a local event in which a number of Gaza car passengers were killed in an accident with an Israeli vehicle. The initial disturbances quickly spread and developed into a large-scale popular uprising throughout the West Bank and Gaza.

One of the new features of the *intifadah* was the involvement of a new generation of West Bank and Gaza Palestinians who grew up under Israeli occupation and were no longer fearful of confronting the Israeli army. The leaders of the uprising succeeded in mobilizing mass support for their tactic of civil disobedience. They also undertook the task of managing various aspects of the *intifadah* and ensuring its continuity. In doing so, the underground leaders of the uprising showed no signs of challenging the PLO's leadership of the Palestinian national movement.

Traditionally, politics in the West Bank has been the domain of the elite. Members of prominent families have controlled local politics in their regions. The three outside powers—the Ottoman Empire, Great Britain, and Jordan—that had a stake in West Bank affairs before 1967 used intermediaries from privileged families to control the West Bank. The arrangement was convenient on both sides. The Ottomans, British, and Jordanians found it easier to deal with a few widely recognized leaders than to promote mass participatory politics. Those arrangements met the interests of the local elite who had no desire to widen the circle of political participation.

Until the 1967 Arab-Israeli war, elite control of local politics remained a primary feature of West Bank political life. Thus at first glance it seemed that Israel's occupation of the West Bank would provide the local elite with an opportunity to increase political assertiveness and independence. Instead, members of the elite were overcome by political torpor. Over the next two decades West Bank politics became so complex that the tradition of elite consensus and control of local politics gradually diminished.

Two sets of factors—the emergence of mass politics and the vulnerability of local politicians to outside pressures and manipulation—gradually reduced the centrality of the elite in West Bank politics. After 1967, the West Bank political arena broadened substantially. Conspicuous growth in higher education, exposure to mass media, labor mobility, and the emergence of new, mass-based social forces brought far-reaching changes in the West Bank social fabric. In particular, the expansion of university education, the politicization of the student movement, the formation of several youth, women's, and professional organizations, Israel's licensing of several Arabic newspapers, and labor mobility resulting from employment inside Israel widened participatory politics. In turn, political participation led both to the mobilization of the mass public and the emergence of new social and political forces. The consolidation of the communist movement, the radicalization of the student population, and the resurgence of Islam in the late 1970s undercut the tradition of elite supremacy.

With the politicization of the masses, the influence and authority of conservative politicians were seriously weakened. Members of traditionally prominent families became extremely insecure and defensive. Yet the traditional politicians were not the only political group affected by these socioeconomic changes. The more educated, younger, and more professionally oriented pro-PLO politicians also had difficulty in building up their legitimacy and authority. Students, the communists, labor unions, and women's organizations were particularly suspicious of the local elite's activities and moves.

The ascendancy of new social forces in the West Bank defined the outer limits of the local elite's political behavior and narrowed the opportunities for the elite to serve as intermediaries between outside forces and the local populace. Politics in the West Bank was no longer the exclusive preserve of the elite. They became only one of several political forces operating at the local level.

The Focus on Ideology

Over the last two decades West Bank politics focused increasingly on ideological issues. The new social forces invoked Palestinian nationalism, Marxism-Leninism, and Islamic fundamentalism to broaden their popular appeal and to compete with the established elite. As ideological credentials became a potent instrument in establishing the legitimacy of the new social forces, the old pro-Jordanian political order was seriously challenged. The mass-based organizations' preoccupation with ideological issues severely constrained politicians' freedom of maneuver and diplomatic flexibility.

The new social and political forces cultivated outside sources to advance their power positions. They found their natural allies in the differing factions within the PLO. Those alliances complicated the configuration of power in the occupied territories, severely constrained Jordan's opportunities in the West Bank, and deepened political divisions and fragmentation in the area. While the new social forces have not yet developed a full-fledged, strong, and unified leadership, they have become vocal and powerful and must be reckoned with on the local scene. For they are capable of complicating the policies of external players—particularly policies that do not conform to their political preferences and interests.

By the end of 1987, the grounds were established for a new phase in the political activism of the new social forces in the West Bank. On December 9 of that year, a youth uprising erupted in the Gaza Strip and soon after spread to several West Bank towns, villages, and refugee camps. Though demonstrations and strikes were common events in the occupied territories, the 1987–88 wave of unrest was unusually intense, persistent, and pervasive. Youth drawn from the middle and high school levels were the primary players in these riots, in contrast to the well-organized groups of university students who had launched the 1970s demonstrations. The net effect of the youths' rebellion was a further consolidation of the role and influence of the new social forces on the West Bank political scene.

Developments in the Middle East have left a deep imprint on West Bank politics. Ideological shifts in the Arab world and changes in the regional balance of power have echoed among West Bank Palestinians. With the defeat of the Arab countries in the 1967 war and the death of Egyptian President Gamal Abd al-Nasser three years later, the ideology of pan-Arabism began to lose its force. As the PLO grew in power, Palestinian national consciousness replaced Arab nationalism as the ideological focus for the West Bank urban elite. Likewise, Menachem Begin's settlement policies, the Camp David Accords and the Israeli-Egyptian peace treaty, the Islamic revolution in Iran in 1979, Israel's invasion of Lebanon in 1982, and the signing of an agreement for joint diplomatic action between Jordan and the PLO in February 1985 were major events that had a significant bearing on the shaping of political opinion among West Bank inhabitants.

Dependence on Outside Forces

West Bank Palestinians have always envisaged themselves as an integral part of the larger Palestinian and Arab communities. But a growing sense of psychological, political, and physical vulnerability to Israel has made them turn to outsiders for political leadership and ideological guidance. The local elite's lack of resources and the region's economic dependence on outside forces—whether Jordan, the PLO, Israel, or the Arab countries—have obstructed the emergence of a viable local leadership.

Since 1967, the elite have been reluctant to promote their own autonomous leadership of the West Bank or to take the initiative on behalf of their constituents. West Bank leaders, unwilling to seek separate solutions to their territory's problems, have looked for outside help to put an end to Israel's military occupation. They have thus become subject to fluctuations in the political influence and political fortunes of the outside players they follow. Periods of demoralization and political resignation in the occupied territories have paralleled times of political disarray and fragmentation among Arab countries in general, and in the PLO in particular, as well as the frequent periods of strained Jordanian-Palestinian and Palestinian-Syrian relations.

The main external powers that have sought to advance their interests in the West Bank are Jordan, the PLO, and Israel. The conflicting interests of these three have only served to deepen disunity and fragmentation among the ranks of the local elite. Indeed, the net effect of their policies has been to weaken the position of the traditional politicians without allowing for the emergence of a new, viable leadership. In their attempt to affect West Bank internal political dynamics, Jordan, the PLO, and Israel have not confined their competition to the manipulation of economic resources and inducements. They have frequently used coercive techniques to penetrate and weaken the sphere of influence of the rival actors.

In the late 1960s and 1970s, the PLO offered itself as a reference point and source of political and ideological inspiration for West Bank Palestinians. Its ideological and political ascendancy diminished the incentives of local politicians to develop autonomous political institutions. The PLO leaders discouraged the emergence of an independent leadership in the occupied territories that might threaten the PLO's status as sole and legitimate representative of the Palestinian people. The organization's lack of a territorial base gave its leaders reason to fear local groups that would compete with the PLO for recognition and legitimacy.

To preserve its privileged status, the PLO expected complete loyalty from the West Bank elite. Moreover, PLO leaders confined the duties of local politicians to generating support for the PLO and its goals. The organization created its own mass-based institutions and structures, especially among youth, workers, and professionals. These institutions have served to widen the popularity and legitimacy of the PLO and to ensure that the political stands of West Bank elite groups conform with those of the PLO. The PLO leaders frequently demanded that local politicians clear in advance their stands on major political issues. The organization developed the capacity to dispense economic and political rewards to its followers and to employ coercive techniques against its opponents and potential rivals when necessary. Its multiple factions and actors hindered the formation of elite groups and fragmented any that emerged.

The PLO's political influence was not free from challenge. For even though Jordan suffered defeat in the 1967 June war, the Hashemite monarchy continued to have a hand in West Bank politics. The government in Amman used the many resources at its disposal to maintain its influence and that of its followers, especially in the economic and political spheres.

Israel, however, by virtue of its direct control of the territories, has had the most substantial influence on local Palestinian politics. Israel's economic policy—particularly its permitting one-third of the West Bank labor force to be employed inside Israel—has contributed to the erosion of power of the conservative elite in the West Bank. And while Defense Minister Moshe Dayan's policy of noninterference in West Bank domestic affairs temporarily allowed the traditional elite to preserve their privileged position, other aspects of Israel's military policy undermined the elite. The policies of deportation and administrative detention employed in the years following the 1967 war took a heavy toll on traditional, pro-Jordanian politicians. In addition, the Israeli military administration in December 1975 amended Jordan's law governing municipal elections and enabled women and propertyless men to vote, further disturbing the position of the traditional elite.

Although the 1976 election produced a new group of younger, more educated West Bank politicians employed in white-collar professions, Israel's military administration continued to use deportation and town arrests to clear the political arena. Within a few years of the 1976 elections the military government had ousted many municipal leaders. Nor would the Israelis sanction an all–West Bank leadership or political parties and structures that would have given political expression to local demands and interests. In the early 1980s a pragmatic group of politicians emerged that advocated Jordanian-Palestinian diplomatic coordination on West Bank negotiations and the association of the West Bank and Gaza Strip with the East Bank, but the Israeli government refused to make any credible offer to this group in return for political moderation.

The combination of domestic and external factors has worked against the rise of an autonomous West Bank leadership. Instead, West Bankers have looked to outsiders for political guidance and representation. Despite the Palestinians' reluctance to promote their own separate leadership and to break away from the rest of the Palestine community, it can no longer be assumed that they will continue to be politically passive. With the PLO's loss of influence in Jordan and Lebanon, and the fact that the West Bank has repeatedly been the focus of diplomatic initiatives, West Bank Palestinians may seek a more active role for themselves in determining their own future. The 1987–88 uprising demonstrated the growing disillusionment of the West Bank–Gaza Palestinians with the inconclusive diplomatic efforts of the outside players, whether the PLO, Jordan, the Arab countries, or the superpowers. The uprising showed that these Palestinians from now on will not wait for external actors to resolve their predicament. Finally, the uprising suggested a change in the center of gravity within the Palestinian national movement toward the occupied territories and away from the exile communities. Nonetheless, there is no reason to expect the West Bank and Gaza Palestinians to challenge the PLO as their spokesman in any future negotiations.

CHAPTER TWO

The West Bank under Jordan's Rule

🔲 🔲 🔲

FOLLOWING THE establishment of Israel on May 14, 1948, Jordan sent its army across the Jordan River to check the Jewish state's formation. It also set up a military administration over the portion of Palestine that came to be known as the West Bank of Jordan. On March 6, 1949, by royal decree, the military administration was replaced by a civilian counterpart and a year later the West Bank was formally annexed to Jordan. Another royal decree forbade the use of "Palestine" in official documents and the area was formally designated the West Bank. In August of 1950 the legal systems of the two banks of the River Jordan were integrated and a month later the Jordanian dinar became the official currency for the entire country.

To legitimize the integration of the West Bank into Jordan, King Abdullah convened a delegation of West Bank leaders and members of socially prominent families in Amman in October 1948. The assembled politicians called on the king to protect Arab rights in Palestine. On December 1, 1948, a congress of West Bank notables held in Jericho requested that the Jordanian monarch incorporate the West Bank into the kingdom.

With annexation of the West Bank, Jordan's population more than tripled. To the almost 400,000 inhabitants of the East Bank were added about 400,000 West Bank residents and an estimated 485,000 refugees (according to calculations by the United Nations Relief and Works Agency, UNRWA, in August 1950). Approximately 30 percent of the landless refugees lived in twenty-nine refugee camps in the West Bank and the Jordan Valley, a third in villages, and the remainder in towns.[1]

1. Shaul Mishal, *West Bank/East Bank: The Palestinians in Jordan, 1949–1967*

The government in Amman divided the West Bank for administrative purposes into three provinces—Jerusalem in the center, including the towns of Jerusalem, Bethlehem, Ramallah, and Jericho; Nablus in the north, including the towns of Nablus, Tulkarm, and Jenin; and Hebron in the south, including the town of Hebron and a cluster of neighboring villages.[2] A civilian governor appointed for each province was accountable to the Ministry of Interior in Amman, an arrangement that discouraged direct legal ties among the three regions.

The largest of the West Bank units in population was the Jerusalem province, numbering over 344,000 people in the Jordanian census of 1961. The majority of its labor force was employed in service industries or tourism. In addition, more than 50 percent of the West Bank's limited industrial base was located in Jerusalem, while it had the smallest share of agriculture in the West Bank provinces. Because of its urban character, Jerusalem's population tended to be more educated and secular than that of Nablus and Hebron. Jerusalem had the highest concentration of men and women with a high school education. The area also had the largest concentration of Christians.

The city of Jerusalem under Jordan's rule was downgraded to equal political status with Nablus and Hebron, the West Bank's other major towns. Nevertheless, Jerusalem's prominent families were able to preserve their influence and prestige. Their association with the central government in Amman, their prominence in the pre-1948 Palestinian nationalist movement and political life, and their close ties with Jerusalem's religious establishment accounted for their continuing dominance in the city.

The Nablus province, with a population of roughly 342,000 in the 1961 census, was almost as large as Jerusalem but its economy was more balanced. Agriculture, particularly in the Tulkarm and Jenin districts, occupied a central position in the regional economy.

(Yale University Press, 1978), pp. 1–13, and "Conflictual Pressures and Cooperative Interests: Observations on West Bank–Amman Political Relations, 1949–1967," in Joel S. Migdal, ed., *Palestinian Society and Politics* (Princeton University Press, 1980), pp. 169–72.

2. Migdal, *Palestinian Society*, pp. 56–60. See also Sarah Graham-Brown, "Impact on the Social Structure of Palestinian Society," in Naseer H. Aruri, ed., *Occupation: Israel over Palestine* (Belmont, Mass.: Association of Arab-American University Graduates, 1983), pp. 223–27.

For the majority of the population, agriculture was a profitable and productive enterprise. The town of Nablus had a larger concentration of industrial firms and projects than any other West Bank town. Nablus also attracted a large number of teachers, professionals, clerks, merchants, businessmen, and other white-collar workers. In addition, it was a center of political opposition during Jordan's rule over the West Bank.

The Hebron province, with a population of only about 119,000 in 1961, lacked both capital and human resources and was the poorest of the three provinces. With a primarily agrarian economy, the Hebron province accounted for only 10 percent of the West Bank's industrial production. The region's economic hardship led to a high level of migration—between 1952 and 1961, a third of its residents left for the East Bank and the Persian Gulf region in search of employment.

Hebron's citizens were far less modernized than those of Jerusalem and Nablus. The Hebron population was conservative, religious, and traditional, and tribal and familial affiliations were more important than national loyalties. While levels of education were relatively high and occupations fairly diverse in the Jerusalem and Nablus regions, there was a high degree of illiteracy in the Hebron province.

The West Bank area as a whole was primarily rural, without major urban centers (with the partial exception of Jerusalem and Nablus). The economy was based on agriculture, bolstered by income from tourism and by UNRWA payments and remittances from abroad. In all, approximately 85 percent of the West Bank's gross domestic product came from the agriculture and service sectors.

Industries in this agriculturally based economy consisted mainly of olive oil processing plants, soap factories, and handicrafts. In 1965, West Bank industry accounted for only 6.6 percent of the West Bank's gross domestic product. In addition, the Jordanian government chose to place most of its economic development projects in the East Bank. For instance, while in 1948 the East Bank of Jordan lacked an industrial base, by 1965 approximately 74 percent of the country's industrial gross national product was due to activities east of the river. Similarly, in 1966, two-thirds of the government's industrial investment was placed in the East

Bank, even though roughly half the population resided in the West Bank.[3]

Jordan's Integration Policies

Although many West Bank politicians in 1950 looked toward the Hashemite regime to defend and promote their cause, they viewed Palestinian incorporation in the Jordanian polity as a step in the direction of comprehensive Arab unity. Many of them considered the relationship with Jordan transitional, as the Palestinian people awaited the opportunity to reconstruct Arab Palestine. They did not, however, define any time limit for the transitional arrangement.

This perception of a transitional relationship by the West Bank's elite did not conform, however, with the Jordanian government's efforts to completely integrate the Palestinians. To ensure the realization of its objective, Jordan adopted a three-track policy of co-optation, political fragmentation and exclusion, and control of the political opposition.

CO-OPTING PALESTINIAN INTERESTS.   The government strove to incorporate notable local leaders of the West Bank in Jordan's economic and political life. Members of prominent families—the Nashashibi, Salah, al-Dajani, and Nusseibeh families of Jerusalem and the Tuqan, Jayyusi, al-Masri, and Abd al-Hadi families of Nablus and Tulkarm—were appointed to senior governmental posts. They in fact monopolized the ministries of economy, commerce, agriculture, health, and education. Likewise, most of Jordan's ambassadors to foreign countries were drawn from these West Bank families. Members of these families were elected to Jordan's House of Representatives or appointed by the king to the Chamber of the Senate, the upper house of Jordan's parliament. Positions in the civil service were also made available to the West Bank educated class. To facilitate their integration into the system, the government extended full citizenship to West Bank Palestinians

3. Brian Van Arkadie, *Benefits and Burdens: A Report on the West Bank and Gaza Strip Economies since 1967* (New York: Carnegie Endowment for International Peace, 1977), pp. 21–28, especially p. 27; Vivian A. Bull, *The West Bank–Is It Viable?* (Lexington Books, 1975), pp. 94–96; Migdal, *Palestinian Society*, pp. 39–40.

and created quasi-democratic institutions to allow for West Bank participation in Jordan's political processes—half of the seats in the House of Representatives and the Chamber of the Senate were reserved for West Bank representatives.

The institutionalizing of parliamentary elections was intended to give a democratic character to Jordan's political system. Yet, to preserve the political privileges and conservative outlook of its West Bank supporters, the Jordanian government confined the right to vote to taxpaying males who had reached the age of twenty-one, thus disfranchising both men with no property and women. The taxpaying requirement was particularly disadvantageous because Palestinian refugees constituted one-third of Jordan's population. Another government restraint gave the minister of interior the authority to appoint the mayor from among the elected municipal council members.

The West Bank's upper class was not the only target of Jordan's co-optation. Several of Jordan's policies—including the expansion of the educational system and the availability of employment opportunities within the Jordanian bureaucracy—attracted other groups of West Bank Palestinians. Indeed, the high unemployment brought on by the influx of refugees and chronic economic hardship prompted those West Bank Palestinians, particularly refugees, to take advantage of educational opportunities. For many families, the pursuit of education became a primary vehicle for social mobility and an improvement in the quality of their life. Moreover, an increased need for doctors, engineers, lawyers, and merchants in the East Bank and the Persian Gulf region gave purpose to a formal education.[4]

Although the West Bank offered growing employment opportunities for the professional class that Jordan's expanding educational system created, a sizable portion of this group migrated to the East Bank and the Gulf region, thus limiting the number of urban elite remaining in the West Bank. The result was that

4. Graham-Brown, "Impact on the Social Structure," pp. 225–27. For a detailed examination of educational opportunities in the West Bank, see Khalil Mahshi and Ramzi Rihan, "Education: Elementary and Secondary," and Muhammad Hallaj, "Mission of Palestinian Higher Education," in Emile A. Nakhleh, ed., *A Palestinian Agenda for the West Bank and Gaza* (Washington, D.C.: American Enterprise Institute, 1980), pp. 29–76.

Jordan's policy of co-optation primarily served the interests of the large landowners, merchants, and industrialists.

To offset the loss of business and commerce that Palestinian coastal towns suffered in 1948, Jordan provided the West Bank business community an opportunity to use its economic expertise, financial assistance, entrepreneurial skills, and foreign trade experience. West Bank businessmen were encouraged to invest in the East Bank, and West Bank economists were entrusted with the task of managing the Jordanian economy.

In addition to the land, wealth, and skills that gave members of the West Bank upper class influence and patronage among their followers, the elite could draw on their association with the regime in Amman. The upper class served as the Jordanian government's mediator in the West Bank, with the power to intercede on behalf of West Bank constituents with the central government. That link allowed the upper class to dispense material benefits and political rewards.

Jordan's policy of co-optation yielded the intended outcome of integration, for West Bank politicians and businessmen quickly developed a vested interest in the survival of the Hashemite regime. Yet, with Jordan's concentration of its economic development projects in the East Bank, the West Bank politicians could not accrue the economic resources necessary to mobilize mass support, broaden their political legitimacy, and emerge as an independent center of power.[5]

FRAGMENTING WEST BANK POWER.   The power of the elite was further diluted by the Jordanian government's policy of keeping West Bank politics localized and fragmented. Jordan's goal was to prevent the emergence of an all–West Bank political leadership and political institutions. Hence the three provinces of the West Bank were subdivided into seven autonomous administrative districts with limited jurisdiction. These districts were directly responsible to Jordan's minister of interior in Amman. Moreover, instead of Jerusalem being designated the capital of the newly created state, Amman was made both the center of power and the seat of government.

5. Migdal, *Palestinian Society,* pp. 33–43.

Not only was the West Bank politically fragmented, but Palestinian politicians were seldom appointed to highly sensitive political or security-related positions. Only on rare occasions were West Bank politicians appointed to the ministry of defense. The Jordanian government was also selective in its appointment of West Bank citizens to sensitive positions in the army and security force. Those posts were almost the exclusive preserve of East Bank Jordanians.[6] The jobs that West Bank Palestinians filled in the army were in technical and maintenance areas.

CONTROLLING THE OPPOSITION.   Jordanian policy in the West Bank also called for strict control of the country's political opposition. Jordan's 1952 constitution outlawed any political party whose operation and ideology would undermine "public order and security." Between 1949 and 1954, there was no strong political opposition in the West Bank as outside Arab support for opposition was marginal. Further, Arab nationalism (the cornerstone for the political opposition) did not enjoy widespread appeal among the West Bank elite until the second half of the 1950s. Nor did the West Bank elite, with its growing economic dependency on Jordan and feeling of political and psychological vulnerability, reject Jordan's guardianship of the Palestinian question. While some groups criticized certain aspects of Jordan's foreign and defense policies, there was hardly any demand for the separation of the West Bank from Jordan.[7]

In the mid-1950s, however, with the unfolding of favorable political developments in the Middle East, the West Bank's political opposition became vocal and articulate. The Baath party's rising influence in Syria and Gamal Abd al-Nasser's consolidation of power in Egypt resulted in the opposition's attraction to Damascus and Cairo. Opposition leaders began to argue that the attainment of Arab unity was a precondition for the reconstruction of Arab Palestine.[8] As a consequence, the ideology of pan-Arabism became a dominant political norm.

Identification with pan-Arabism enhanced the opposition's po-

6. Mishal, "Conflictual Pressures," p. 177, and *West Bank/East Bank*, pp. 42–45.

7. Mishal, *West Bank/East Bank*, pp. 45, 76–77.

8. See Amnon Cohen, *Political Parties in the West Bank under the Jordanian Regime, 1949–1967* (Cornell University Press, 1982).

litical legitimacy and popularity among the West Bank population. For by manipulating their connections with Cairo and Damascus, opposition leaders were able to gain support among the masses. As their ability to mobilize the West Bank public grew, their strategy diluted Jordan's traditional approach of ruling the West Bank through its affluent class. The opposition's power was further enhanced by Palestinians' increasing identification with external forces.

These developments conflicted directly with the Jordanian government's attempts to broaden its legitimacy by building up local allegiances. Occasionally the Jordanian government was forced to meet some of the opposition's demands. For example, it terminated the Jordanian-British defense treaty and abstained from joining the Western-sponsored Baghdad Pact. Similarly, it did not attempt to shape the outcome of the 1956 parliamentary elections.[9]

West Bank opposition parties were transnational in their political outlook, advocating either Arab nationalism, communism, or pan-Islamic ideologies. All demanded the introduction of constitutional, democratic reforms in Jordan's political system. In particular, opposition leaders argued that the executive should be accountable to the parliament. They further believed that the nonconfidence vote in the government should be based on a simple majority rather than a two-thirds majority. And they demanded that the government not discriminate against West Bank Palestinians in filling senior positions in the army and civil service. They wanted the Jordanian government to allocate more funds for economic development in the West Bank.

The West Bank political opposition did not confine its demands to the domestic scene. Opposition leaders strongly argued for the reorientation of Jordan's defense and foreign policies away from the West. Insisting on the reconstruction of an entirely Arab Palestine, they were also opposed to any political settlement with Israel and resisted the resettlement of Palestinian refugees.[10]

9. Mishal, *West Bank/East Bank*, pp. 56–62.

10. Ibid., pp. 24–34; Amnon Cohen, "Political Parties in the West Bank under the Hashemite Regime," in Moshe Maoz, ed., *Palestinian Arab Politics* (Jerusalem: Jerusalem Academic Press, 1975), pp. 21–49; Uriel Dann, "Regime and Opposition in Jordan since 1949," in Menahem Milson, ed., *Society and Political Structure in the Arab World* (New York: Humanities Press, 1973).

Several leaders of the political opposition, including those from the Baath party and the Arab Nationalist movement, openly called for the overthrow of the king in the second half of the 1950s.

Yet, with the possible exception of the Jordanian Communist party, no political group espoused the formation of a Palestinian state in the West Bank, nor did any party work to promote a separate and distinct national identity for Palestinians. Such ideas were still alien concepts and only began to have political currency after the emergence of the Palestine Liberation Organization (PLO) and the Palestinian resistance movement in the mid-1960s.

West Bankers' Reasons for Maintaining Unity with Jordan

Both pro-Jordanian and opposition leaders lacked the incentive to break away from Jordan and to establish an autonomous political leadership and an independent state. Their political quiescence on these issues was due in part to their ideological disposition as Arab nationalists. A majority of the West Bank elite wanted to retain the unity between the two banks of the Jordan River. They felt that dismemberment of the West Bank from Jordan would be counterproductive and would contradict the dictates of Arab nationalism. In their opinion, the reconstruction of Arab Palestine was a collective Arab responsibility that Palestinians were incapable of achieving on their own.

The urban elite also wished to preserve their political link with Jordan for purely pragmatic reasons. The close association with the East Bank had resulted in the extension of Jordanian citizenship and services to the West Bank population, the absorption of the region's educated, professional, and entrepreneurial class into Jordan's bureaucracy and economic life, and the appointment of West Bank leaders to prominent positions in Jordan's government.

Beyond that, the Jordanian government frequently issued political statements expressing its firm commitment to the integrity of Arab Palestine, and to the right of refugees to return to their homeland. It sometimes used coercive measures in dealing with the opposition, but not always. Indeed, although it held out economic inducements and worked to co-opt the local elite, the

government tried to accommodate several of the opposition political parties, including the Muslim Brotherhood. In attempting to
neutralize opposition groups, it occasionally made political gestures
designed to meet their political demands—the 1952 constitution,
for instance, incorporated several provisions limiting the power of
the executive, thus making it accountable to the parliament. The
government also allowed parliamentary elections.[11]

The Palestinians' deep sense of psychological, political, and
physical vulnerability to Israel increased their reliance on the
Jordanian regime and weakened their incentives to develop autonomous leadership. In addition, Jordan's monopoly of power
and its control mechanisms provided no inducements for the West
Bank elite to act independently.

Harsh security measures and a ban on the formation of political
parties in the West Bank deprived the opposition of a functional,
formal framework to build on, thus inhibiting the development of
its leadership capacities. Lack of an overt party structure also
limited the opposition's potential for recruiting members. And the
harshness of security measures forced many opposition leaders to
go underground or into exile.

Competing external ideological affiliations among members of
the opposition led to its disunity and fragmentation. In addition,
West Bank opposition groups did not possess sufficient instrumental resources, particularly a strong economic base, for mass
mobilization. And while education and external ideological allegiances were the opposition's main assets, these alone were not
sufficient to allow the opposition leadership to emerge as an
areawide political elite.

While the West Bank urban elite accepted their integration into
the Jordanian polity and the West Bank's economic dependency
on the East Bank of Jordan, the relationship could not last. West
Bank leaders envisaged the link with Jordan as a transitional stage
in the search for a solution to the Palestinian question. From this
perspective, the legitimacy accorded the Jordanian regime was
limited. Overwhelmed by grievances that accompanied the establishment of Israel, West Bank Palestinian opposition leaders did

11. Mishal, *West Bank/East Bank*, pp. 43–45.

not believe that Jordan was able to provide them with the leadership necessary to help them recover Palestine. Thus they sought other sources of political identification—pan-Arabism, pan-Islamism, Marxism-Leninism, and, from the mid-1960s, Palestinian nationalism.

CHAPTER THREE

The Traditional Elite after the 1967 June War

🔲 🔲 🔲

WHEN THE Israelis, as a result of the Arab-Israeli war in June 1967, began their military occupation of the West Bank, a new phase in the evolution of political trends among West Bank Palestinians began. On the eve of the war, the West Bank had neither an integrated leadership nor a territorial political structure. Jordan's policies had effectively confined the political influence of prominent, conservative West Bank families to their local towns. The political opposition also had limited and fragmented power. The defeat of both Egypt and Syria, the two pan-Arab regimes in the war, demoralized followers of both the Arab Nationalist movement and the Baath party in the West Bank. After 1967 the supporters of the Arab Nationalist movement transferred their allegiance to the Popular Front for the Liberation of Palestine, the heir of the Arab Nationalist movement. The Muslim Brotherhood remained dormant until the late 1970s. And the Jordanian Communist party, which later played an active role in West Bank politics, was in a state of disarray following the 1967 war, with many of its activists either in jail or exiled.

In such a weak political setting, it was natural that the conservative elite who had dominated West Bank political life during Jordan's rule assumed leadership of the movement protesting Israel's military occupation. Their economic wealth both in land and in capital, their religious and social preeminence in West Bank society, and their monopoly of higher education were valuable assets that worked to preserve the authority and influence of these pro-Jordanian politicians. The Israeli government's decision to maintain the municipal apparatus in the West Bank gave them another channel for continuing influence. Their intercession on behalf of their local constituents before 1967 provided them with a degree of legitimacy and recognition among the local populace.

Leaders of Protest

With the advent of the Israeli military regime, the West Bank politicians assumed the unaccustomed role of protesting government policies. The change was due in part to the disappearance of the political influence, power, and prestige that the traditional elite had derived from their close association with the Jordanian regime. In addition, the political interests of the West Bank leaders were no longer confined to their own towns and districts. Indeed, after the war, their activities assumed a West Bank–wide dimension. Thus, whatever their political persuasions, the West Bank's leaders united to protest military occupation. The traditional elite thus provided guidance, leadership, and inspiration for the civil disobedience that erupted soon after the war.

In the initial years, these leaders came mostly from the Jerusalem area, as they had the most to lose from Israel's occupation of their city. Jerusalem's politicians issued a number of statements condemning Israel's occupation of the West Bank and annexation of Jerusalem. On July 24, 1967, twenty-odd leaders, including Anwar Nusseibeh (Jordan's former defense minister), Rouhi al-Khatib (deposed mayor of Jerusalem), and Abd al-Hamid al-Saiyih and Hilmi al-Muhtasib (Islamic religious dignitaries), met in Al-Aqsa Mosque and issued a statement. Three weeks later, 100 dignitaries issued another statement,[1] and on October 4, 129 public figures representing various political opinions still another. All of the statements condemned Israel's annexation of East Jerusalem and asserted the Arab and Islamic character of the city.[2]

1. *Al-Dustur* (Amman), August 16, 1967.
2. On the West Bank's reaction to Israel's military occupation, see Ann Mosely Lesch, *Political Perceptions of the Palestinians on the West Bank and the Gaza Strip,* Special Study 3 (Washington, D.C.: Middle East Institute, 1980), pp. 31–35; Ibrahim Dakkak, "Back to Square One: A Study in the Re-emergence of the Palestinian Identity in the West Bank, 1967–1980," in Alexander Schölch, ed., *Palestinians over the Green Line: Studies on the Relations between Palestinians on Both Sides of the 1949 Armistice Line since 1967* (London: Ithaca Press, 1983), pp. 70–71; Moshe Shemesh, "The West Bank: Rise and Decline of Traditional Leadership, June 1967 to October 1973," *Middle Eastern Studies,* vol. 20 (July 1984), pp. 290–300; Rafik Halabi, *The*

Another step taken to resist the Israeli military regime was the Arab Municipal Council of Jerusalem's rejection of an offer by its Israeli counterpart to integrate the two communities. Likewise, a number of judges and the lawyers' union declared an open strike to protest the transfer of the court of appeals from Jerusalem to the neighboring town of Ramallah. The teachers' union also went on strike to oppose the changes that Israel planned to introduce into the school curriculum.

More significant, however, was the establishment of the Islamic Supreme Council and the Higher Committee for National Guidance, both of which played a leading role in the civil disobedience movement. Neither was formed in response to external demands, but rather because of the urgent need to rectify deficiencies inherited from Jordan's rule over the West Bank. Both institutions were attempts by the West Bank urban elite to create structures that would give political expression to the interests of the local populace.

The Islamic Supreme Council, created by the leaders who met at Al-Aqsa Mosque a month after Israel's annexation of Jerusalem, was set up to protest Israel's annexation policy, defend Islamic holy places in Jerusalem, and preserve its Arab and Islamic character. In addition to five religious dignitaries, the council included thirteen prominent pro-Jordanian figures and five representatives of the political opposition (three Baathists, a communist, and a representative of the Arab Nationalist movement). Abd al-Hamid al-Saiyih was chosen as chairman of the council and Hilmi al-Muhtasib as deputy. The council became even more pro-Jordanian after Israel's deportation of the leaders of the political opposition and the appointment, in May and September of 1969, of fifteen new members with pro-Jordanian leanings.[3]

The political activities of the Islamic Supreme Council within the civil disobedience movement subsided significantly with the deportation of al-Saiyih on September 23, 1967. The new chairman,

---

West Bank Story, trans. Ina Friedman (Harcourt Brace Jovanovich, 1982), pp. 29–73; Mahdi Abd al-Hadi, *The Palestinian Question and Proposals for Political Solutions, 1934–1974* (in Arabic) (Beirut: Al-Maktabah al-Asriyah, 1975), pp. 324–61.

3. Dakkak, "Back to Square One," p. 72; Uzi Benziman, *Jerusalem: A City without Walls* (in Arabic), trans. Muhammad Madi (Jerusalem: Abu Arafeh Agency, 1976), p. 83.

al-Muhtasib, preferred to confine the activities of the council to administrative functions.

In contrast to the religious and public character of the Islamic Supreme Council, the Higher Committee for National Guidance served as a semiclandestine political apparatus. The Higher Committee, founded after four members of the Islamic Supreme Council were deported on July 30, 1967, primarily strove to provide leadership for the protest movement. It urged local citizens to demonstrate and strike and to refrain from cooperating with the Israeli military regime. The committee was assisted in its work by a number of local committees that were formed in major West Bank towns.[4] The majority of members of the Higher Committee, like the Islamic Supreme Council, were pro-Jordanian. However, both communists and the representatives of the Arab Nationalist movement played leading roles in the operation of the Higher Committee. Following the deportation of al-Saiyih, who served as chairman of the Higher Committee as well as the Supreme Council, Rouhi al-Khatib, the former mayor of Jerusalem, served as chairman of the Higher Committee until March 7, 1968, when he was deported by the Israelis. The leadership was then jointly assumed by three Jerusalem dignitaries, lawyers Abd al-Muhsin Abu Maizer and Kamal al-Dajani and Saad al-Din al-Alami, the head of the Islamic religious court in Jerusalem.

Loyalty to Jordan

West Bank politicians stressed the inseparable unity of the West Bank with Jordan and the restoration of Jordan's sovereignty over the occupied territories. Indeed, an overwhelming majority of them expressed opposition to suggestions that an independent Palestinian state or autonomy for the occupied territories be established. Nearly all West Bank politicians argued that such a Palestinian entity would become isolated from the rest of the Arab world and would be dependent on Israel. Thus the reconstitution of Jordanian sovereignty over the West Bank was viewed as a necessity for generating international pressure on the Jewish state. As the former mayor of Nablus, Hamdi Kanan, commented, "I was convinced that pursuing a solution to the Palestinian problem

4. Dakkak, "Back to Square One," p. 71; Halabi, *West Bank Story*, pp. 38–40.

through Jordan was the best option open to my people."[5] Moreover, from the perspective of West Bank politicians, passage of United Nations Security Council Resolution 242 increased Jordan's chances of recovering the occupied territories.

The diplomatic alliance between King Hussein and President Nasser of Egypt following the 1967 June war reinforced the West Bank politicians' belief in a pan-Arabist solution to the Palestinian question. They continued to perceive the question as an Arab issue and argued that only a united Arab effort could rescue the Palestinians from their predicament. Few politicians envisaged any direct, political role for themselves in ending Israel's military occupation. Instead, they continued to rely on Jordan and other Arab regimes to settle pan-Arab problems. Their position coincided with that of the Israeli Labor government, whose official stand was predicated on an interstate solution to the Palestinian question, where the future of the occupied territories would be determined in direct Israeli-Jordanian negotiations.

Jordan's political influence in the West Bank had not then been challenged by the Palestine Liberation Organization (PLO). The Palestinian resistance movement, struggling for Arab and Palestinian recognition, had failed to establish a political and military infrastructure for itself in the occupied territories. In the spring and summer of 1969, the pro-PLO military cells were dealt a heavy blow when the Israeli government discovered and arrested PLO commandos.

For a variety of practical reasons, the reconstruction of legal links between the West Bank and Jordan seemed desirable. Jordan was the only gateway for West Bank Palestinians to the rest of the Arab world and was a market for West Bank agricultural produce. West Bank inhabitants held Jordanian passports, and students had to pass the Jordanian general examination before entrance into universities. Familial, social, economic, and cultural ties between the people on the two sides of the Jordan River were strong. And Israel's open-bridge policy, which facilitated the flow of people and goods from the West Bank eastward, allowed Jordan to preserve its political and economic influence among the local populace.

Soon after the June war ended, the Jordanian government

5. Quoted in Halabi, *West Bank Story,* p. 60.

extended financial assistance to the Islamic religious establishment, the municipalities, chambers of commerce and industry, the public school system, and charitable organizations in the West Bank and to former Jordanian government officials, members of parliament, and bureaucrats. For example, the government provided approximately 25 percent of the West Bank's municipal budgets. It also transferred a quarter of a million dollars to the West Bank to sustain the strikes held by lawyers, judges, and teachers. Between eight thousand and ten thousand former civil servants and bureaucrats remained on Jordan's payroll and some of them continued their civil service after the Israeli occupation of the West Bank.[6]

Dissenting Views

Despite the desire of the overwhelming majority of the West Bank urban elite to return their territory to Jordanian sovereignty, dissenters began to speak out. A number of politicians argued that returning the West Bank should have a political cost to Jordan. In particular, they demanded constitutional reforms in Jordan's political system that would limit the king's power and make him accountable to the parliament. Hamdi Kanan, a principal proponent of constitutional reform, argued for a federal union between the West Bank and Jordan rather than reintegration into the East Bank. These political demands were prevalent between 1968 and 1970, when the Palestinian military and political presence in Jordan was still viable.[7]

As military confrontation between Jordan and the PLO grew, and the political influence of the Islamic Supreme Council and the Higher Committee for National Guidance waned, a minority of West Bankers, particularly among the young, began to argue for launching military operations against Israeli targets. The Popular Resistance Front tried to organize underground military cells and initiate military attacks against Israeli civilian and military targets. Its members were mostly local communists and followers of the Arab Nationalist movement who, in the wake of the 1967 June

6. Ibid., pp. 59–61; Clinton Bailey, "Changing Attitudes toward Jordan in the West Bank," *Middle East Journal*, vol. 32 (Spring 1978), pp. 156–58.

7. Bailey, "Changing Attitudes," pp. 158–61; Lesch, *Political Perceptions*, p. 40; *Al-Quds* (Jerusalem), January 2 and 9, 1969, February 13, 1970.

war, had become ardent supporters of the Popular Front for the Liberation of Palestine. The front's activities nearly ceased, however, after the Israeli army arrested many of its members in February and September of 1969.

One group of West Bank politicians, on reconsidering the West Bank's transitional relationship with Jordan between 1950 and 1967, began to advance the case for a separate and distinct Palestinian political entity. From their perspective, the 1967 war not only undermined the pan-Arab approach to the resolution of the Palestinian question, but it also posed a challenge to the status of the West Bank–Jordan relationship. The Israeli occupation had ended the temporary political arrangement that had been established between the two banks of the Jordan in 1950.

A number of politicians sought to forge an indigenous Palestinian leadership in order to fill the political vacuum left by the war and to develop local initiatives to resolve the Palestinian question.[8] Shortly after the war, thirty West Bank politicians proposed to resolve the Palestinian question through a process in which Israel would allow the Palestinians to form an independent state. In return, the West Bank Palestinians would sign a peace treaty with Israel and recognize Israel's pre-1967 borders. This group of politicians advocated calling a popular congress to discuss these ideas and convening a constituent assembly to elect a new Palestinian leadership. The primary task of the leaders would be to initiate direct negotiations with Israel in order to settle the Palestinian question.

To demonstrate their peaceful intentions toward Israel, these proponents of a Palestinian state renounced the use of violence as an instrument for settling national grievances. They envisioned a process of creating a separate Palestinian state that would begin with the Israeli army's withdrawal from the West Bank. Next the occupied territories would be placed under United Nations supervision for a transitional period. During the transition the West Bank Palestinians would prove to the Israelis that once they gained

8. See Lesch, *Political Perceptions*, pp. 40–41; Bailey, "Changing Attitudes," pp. 158–59; Shemesh, "West Bank," pp. 300–03; Dakkak, "Back to Square One," pp. 71, 73; Abd al–Hadi, *Palestinian Question*, pp. 324–61; Shlomo Gazit, "Early Attempts at Establishing West Bank Autonomy (The 1968 Case Study)," *Harvard Journal of Law and Public Policy*, vol. 3 (1980), pp. 129–53.

their independence, they would not threaten Israel's security. This period of autonomy would also have the advantages of freeing the local population from Israel's direct military control and halting Palestinian emigration. Finally, in a third phase, a popular referendum would be conducted in the occupied territories to allow the local population to determine its own future.

While hostility to the Jordanian regime was a motivating force behind many politicians' desire for a Palestinian state, others believed that autonomy would ensure a quick withdrawal of the Israeli army from the West Bank, simultaneously putting an end to their subjugation to Jordanian sovereignty. Those who promoted autonomy charged that material interests were behind the calls of pro-Jordanians to reunite the West Bank with the East Bank.

Among the main advocates of a separate Palestinian entity were Muhammad Ali al-Jabari (mayor of Hebron), Aziz Shihadah (a Christian lawyer), Hamdi al-Taji al-Farouqi (a medical doctor), and Musa al-Alami (a veteran politician). They had attracted to their views such young journalists and writers as Muhammad Abu Shilbaya and Jamil al-Hamad from the Jerusalem-Bethlehem area.[9] Al-Jabari, who had served as minister of education in the Jordanian government, proposed a five-year transitional period after an Israeli withdrawal, then a referendum on the question of forming a Palestinian state along the lines of the 1947 United Nations partition plan. Al-Jabari's interest in autonomy stemmed from his conviction that this plan was the most feasible for a "transitional solution."[10] He repeatedly requested that the West Bank military governor allow the convening of a conference for West Bank mayors to discuss the question of self-government.

A lack of enthusiasm for his ideas among the Palestinians prompted al-Jabari to demand that Israel impose autonomy unilaterally on the local population so that West Bank politicians would avoid being perceived as "collaborators." Under this revised plan, the West Bank military governor would appoint the mayors

9. For elaboration of the views of some of these politicians, see Abd al-Hadi, *Palestinian Question,* pp. 324–61; *Al-Quds,* November 24 and 25, 1970; Shemesh, "West Bank," pp. 300–01.

10. On al-Jabari's political views, see Gazit, "Early Attempts," p. 149; Halabi, *West Bank Story,* pp. 70–71; Moshe Maoz, *Palestinian Leadership on the West Bank: The Changing Role of the Arab Mayors under Jordan and Israel* (London: Frank Cass, 1984), pp. 95–99; Shemesh, "West Bank," p. 301.

as governors in their districts and expand their municipal juris-
dictions. Al-Jabari's ambition to be appointed head of a West Bank
autonomy council met with opposition both in the Israeli government and among rival politicians in the Bethlehem district. The
Israelis offered him the governorship of Hebron on the grounds
that al-Jabari did not enjoy West Bank–wide political support, and
the politicians from the Bethlehem, Ramallah, and Jericho regions
wanted to have their own autonomous councils.

With mounting criticism of his views and threats on his life, al-
Jabari's commitment to the idea of a separate Palestinian state
began to wane. He eventually supported King Hussein's plan for
a United Arab Kingdom when that was proposed in March of
1972.[11]

Like al-Jabari, Hamdi al-Taji al-Farouqi began to publicize his
views shortly after the 1967 war. He at first advocated creation of
a Palestinian state alongside Israel in accordance with the 1947
United Nations partition plan. Al-Farouqi was also in favor of
placing the West Bank under United Nations and Arab League
supervision. He further suggested that, after five years, the Palestinians set up their own independent state with Jerusalem as its
capital.

In response to the PLO's mounting criticism of the advocates
of a West Bank–Gaza state, al-Farouqi called for the establishment
of a secular democratic state in all of Palestine, a proposal that was
advanced by the PLO. After the Jordanian-Palestinian civil war of
September 1970 and the subsequent expulsion of the PLO's troops
from Jordan, al-Farouqi abandoned his support of such an idea.
Like al-Jabari, he responded favorably to King Hussein's United
Arab Kingdom plan and argued for the confederation of a West
Bank Palestinian state with Jordan.

Aziz Shihadah called on Israel to recognize the Palestinian right
of self-determination and to help West Bank Palestinians form an
independent state. Because Jordan appeared to be incapable of
extricating the West Bank from Israel's military control, Shihadah
urged his fellow Palestinians to take the initiative. He proposed
the convening of a popular congress for Palestinians inside and
outside the occupied territories to elect leaders and promulgate a

11. On the change in al-Jabari's views, see *Al-Quds*, December 7, 1973.

new Palestinian constitution. And to deal with Jordanian criticism of the idea of a separate Palestinian entity, Shihadah espoused a confederation of the Palestinian state with Jordan. However, for reasons of personal safety, Shihadah stopped discussing his views publicly during most of 1969 and 1970.[12]

Writing in *Al-Quds*, the journalist Muhammad Abu Shilbaya articulated a number of arguments in favor of an independent Palestinian state.[13] Abu Shilbaya saw the need for a transitional period before the establishment of a full-fledged Palestinian state that would allow for the return of refugees, the issuing of passports, the formation of political parties, and the convening of a constituent assembly.

ISRAEL'S VIEWS ON AUTONOMY. While the proposals for a Palestinian entity were imaginative, they challenged the prevailing political consensus in and outside the occupied territories concerning a resolution of the Palestinian question. And they sharply clashed with the positions held by the three external actors (Israel, the PLO, and Jordan) who over the years had profoundly affected the evolution of West Bank political thinking. Although the proponents of autonomy sought a peace treaty with Israel and tried to elicit Israel's support for the establishment of a Palestinian state, the Israeli government appeared hesitant to treat their proposals seriously. Indeed, Israel's flirtation with these ideas was part of the search for a solution to the West Bank issue through dialogue with representatives of the local population. The officials who pursued this approach seemed to believe that they should bring about a solution that would reflect Israel's victory in the 1967 war. The prospects of Israel's indefinite military presence in the West Bank made the idea of autonomy appealing, since local administration would be in the hands of West Bankers, reducing tension between Israelis and Palestinians, and the army would not have to exercise direct military control over the lives of the local populace.[14]

12. Shemesh, "West Bank," p. 300; Aziz Shihadeh, "Freedom from Outside Influences," *New Outlook*, vol. 12 (November–December 1969), pp. 41–43.

13. *Al-Quds*, October 29, 1970. See also Muhammad Abu Shilbaya, "No Peace without a Free Palestinian State" (in Arabic) (pamphlet, Jerusalem, 1971); Lesch, *Political Perceptions*, p. 41.

14. Gazit, "Early Attempts," pp. 129–53.

Yet Israel's interest in the autonomy scheme was half-hearted, as evidenced by the military government's failure to authorize any of the political meetings requested by advocates of a Palestinian state. Israel also prevented the emergence of a West Bank political leadership and the formation of political institutions for the articulation of West Bank interests. Moreover, Israel's narrow interpretation of the concept of autonomy conflicted with the idea of self-government in a transitional period that would culminate in an independent state. The Israeli interpretation of Palestinian autonomy envisioned a civilian administration under Israeli supervision, with Jerusalem and the Gaza Strip excluded from the political arrangements, and Israeli control of foreign and defense policy.

Israel's wavering attitude toward Palestinian autonomy appears to have been a response to the evolving political consensus in favor of United Nations Security Council Resolution 242. Preferring an interstate solution in which Jordan would be Israel's negotiating partner for the future of the West Bank, the Israeli government may have flirted with the advocates of a Palestinian entity to put pressure on King Hussein to move ahead with negotiations.

ARAB VIEWS OF A SEPARATE ENTITY.   Another constraint on the possibility of a Palestinian entity was the opposition of both Jordan and the PLO. Each warned against the formation of a Palestinian state and accused the proponents of autonomy of being defeatists, traitors, and puppets of Israel. For Jordan, a self-governing West Bank would undo the two-decade legacy of its rule over that region and contradict its claim of sovereignty. The Jordanians, furthermore, viewed the Palestinian question as an Arab issue, which could not be settled through a local West Bank initiative.[15]

For the PLO, the idea of establishing a West Bank–Gaza Palestinian state was not yet perceived as a sign of Palestinian nationalism. Indeed, it appeared reactionary when compared with the goal of liberating all of Palestine through armed struggle and popular warfare.[16] The opponents of a Palestinian state contended

15. Bailey, "Changing Attitudes," p. 159.
16. Munir Shafiq, "Why Do the Palestinians Reject the Proposal of a Palestinian State in the West Bank and Gaza Strip?" (in Arabic), *Shuun Filistiniya*, March 1972,

that such a state would be politically and economically unviable and a puppet in the hands of Israel. The leaders of such a state would be drawn from the traditional elite, and the "real revolutionaries and fighters" would have no place. And recognition of Israel by such a state would liquidate the Palestinian question and fragment the Palestinians.

A third obstacle to the idea of a separate Palestinian state lay in a hostile domestic environment. The suggestion of signing a peace treaty with Israel in return for a Palestinian state found almost no support among the urban elite, even though the Arabs had so recently been humiliated in the 1967 war. On the contrary, proponents of this idea quickly lost any political credibility or legitimacy they may have had. With the possible exception of al-Jabari, with his power base in the Hebron district, none of the advocates of a separate Palestinian entity enjoyed any widespread political legitimacy or following. Nor had they any resources for recruiting and mobilizing mass support.

Thus, the prevailing pan-Arab and pro-Jordanian trends in the occupied territories led to sharp criticism of the idea of a separate Palestinian entity. The overwhelming majority held that the Palestinian question was an Arab issue and that its resolution was a collective Arab responsibility. The statement issued on October 4, 1967, by 129 West Bank politicians denounced the notion of forming a separate Palestinian entity, pronouncing it a mechanism to perpetuate Israel's military occupation. It contended that an Israeli-sponsored Palestinian entity would be isolated from the Arab world, would be economically weak, and would lack domestic political legitimacy. It also expressed the belief that the only feasible solution was to return the West Bank to Jordanian sovereignty.

The idea of a Palestinian state or self-government in the occupied territories thus failed because it ran against the prevailing wisdom and political consensus. Formation of a West Bank Palestinian state had not yet become an objective of the Palestinian nationalist movement, nor was it considered conducive to the long-term goal of establishing a democratic, secular state in all of Palestine. The idea, according to Ann Lesch, a pioneering writer on West Bank

---

pp. 65–73. See also Nabil Shaath, "The Palestine of Tomorrow" (in Arabic), *Shuun Filistiniya*, May 1971, pp. 5–23; Ghassan Kanafani, "The Ghost of a Palestinian State" (in Arabic), *Al-Hadaf*, March 6, 1971.

politics, was "still premature and heretical."[17] Yet it was the precursor of a trend in the PLO that began to be discernible in the mid-1970s.

The Disappearance of Old Illusions

Between 1970 and 1973, political inactivity and a mood of resignation prevailed among the West Bank urban elite. The inconclusive outcome of the civil disobedience movement against the Israeli military occupation by 1969 had contributed significantly to this state of affairs. Israel's punitive measures—including the policies of deportation, administrative detention, imprisonment, demolition of houses, and restriction of political activity—exhausted the energies of West Bank politicians and resigned them to the fact that occupation would not end soon.[18]

Between September 1967 and December 1970, the Israeli government deported 514 Palestinians from the occupied territories, some of whom were religious dignitaries, mayors, professionals, teachers, leaders of the political opposition, and pro-Jordanian politicians from the West Bank. The policy of deportation took a heavy toll on Jerusalem politicians, who in the first three years of occupation had provided the ideological and political leadership for the protest movement. This was not a coincidence; Israel's policy was aimed at depleting the holy city of its political leadership and undermining the political standing of the leaders in the Palestinian community. The net effect of the policy was to shift political activities and leadership to other West Bank towns.

Disappointing results of the PLO's strategy of armed struggle also contributed to the political inactivity in the West Bank. By 1970, the military cells within some of the PLO's factions in the occupied territories had been discovered and suppressed, while infiltration by Palestinian commando groups from the East Bank into the occupied territories to attack Israeli targets had been

17. *Political Perceptions,* p. 41.

18. Ann Lesch, "Israeli Deportation of Palestinians from the West Bank and the Gaza Strip, 1967–1978," *Journal of Palestine Studies,* vol. 8 (Winter 1979), pp. 101–31, (Spring 1979), pp. 81–112; Michael Adams, "Israel's Treatment of the Arabs in the Occupied Territories," *Journal of Palestine Studies,* vol. 6 (Winter 1977), pp. 34–39.

halted. The commando groups had established military bases in the East Bank of Jordan after the defeat of the Arab armies in the 1967 war. In response to Palestinian attacks in the following years, the Israeli government had retaliated against Jordanian population centers and economic projects. The commando groups' activities, together with their growing popularity inside Jordan, culminated in a large-scale confrontation with the Jordanian army in September 1970. By July 1971 King Hussein's troops had ended the PLO's military and political presence in Jordan; the PLO was no longer able to establish direct contact with West Bank Palestinians. Moreover, the outbreak of the civil war not only ruptured Palestinian-Jordanian relations but weakened the viability of the Eastern Front—Syria, Jordan, and the PLO—as a challenge to Israel's occupation of the West Bank.

Similarly, the Palestinian resistance movement failed to establish itself as a viable political force among West Bank Palestinians. The Islamic Supreme Council, for example, confined itself to issuing an appeal to both sides in the Jordanian-Palestinian civil war to stop fighting. It abstained from condemning Jordan or expressing strong sympathy for the PLO.

The PLO's political weakness among the Palestinian inhabitants of the occupied territories was a direct reflection of its lack of interest in West Bank politics. As a national liberation movement, the PLO was primarily interested in liberating all of Palestine through military means. Accordingly, it failed to see any need to build a political constituency in the West Bank. Thus when its political and military headquarters in Jordan were dismantled, the PLO concentrated on its struggle to secure a new haven in Lebanon.

The sense of political paralysis among West Bank politicians was exacerbated by the failure of Egypt's "war of attrition" in 1969 and 1970 as well as the death of the Egyptian president in September 1970. Nasser's death and rivalries among the Arab countries during this phase shattered the hopes of West Bank Palestinians for a pan-Arab military solution to their predicament.[19] The ousting of the Syrian Baath party's left wing from power in November 1970 reinforced the growing disillusionment of West Bank politicians with the Arab countries' ability to end Israel's military occupation.

19. *Al-Quds,* September 29 and 30 and October 1, 5, 15, 17, and 18, 1970.

The 1970 Palestinian-Jordanian civil war left bitter feelings against Jordan among some West Bank politicians and the general public. The hostility, however, did not immediately discredit the conservative elite in the West Bank whose power depended on connections with Jordan. It did lead eventually to their demise and the emergence of a new nationalist leadership in the mid-1970s.

The political indifference is evident from the West Bank elite's reaction to King Hussein's plan for a United Arab Kingdom and to the conduct of the 1972 municipal elections. The king's plan for the resolution of the Palestinian question, released on March 15, 1972, promised Palestinians in the occupied territories self-government within the framework of a federal state. Each of the two autonomous entities within this state—the West Bank and East Bank of Jordan—would have its own local parliament and government. Foreign policy, defense, and the preservation of the union would be the prerogatives of the federal government headed by the king.[20]

The timing of the plan seems to have been politically dictated. Jordanian officials may have thought that chances were good that the king's plan would be well received in the occupied territories. The PLO, after all, was politically weak and its military infrastructure in Jordan had been obliterated. The West Bank population was becoming increasingly frustrated. Launching the plan might improve Jordan's image in the occupied territories, and it would enhance the chances of reelecting pro-Jordanian politicians in the 1972 municipal elections.[21]

To give his plan political credibility and currency, the king created a ministry for the occupied territories and increased the amounts of financial assistance for West Bank institutions and municipalities. The government released a number of political and security prisoners arrested during and after the 1970 civil war. King Hussein appointed Zaid al-Rifai, of Palestinian descent, as prime minister and increased the number of Palestinian ministers in the cabinet. He also authorized formation of the National Union

20. Bailey, "Changing Attitudes," p. 161; for the text of the plan, see *Al-Quds*, March 16, 1972.
21. Bailey, "Changing Attitudes," pp. 160–61.

political party and appointed Mustafa Dudin, from the Hebron region, as its chairman.

It was not hostility emanating from the West Bank that caused the failure of the United Arab Kingdom plan; its ultimate demise was brought about by opposition from the PLO, the Arab countries, and Israel. Indeed, the West Bank urban elite's attitude toward the plan was ambivalent, for they neither rejected it outright nor gave it an enthusiastic reception. Though they criticized the political regime, the West Bank elite continued to value the close social, familial, economic, and cultural ties with Jordan. And a host of benefits accruing from their links with Jordan also prompted the West Bank politicians' acceptance of the centrality of Jordan to their lives. As Mayor Kanan of Nablus commented, "If we find this federation plan acceptable, it is not out of love for the King or his regime."[22] On March 20, 1972, *Al-Quds* urged the West Bank population to study carefully the king's plan and not to reject it outright. The paper felt that the plan was designed to end Israel's military occupation and to restore Arab sovereignty over Jerusalem.[23]

The 1972 Municipal Elections

The 1972 municipal elections furnish additional evidence of the sense of political despondency in the West Bank. They also provide a clear example of the intense competition among Israel, Jordan, and the PLO as each attempted to shape political developments and postures in the occupied territories to suit its own preferences and interests.

On November 26, 1971, the military government disclosed its plan for conducting municipal elections in the West Bank in the early spring of 1972.[24] The Israeli government hoped that a more cooperative group of mayors and municipal council members would be elected. Such an outcome seemed feasible in view of the

22. *Al-Quds*, March 14, 1973, quoted in ibid., p. 161.
23. Bailey, "Changing Attitudes," p. 161.
24. On the 1972 municipal elections, see Lesch, *Political Perceptions*, pp. 43–47; Shemesh, "West Bank," pp. 303–14; John P. Richardson, *The West Bank: A Portrait*, Special Study 5 (Washington, D.C.: Middle East Institute, 1984), pp. 83–84; Maoz, *Palestinian Leadership*, pp. 101–13.

growing frustration and political alienation of the West Bank
population that the Jordanian-PLO rift and the general disarray
in the Arab world had caused. By conducting municipal elections,
the Israeli government would demonstrate its liberal rule over the
West Bank. It could point to the "benevolent nature" of its
occupation and contest the Arab countries' charges that Israel was
violating Palestinian human and civil rights.[25]

The announcement that municipal elections would be held
caused confusion in the ranks of the Jordanian government. Rouhi
al-Khatib and Nadim al-Zaru, the deported mayors of Jerusalem
and Ramallah, advised the Jordanian government to oppose the
elections. The government did so from fear that the elections
would give a sense of legitimacy to Israel's occupation of the West
Bank. It was also concerned that Israel's real aim might be to bring
proponents of autonomy into power. Such a move, if successful,
would threaten Jordan's claim of sovereignty over the West Bank
and erode the power position of the traditional elite.[26]

By January, Jordan's political posture had undergone a decisive
shift, for the government came out in favor of holding the elections.
The Israeli government's determination to conduct the elections
on time had convinced the Jordanian government that any attempt
to obstruct them would be futile. Jordan's opposition would serve
only to undermine its political credibility among the West Bank
population. Similarly, Israel's threat to appoint its own officers as
mayors, should the elections fail to take place, posed a host of
complex problems in Jordan's official dealings with West Bank
towns. Not only would Jordan be unable to extend financial
assistance to Israeli-run municipal councils, but it would be unable
to continue its coordination with West Bank mayors in the areas
of city planning and budgeting.

Jordan's attitude shifted too because of its concern to preserve
its political control in the occupied territories. If its followers
boycotted the elections, then it was possible that the proponents
of self-government could win. Moreover, in the battle for custodianship of the Palestinian question and control of the occupied

25. Maoz, *Palestinian Leadership*, p. 103.
26. For Jordan's initial reaction to the elections, see *Al-Dustur*, December 9,
1971; Said Hammud, "The Municipal Elections in the Occupied West Bank" (in
Arabic), *Shuun Filistiniya*, April 1972, pp. 8–14.

territories, the Jordanian government was not keen on adopting a position identical to that of its rival, the PLO. The election of pro-Jordanian mayors would provide a clear sign of Jordan's continued political legitimacy in the occupied territories and strengthen King Hussein's position vis-à-vis that of the PLO in the Arab world.

Unlike Jordan, the PLO was uncompromising in its opposition to elections. Its executive committee urged West Bankers in early February 1972 to refrain from voting and warned potential candidates against involvement in the municipal elections. Holding elections under conditions of occupation was illegal, the committee claimed. Engagement in such a political process would undermine the PLO's objective of liberating all of Palestine through armed struggle, and the PLO reminded West Bank citizens that the only mode of operation should be resistance to Israel's military occupation and absolute noncooperation with the enemy.[27] However, after the first round of elections in March of 1972, some PLO followers opted to support incumbents during the second round of elections, in May.

In its quest to become the exclusive representative of Palestinian interests and national aspirations, the PLO stood against any opportunity for the West Bank traditional elite to renew their political legitimacy or to help Jordan revive its claims of sovereignty over the territories. King Hussein's announcement of his United Arab Kingdom plan intensified the PLO's fears, and municipal elections threatened the victory of "local collaborators" who would then cooperate with the "enemy" in implementing autonomy.

The conflicting priorities and interests of Israel, Jordan, and the PLO so perplexed the local leaders that the mood of political resignation deepened. Some incumbents and their followers opposed holding the elections for fear they might lose their municipal seats to the "radicals." Others suspected that advocates of autonomy would win the elections with the help of the military government. And politicians sympathetic to the PLO opposed the elections.

The local communists did not support the municipal elections since they believed that conservative politicians would remain in

27. Munther Anabtawi, "On the Occasion of the Municipal Elections in the West Bank: Israel's Ping-Pong Game" (in Arabic), *Shuun Filistiniya*, April 1972, pp. 15–27.

control of the municipal councils.[28] It was also at this time that local communist leaders began to reconsider their links with Jordan and to rearticulate their views on the establishment of an independent West Bank–Gaza Palestinian state.[29]

One small group of politicians openly favored holding the elections. They were mostly supporters of a separate Palestinian entity. Hamdi Kanan, the main figure in this group, contended that neither the incumbent mayors, Jordan, nor the PLO truly represented the interests and needs of the local populace.[30] In his opinion, a new generation of leaders had emerged since the municipal elections in 1963. Kanan concluded that because of Israel's occupation, the role of the municipalities was no longer solely administrative; it was becoming increasingly political. Thus elections could bring about a new, better-qualified leadership to fulfill the changing political needs of the municipalities and meet the exigencies of Israel's military occupation.

Whatever the arguments for or against municipal elections, the Israeli government was resolved to hold them on time. The PLO's opposition added a sense of urgency, as the elections came to be seen as a test case for Israel's control of the West Bank. To ensure the participation of the local populace, the military government threatened to appoint Israeli officers as mayors and to impose economic sanctions on towns whose politicians were boycotting the elections.

On March 28, 1972, the first round of elections took place in the northern towns of the West Bank, and on May 2 the second round took place in central and southern towns. Out of the 23 mayors, 15 were new; and out of 192 contested municipal seats, 108 were filled by new members. The fact that more than half of the municipal seats were occupied by new members did not, however, indicate the emergence of a new brand of politician.

28. *Al-Watan*, the communist underground publication, in its issues of December 1971 and March 1972 provided an exposition of the communists' political stands.

29. Following the successful first round of elections in West Bank northern towns, the communists tempered their opposition. Indeed, they asked their followers to participate in the second round of the elections, which were to take place in the southern towns, so as to keep the incumbents in office. The relationship between the communists and Jordan is explored in chap. 5, below.

30. See his articles in *Al-Quds*, August 1, 1971, and *Al-Anba*, February 11, 1972.

Indeed, the majority of those elected were conservative and traditional—only 3 percent were below the age of thirty and 47 percent between thirty and fifty years old; the remainder were over fifty. Only 10 percent had some form of college education, 25 percent had high school training, and 65 percent were illiterate or had only some elementary education. A quarter of the members were white-collar workers, the remainder landowners, merchants, and businessmen.[31]

The conservative composition of the councils elected in 1972 can in part be attributed to Jordan's municipal law, passed in 1955, that allowed only men who had reached the age of twenty-one and who paid taxes on their property to vote.[32] The exclusion of women and of all men who were propertyless would ensure the survival of the traditional elite. For those taxpayers who could vote, considerations of clan loyalty, family connections, and economic interest as well as the wealth, social position, and age of the candidate played a crucial role in determining voting behavior.

The 1972 elections also revealed the pro-Jordanian political disposition of West Bank voters. The elections indicated that the PLO's influence was still limited within the occupied territories and that pro-PLO politicians did not enjoy widespread popular support. A few of the mayors elected eventually revealed Palestinian nationalist aspirations and pro-PLO political stances. Three of them—Karim Khalaf of Ramallah, Abd al-Jawad Salih of Al-Birah, and Hilmi Hanoun of Tulkarm—together with activists in the Baath party and the local communists became the core of the new nationalist leadership that emerged after the 1973 October war.

Waning Influence

In addition to the residual influence of the conservative pro-Jordanian elite and the built-in bias of municipal election law, the prevailing sense of political passivity on the part of the West Bank elite accounted for the elections' outcome. Municipal council members repeatedly asserted that they did not intend to engage in politics but would confine their activities to administrative affairs.

31. Maoz, *Palestinian Leadership,* pp. 105–06; Shemesh, "West Bank," p. 313.
32. Shemesh, "West Bank," p. 309.

Political issues were not highlighted in the election campaign. Indeed, it was much later that the office of mayor became highly politicized. And although the Israeli government insisted on holding elections, it discouraged advocates of autonomy from operating freely. Al-Jabari was barred, for instance, from convening a conference of West Bank mayors to discuss opening direct talks with the Israeli government on the future of the occupied territories within the framework of a federation with Jordan.

After the 1972 elections, the political preeminence of the pro-Jordanian traditional elite began to wane. Among the forces that began to emerge inside and outside the occupied territories was a new elite with nationalist aspirations. The consolidation of the local communists' political power, the expansion of university education, the radicalization of the student movement, and the expansion of the West Bank working class, all served to diminish the domination of the traditional elite in West Bank politics. The new forces widened the circle of participatory politics in the West Bank.

CHAPTER FOUR

The Ascendancy of the Pro-PLO Urban Elite

🏳 🏳 🏳

ALTHOUGH THE traditional politicians in the West Bank carried the municipal elections of 1972, those elections revealed the dearth of political activity and the sense of political resignation among the urban elite. By the mid-1970s, conservative politicians seldom expressed support for King Hussein's regime or demanded the restoration of Jordanian sovereignty over the West Bank. And the Islamic Supreme Council, Jordan's main power center in the occupied territories, had already begun to lose control of West Bank politics.

At the same time that Jordan and its followers were going through a crisis in political influence, the political clout of the Palestine Liberation Organization (PLO) and advocates of Palestinian nationalism was on the rise. Mayors Karim Khalaf of Ramallah, Abd al-Jawad Salih of Al-Birah, and Hilmi Hanoun of Tulkarm, together with the local communists, had begun to argue in support of a distinct Palestinian national identity and the creation of a West Bank–Gaza Palestinian state. And they supported the PLO as the representative of Palestinian national interests. The licensing of two Arabic dailies, *Al-Fajr* and *Al-Shaab*, in the spring of 1972 gave a boost to the rising nationalistic Palestinian leadership. The two papers were strongly anti-Hashemite and both advocated the formation of a PLO-led Palestinian state.[1] The pro-Jordanian daily *Al-Quds* disclosed a growing West Bank disillusionment with King Hussein's regime.[2]

Propagation of the idea of a Palestinian state by the rising new politicians was no longer viewed as defeatist and reactionary. On

1. *Al-Fajr*, July 29, 1972, September 22 and 29, 1973; *Al-Shaab*, August 23, 1972, February 12, March 10, and June 10, 1973.
2. *Al-Quds*, September 27 and December 12, 1970, April 8, 1971.

the contrary, it became quite popular among the West Bank–Gaza population.[3] Indeed, following the 1973 October war the concept was pursued vigorously by the rising new elite.

The Demise of the Pro-Jordanian Elite

Why did a political shift from an essentially traditional pro-Jordanian attitude to a more nationalist pro-PLO posture take place? Certainly, it was neither sudden nor surprising, as it came in response to major regional shake-ups unleashed by the 1967 June war. The gradual demise of the West Bank traditional elite can be traced to several political realities that affected the assets and resources of Jordan, the PLO, and Israel.

After Israel's occupation of the West Bank, the conservative politicians no longer had direct access to the center of government.[4] Before 1967, these politicians could dispense material benefits and political rewards that flowed from Amman and intercede on behalf of their followers with the central government. After the war, such privileges could not be honorably derived by maintaining close ties with the occupying power.

The links with Jordan that had provided the traditional elite's social and political prominence in the West Bank worked to their detriment after Israel's military occupation began. For example, the Jordanian army's quick and humiliating defeat not only dishonored the regime but also its clients in the occupied territories. And the growing tension between the PLO and Jordan, which culminated in the eviction of the PLO from Jordanian territories in July 1971, brought embarrassment to West Bank conservative politicians. The 1970 civil war ruptured Palestinian-Jordanian relations, but the death of Gamal Abd al-Nasser, the charismatic president of Egypt, shattered the traditional elite's belief in an Arab solution to their problems. Indeed, their hopes that the Jordanian monarch would extricate them from Israel's military

3. The rise of the PLO had a significant impact on the popularity of the concept of a Palestinian state because the PLO was a primary supporter of the idea and was itself considered legitimate by the Arab countries.

4. Mark Heller, "Politics and Social Change in the West Bank since 1967," in Joel S. Migdal, ed., *Palestinian Society and Politics* (Princeton University Press, 1980), pp. 195–99.

occupation began to fade; meanwhile, Israel deepened its presence in the occupied territories.

It was Jordan's failure to join the 1973 October war, which restored pride to the Arabs and boosted their morale, that dealt a serious blow to its influence in the occupied territories. Jordan lost its moral claim to restore its sovereignty over the West Bank and to speak in the name of the Palestinian people. It lost prestige and influence also because of its exclusion from the disengagement agreements that Egypt and Syria concluded with Israel between 1973 and 1975. Jordan's problems were compounded by the PLO's political ascendancy and the growth of Palestinian nationalism among the West Bank urban elite.

Nor did King Hussein's efforts to arrest the eroding influence of his followers in the West Bank bear fruit. In a move designed to enhance the diminishing power of the Islamic Supreme Council, the Jordanian government appointed the council's head as chief of the religious courts in the West Bank. The Islamic court of appeal in Jerusalem was given responsibility for restoring the Al-Aqsa Mosque and the Dome of the Rock.[5] And the government resumed financial assistance, which had been suspended in 1970, to West Bank municipalities, civil servants, and teachers.[6]

These measures failed, however, to preserve the fading influence of the traditional elite or to arrest the rising power of the new elite and the mounting support for the PLO. Often, traditional leaders felt compelled to express publicly their support for the PLO and to desist from openly identifying with Jordan or advocating the restoration of Jordanian sovereignty over the West Bank.[7]

Israel's economic policy following the 1967 June war also undermined the economic base, and thus the political authority, of the traditional elite. Some measures such as the open bridge policy allowing for the flow of goods and people tempered the adverse effects of Israel's economic restrictions; it allowed large

5. Ibrahim Dakkak, "Back to Square One: A Study in the Re-emergence of the Palestinian Identity in the West Bank, 1967–1980," in Alexander Schölch, ed., *Palestinians over the Green Line: Studies on the Relations between Palestinians on Both Sides of the 1949 Armistice Line since 1967* (London: Ithaca Press, 1983), p. 72.

6. *Al-Quds*, February 13, 1975; *Maariv*, November 23, 1974.

7. See interviews with Hamdi al-Taji al-Farouqi and Amin al-Khatib, *Al-Quds*, December 10, 1973, and with Hamdi Kanan, ibid., November 28, 1973. See also ibid., December 4, 1973, October 16, 1974.

landowners to export their agricultural products to the East Bank and the government in Amman to give financial aid to its power centers in the occupied territories. But the unrestricted flow of industrial and agricultural goods from Israel into the West Bank suffocated local markets and discouraged local businessmen from investing their capital in economic projects. The Israeli government's refusal to invest in or develop a West Bank economic infrastructure made matters even worse.

More detrimental to the economic interests of the traditional leaders, however, was the Israeli government's decision to let West Bank workers seek employment inside Israel. By 1974 the appeal of higher wages had attracted almost a third of the West Bank labor force—mostly peasants—to jobs in Israel. The transfer of such a sizable share of the labor force caused an acute scarcity of workers in the West Bank's agricultural and industrial sectors. Many peasants left their villages and land, which forced local businessmen and landowners to raise the wages of West Bank workers to match those in Israel.[8]

The older politicians were no longer the commanding presence in the local employment market. Land and capital, the two main vehicles for the traditional politicians' authority, lost some of their importance and appeal to local workers and peasants. The local elite's opportunity to find jobs for relatives, friends, and followers in the government also disappeared with the severance of the West Bank from Jordan.[9]

With the opening of the Israeli market, West Bank workers were no longer dependent for their livelihood on the West Bank business and commercial class. The standard of living of the growing West Bank working class improved significantly.

8. Vivian A. Bull, *The West Bank—Is It Viable?* (Lexington Books, 1975), pp. 117–23; Brian Van Arkadie, *Benefits and Burdens: A Report on the West Bank and Gaza Strip Economies since 1967* (New York: Carnegie Endowment for International Peace, 1977), pp. 60–61, 73; Sarah Graham-Brown, "The Economic Consequences of the Occupation," in Naseer H. Aruri, ed., *Occupation: Israel over Palestine* (Belmont, Mass.: Association of Arab-American University Graduates, 1983), pp. 205–12; Emile Sahliyeh, "West Bank Industrial and Agricultural Development: The Basic Problems," *Journal of Palestine Studies,* vol. 11 (Winter 1982), pp. 61–62; Jamil Hilal, *The West Bank: Social and Economic Structure (1948–1974)* (in Arabic), Palestine Books, 60 (Beirut: Palestine Liberation Organization Research Center, 1975), pp. 177–302.

9. Heller, "Politics and Social Change," pp. 196–97.

As conditions improved, the existing labor unions expanded and new ones sprang up. The relative economic prosperity of the West Bank allowed workers and peasants to give their children the opportunity to seek higher education. This led to the establishment of several new universities, and higher education ceased to be a monopoly of the elite and the rich. Gradually, modern norms—college education and professional achievement—began to replace the traditional criteria for social stratification. The persistence of clan loyalty, familial connection, and deference to age and land possession was intrinsic to the continued viability of the traditional elite, and as these ties weakened, so did the influence of the traditional elite.

The impact of socioeconomic change extended to the political realm. The expansion of the student movement and labor unions widened the circle of participatory politics in the West Bank. Rather than identifying with Jordan and the traditional elite, the new organizations followed the ideologies of Palestinian nationalism, Marxism-Leninism, and Islamic fundamentalism. Beginning in the mid-1970s they succeeded in curbing significantly the influence of the older politicians.

The failure of the pro-Jordanian politicians to mobilize the masses put those politicians at a major disadvantage in their confrontation with the new nationalist elite. Before 1967, Jordanian support ensured the longevity of the conservative leaders. The disorganization, disunity, and exclusion of the political opposition during Jordan's rule contributed to the pro-Jordanian politicians' lack of interest in widening their base of popular support.

The final demise of the conservative politicians arose in large part from Israel's deportation policy and restrictions on political activity. Of the 514 West Bank figures known to have been deported to Jordan between September 1967 and December 1970, many were from the pro-Jordanian elite. The Israeli government did not tolerate the rise of an all–West Bank leadership and political institutions. It harassed the members of the Islamic Supreme Council and the Higher Committee for National Guidance and obstructed the formation of political parties and associations. The jurisdiction of mayors was confined to their towns, and they were banned from engaging in politics.[10] Moreover, the Israeli Labor

10. Nimrod Raphaeli, "Military Government in the Occupied Territories: An

government, preferring an interstate solution with Jordan, discouraged proponents of a separate Palestinian entity.

In addition to Israel's restrictive policies, the persistence of traditional rivalries among the West Bank's major towns and families limited the capacity of conservative politicians to coordinate their political activities and create political frameworks. Rivalries between Hebron and Bethlehem and between Hebron and Nablus impeded any comprehensive discussion of autonomy for the West Bank.

A New Nationalist Elite

With the majority of the conservative elite alienated from the general public, most of the seats in the 1976 municipal elections went to new leaders. The new elite differed from the traditional politicians in age, education, occupation, source of wealth and status, and political orientation. The new politicians were younger and better educated. They were lawyers, engineers, pharmacists, teachers, writers, journalists, leaders of labor unions, members of professional associations and of women's organizations. Unlike the working class, the intelligentsia and professionals were hurt by Israel's occupation of the West Bank. Their political affiliations were with the Arab Nationalist movement, the Baath party, and the Jordanian Communist party, and many had been leaders of the political opposition during Jordan's reign over the West Bank.

Unlike the older leaders, the new elite derived their political legitimacy and influence from their identification with the PLO and its belief in Palestinian nationalism. Yet they came from much the same socioeconomic stratum as the old elite. The prominent politicians of the West Bank continued to come from well-to-do and socially prominent families. They had no economic and social agenda that differentiated them from the older generation. Their distinctiveness stemmed from their ideological orientation and political rhetoric.

Political competition between the two camps thus turned on narrow ideological questions. Debate focused on national and

Israeli View," *Middle East Journal*, vol. 23 (Spring 1969), pp. 177–90; Migdal, *Palestinian Society*, pp. 45–50; Michael Adams, "Israel's Treatment of the Arabs in the Occupied Territories," *Journal of Palestine Studies*, vol. 6 (Winter 1977), pp. 34–39.

political issues, including the intensity of the opposition to Israel's military occupation and the degree of assertion of a separate Palestinian identity and interest. And the question of which outside actors should play the dominant role in West Bank affairs figured heavily in the ideological debate. Neither camp addressed fundamental questions of social change—economic development, the role of women, or the place of religion in society.

Their narrow class interest accounted for their political weakness. And their narrow ideological focus left the way open for the emergence of new political trends such as Islamic fundamentalism and communism and the radicalization of the student movement. Both the old and the new elite groups suffered from the pressure and intervention of outside players. The old elite was dependent on Jordan's material support, the new politicians on the PLO's ideological and organizational abilities, for their legitimacy and influence.

By advocating Palestinian nationalism and identification with the PLO, the new elite sought to develop a new point of reference and sense of political allegiance. They invoked new political symbols in the hope of offering a more promising avenue for political salvation. Besides, these symbols were a source of political influence and legitimacy that reached far beyond the domain of local politics.

The new elite's strong sense of Palestinian nationalism prompted its members to express anti-Hashemite sentiments and to reject Jordan's claims of representing Palestinian interests. Emboldened by the military and political outcomes of the 1973 October war and the designation by the Arab League of the PLO as the sole representative of the Palestinian people the year after, the new elite openly opposed the Israeli military government. Its members encouraged the wave of demonstrations and strikes that took place between the fall of 1975 and spring of 1976.[11]

The new politicians sought to widen their base of popular support and legitimacy by creating new political structures and manipulating existing mass organizations. In 1973 they established

11. Moshe Maoz, *Palestinian Leadership on the West Bank: The Changing Role of the Arab Mayors under Jordan and Israel* (London: Frank Cass, 1984), pp. 108–17; Ann Mosely Lesch, *Political Perceptions of the Palestinians on the West Bank and the Gaza Strip*, Special Study 3 (Washington, D.C.: Middle East Institute, 1980), pp. 54–71.

the Palestine National Front (PNF) which existed until 1977, and in 1978 the National Guidance Committee which lasted until 1982. These two institutions articulated the interests and demands of Palestinians in the occupied territories and organized civilian resistance to Israel's military occupation. The new politicians used these organizations to rally support for the PLO and to formulate political positions consonant with those of the PLO and promote their adoption by the organizations. By doing so, the West Bankers hoped to affect the formulation of PLO policies and political orientation.

The new elite also sought to dominate local governments and discredit the traditional politicians. In the 1976 municipal elections they defeated most of the traditional pro-Jordanian notables. Members of the new elite worked with labor unions, student councils, and women's organizations to mobilize and expand their activities. West Bank communists were active in many of these mass organizations. The primary medium for the dissemination of the new elite's political ideas was the press. The licensing of *Al-Fajr* and *Al-Shaab* gave the West Bank press a Palestinian nationalist dimension and orientation. The two Arabic newspapers played an active role in accelerating the growth of a Palestinian national consciousness and in fostering support for the PLO. They called for the formation of an independent Palestinian state in the occupied territories and proclaimed the PLO as the sole legitimate representative of the Palestinian people.[12]

Some of the new elite even attempted to solicit support among Israel's leftist parties and academic community. Others tried to make use of Israel's legal system by appealing to its supreme court to protest land expropriation, the construction of settlements, and deportation orders.

THE PLO'S ASSUMPTION OF LEADERSHIP.   The new elite were never able to develop an autonomous leadership. With recognition of the PLO in 1974 by the Arab League and the United Nations General Assembly, that organization became accepted as the exclusive representative of the Palestinian people. This advanced the

12. See, for example, *Al-Fajr*, July 28 and September 22 and 29, 1973. See also *Al-Shaab*, August 23, 1972, February 12, March 10, and June 12, 1973.

stature of the PLO among West Bank Palestinians while diminishing the incentive to develop an indigenous leadership. The PLO's semblance of statehood, attained through its political and military activities in Lebanon in the 1970s, made it the center of gravity and attraction to Palestinians everywhere. Especially for those in the occupied territories, the organization—with its ideology of Palestinian nationalism—was an appealing alternative to the temporary political arrangement between the West Bank and Jordan established in 1950.

As a quasi-government with substantial financial resources, the PLO was able to offer material benefits and political rewards to reinforce its status in the occupied territories. Periodically the organization resorted to coercion and intimidation to silence its opponents and warn potential collaborators. The most blatant reminders were the assassinations of Abd al-Nur Janho, Hashim Khuzandar, and Yusif al-Khatib in 1978, 1979, and 1981, respectively.

The leaders of the PLO were, understandably, not keen on seeing the emergence of local leaders in the West Bank. They preferred their supporters to confine their roles to generating support for the Palestinian cause, leaving the question of representation of Palestinian interests to the PLO. In 1974, as a sort of diplomatic engagement, the PLO began actively working to mold the political attitudes of West Bank Palestinians. Its political ascendancy both in and outside the occupied territories thus worked to diminish the propensity of the West Bank's new elite to develop an independent leadership.

In early 1973, to ensure the integration of West Bank Palestinians into the PLO, the Palestine National Council (the governing organ of the PLO) had endorsed the idea of forming a national front that would serve as a political voice for the PLO inside the occupied territories. A year and a half later, the council adopted the concept of establishing a national authority in the West Bank and Gaza Strip,[13] as a transitional goal en route to establishing a state in all of Palestine. One hundred seats in the National Council were assigned to representatives from the occupied territories and on

13. This concept was further defined in 1977, during the thirteenth session of the Palestine National Council.

occasion West Bank deportees were appointed to the PLO's executive committee. For instance, Abd al-Jawad Salih, mayor of Al-Birah, Hanna Naser, president of Bir Zeit University, the Reverend Ilya Khury from Jerusalem, Fahd al-Qawasmah, mayor of Hebron, and Muhammad Milhim, mayor of Halhoul, served on the executive committee in the late 1970s and early 1980s.

ISRAEL'S RESTRICTIVE POLICIES. While the PLO's political ascendancy removed the West Bank Palestinians' incentive to opt for an indigenous leadership, the policies of various Israeli governments in the 1970s and 1980s also prevented the crystallization of an effective leadership. After their election in 1976, West Bank mayors and council members were subjected to all types of harassment, restriction, and intimidation. On May 2, 1980, the mayors of Hebron and Halhoul were deported to Lebanon, and a month later the mayors of Ramallah and Nablus were maimed by bombs placed in their cars by Israeli settlers. In July, town arrest orders were imposed on several West Bank and Gaza politicians. During the spring and summer of 1982, eight mayors were removed from office and the National Guidance Committee was outlawed. Israeli settlers' provocations in Islamic mosques in Hebron and Jerusalem, intensification of the construction of Jewish settlements and land expropriation, and the coming of the Likud to power in May 1977, with its invocation of religious claims to rationalize Israel's permanent control over the territories, pushed the West Bank urban elite to look toward the PLO for political leadership.

The Palestine National Front

The new generation of politicians chose a political framework to express their ideas that would enable them to replace the traditional leaders and offer stiff resistance to Israel's military occupation. The political structure, the Palestine National Front (PNF), came into existence during the summer of 1973. The new elite presented the PNF as a politically modernizing organ that would fill the vacuum left by the erosion of the pro-Jordanian leaders' influence and political weight.

The PNF was the second serious attempt by the local elite to establish a political structure for the West Bank. The Islamic

Supreme Council and the Higher Committee for National Guidance had earlier advocated the restoration of Jordanian sovereignty; the PNF, in contrast, espoused the right of self-determination and the formation of an independent Palestinian state. The PNF's ideas reflected the prevailing mood in the occupied territories following the 1973 October war. The era of political inactivism and calls to restore Jordanian sovereignty had come to an end.

The founders of the PNF saw it primarily as a means of organizing political opposition to Israel's military occupation. They also were guided by the experience of other countries that had been subjugated to colonial rule. The aim of the front, they contended, was the unification of all existing political groups and forces in the occupied territories against Israel, irrespective of their political and ideological orientations. As Mayor Salih of Al-Birah, a prominent member of the PNF, put it, "Following the war, we felt that we needed a collective leadership so that our political stands and resistance to the military occupation would not be individualistic."[14]

Because the civil disobedience movement had clearly failed by 1970, the new elite felt a need to develop an indigenous leadership to deal with the exigencies of daily living under military occupation. Moreover, they envisaged the PNF as a collective self-defense mechanism against Israel's settlement policy and land expropriation. It would also protect the West Bank from Jordan's renewed interest in reestablishing its sovereign rights.

Members of the new elite were convinced that solid backing from the occupied territories was necessary to make the PLO's diplomatic role credible and to frustrate Jordan's ambitions. They were determined to extend the PLO's message among West Bank Palestinians and, while not posing as an alternative to the PLO, to articulate West Bank political demands and wants. They meant to secure a policymaking role for the West Bank urban elite in the PLO and have some influence on its political orientation.[15]

THE PNF'S PROGRAM.   The PNF made its public debut in August 1973.[16] (There was some dispute over who started the front—the

---

14. Interview in *Al-Mustaqbal,* November 1979.
15. Dakkak, "Back to Square One," p. 90.
16. Lesch, *Political Perceptions,* p. 53.

PLO's followers contended that the PNF was established in response to an appeal by the eleventh session of the Palestine National Council in January 1973, the communists that the PNC's resolution was in response to an initiative early in 1972 from within the occupied territories.)[17] It was a broad coalition of political and social forces in the West Bank and Gaza, including followers of Fatah, the Democratic Front for the Liberation of Palestine, the Baath party, and the Jordanian Communist party; representatives from labor unions, professional associations, student councils, and women's organizations; intellectuals; merchants, landowners, and peasantry; and leaders of the Islamic religious establishment.[18]

Supporters of the Popular Front for the Liberation of Palestine (PFLP) did not join the PNF. The PNF goal of establishing a West Bank–Gaza Palestinian state clashed sharply with the Popular Front's basic tenet of liberating all of Palestine through armed struggle.[19] Popular Front supporters felt that the 1973 October war had not brought a fundamental change in the regional balance of power that would favor the realization of Palestinian national rights. Nevertheless, the Popular Front coordinated its activities and political stands with those of the PNF's central committee,[20] and followers of the Popular Front maintained close ties with the PNF.

All of the political forces in the ranks of the Palestine National Front were expected to honor and implement its political program. Yet individual factions could broaden their separate power bases in the occupied territories.

The two main themes of the PNF's political program and activities between 1973 and 1977 were resistance to Israel's military occupation and the assertion of a distinct Palestinian national identity.[21] The founders described the program as both revolu-

17. Dakkak, "Back to Square One," p. 75.

18. Lesch, *Political Perceptions*, p. 53. See also Isam Ahmad al-Fayiz, *The Hashemite Regime: National Rights of the Palestinian People* (in Arabic) (Beirut: Ibn Khaldun, 1974), pp. 111–12.

19. Lesch, *Political Perceptions*, p. 57. See also Faisal Hourani, *Palestinian Political Thought, 1964–1974: A Study of PLO Basic Documents* (in Arabic) (Beirut: Palestine Liberation Organization Research Center, 1980).

20. Dakkak, "Back to Square One," p. 76.

21. For the text of the Palestine National Front's political program, see *Al-Hadaf*, September 29, 1973.

tionary and realistic. They were convinced that attention could be paid simultaneously to the immediate concerns of the Palestinians and to their long-term national aspirations. The program combined resistance to Israel's military occupation with diplomatic efforts rather than armed struggle as the means to achieve the more limited Palestinian political objectives.

The revolutionary part of the program underlined the need to step up local Palestinians' opposition to Israel's military occupation. It was hoped that protests would bring about withdrawal of the Israeli army from the West Bank and end the policy of land expropriation and construction of Jewish settlements. The program also advocated a strengthened West Bank local economy, with safeguards against the flow of Israeli agricultural and industrial products. It addressed the need to preserve a separate Palestinian national identity and cultural ethnicity and to defend Islamic holy places in Jerusalem and elsewhere in the West Bank.

POLITICAL ACTIVITIES.   Followers of the PNF argued that the struggle against Israel should not be limited to military means and they confined their actions to passive resistance. They did not hesitate to defame local collaborators, spell out political demands, publish statements, distribute leaflets and petitions, and speak out on political issues. And they asked the local populace to hold strikes, demonstrations, and sit-ins to protest land confiscation and construction of Jewish settlements.

During the 1973 October war, PNF leaders unsuccessfully appealed to West Bank workers to boycott employment inside Israel.[22] Following the war, the organization's passive resistance activities became more frequent and visible. In December the front called on workers not to participate in the Histadrut elections (Israel's labor federation),[23] an appeal that was heeded. A similar appeal was made to Jerusalem businessmen and merchants to abstain from paying Israeli taxes.[24]

22. "Let Us Contribute to the War of Liberation" (in Arabic) (leaflet, October 14, 1973).

23. Lesch, *Political Perceptions*, p. 54; "No, We Will Not Vote" (in Arabic) (leaflet, December 19, 1973).

24. Dakkak, "Back to Square One," p. 76; "Let Us Not Pay Taxes to the Zionist Bandits" (in Arabic) (leaflet, December 24, 1973).

In March 1974 the front published a statement in support of a strike by Palestinian prisoners in Israeli jails. In the same month, PNF activists invited five hundred dignitaries from the West Bank and Gaza Strip to a conference in Jerusalem organized to protest Israel's policy of demolishing houses, administrative detention, imprisonment, deportation, and land expropriation.[25]

Front activists were determined to frustrate all political initiatives that would not realize Palestinian national rights of self-determination and statehood. Article 3 of the program spoke of the front's resolve to frustrate all "conspiratorial plans" aimed at "liquidating the Palestinian cause." The front played a leading role in the civil disobedience in the fall of 1975 and winter and spring of 1976 protesting the Allon Plan, which envisaged returning sizable portions of the West Bank to Jordan, and the Civil Administration Plan of Israeli Defense Minister Shimon Peres, a federation proposal that promised West Bank and Gaza Palestinians jurisdiction over their civilian affairs but left finance, security, and foreign policy in the hands of the Israeli army.[26] Mayor Hilmi Hanoun of Tulkarm summarized the PNF's objection: "Civil administration in the shadow of occupation is against our interest. We do not think about civil administration but about complete [Israeli] withdrawal from the occupied lands."[27]

The PNF used West Bank organizations to marshal opposition to the Civil Administration Plan. And in the 1976 municipal elections its leaders worked to bring into office pro-PLO politicians who would resist the introduction of civil administration.

SUPPORT FOR THE PLO.   In opposing King Hussein's interest in restoring Jordan's sovereignty over the occupied territories, the front's political program acknowledged the PLO as the sole legitimate representative of the Palestinians and underlined the right of the organization to speak in the name of the PNF in any peace talks. In October 1974, PNF leaders forwarded a petition signed by 180 West Bank and Gaza Strip dignitaries to the Arab Summit Conference in Rabat proclaiming the PLO as the sole legitimate

25. Lesch, *Political Perceptions*, p. 57.
26. Ibid., pp. 65–66.
27. *Al-Fajr*, October 26, 1975, quoted in ibid., p. 67.

representative of the Palestinian people—an act that strengthened the PLO's case against Jordan.

The PNF regarded itself as an integral part of the Palestinian and Arab national liberation movements and urged the PLO to consolidate its ties with progressive Arab regimes and the socialist camp. The revolutionary aspects of the PNF's program won it political legitimacy and popular support in the occupied territories and helped reinforce the PLO's diplomatic gains internationally. Yet the PNF's most salient contribution lay in its realistic approach to finding a solution to the Palestinian question. Leaders of the PNF believed the restoration of Arab pride and fighting honor during the 1973 October war furnished a golden opportunity to realize Palestinian national rights through diplomatic means. In a letter to the PLO's executive committee in early December 1973, they urged the PLO to participate in the proposed Geneva conference and to support the 1947 United Nations partition plan.[28] In early 1974 a PNF delegation again appealed to the executive committee, warning that the PLO's failure to participate in the peace conference would only allow Jordan to reestablish its claim of sovereignty over the occupied territories. They reminded PLO leaders that the Arab countries would acquiesce to Jordan's new role and that the PLO would be isolated internationally, thus jeopardizing its right of representing Palestinian national interests.

The PNF's central committee appealed to the PLO's executive committee to formulate a policy within the realm of what was possible, not what ought to be. It urged PLO leaders to make use of the emerging international consensus favoring a diplomatic solution to the Palestinian question. The front also demanded that the formation of a Palestinian state in the West Bank and Gaza Strip be accepted by the various PLO factions and that international Arab support for such a state be solicited.

The front reminded the PLO leaders that most of the world

28. On the front's political attitudes, see the Palestine National Front's letter to the PLO's executive committee, December 1, 1973, reprinted in *Journal of Palestine Studies*, vol. 3 (Spring 1974), pp. 187–91. See also "Guidelines on the Road" (in Arabic) (leaflet, December 12, 1973); "Landmarks on the Road" (in Arabic) (leaflet, January 1974); Dakkak, "Back to Square One," p. 77; Lesch, *Political Perceptions,* pp. 57–58.

community did not support the objectives of either liberating all of Palestine or dismantling Israel. On the contrary, they recognized Israel's right to exist and therefore would not support its destruction. Such immutable facts warranted Palestinians' both lowering their political expectations and abandoning their maximalist demands. Advocacy of extremist positions, they argued, would only help to perpetuate Israel's occupation of the West Bank. The PLO had won its diplomatic gains in the mid-1970s only after the organization had shown an interest in a political solution to the Palestinian question. Thus, the PNF appealed repeatedly to the PLO to coordinate its activities with Egypt and Syria, as well as the other Arab countries.[29] It urged, once again, a pan-Arab solution to the Palestinian question.

The PNF leaders, wary of the PLO's objective of liberating all of Palestine, were convinced that the formation of a West Bank–Gaza Palestinian state would help end the state of belligerency between Israel and the Arab countries and Israel's aggressiveness. An era of cooperation and mutual understanding between Israelis and Palestinians could ultimately lead to the creation of a secular democratic state for both Jews and Arabs in Palestine. Such an outcome could be brought about—if at all—only through the use of peaceful means on both sides.

The PNF's views on the solution of the Palestinian question appeared more realistic, less dogmatic, and less rigid than those of the PLO in the mid-1970s (eventually the PLO adopted a similar stand). Undoubtedly, the hardships of living under occupation accounted for the more realistic political demands and expectations of West Bank Palestinians. But the pragmatic approach of the PNF also mirrored the political preferences of the communists, the most influential political force within the front. For instance, the PNF's advocacy of a two-state solution for the Palestinian-Israeli problem was a translation of the communists' long-held political position. The abstention of hard-line groups, particularly the Popular Front, also meant that the PNF could take a pragmatic stand.

Formidable obstacles stood in the way of implementing the

29. Joint Arab action in the imposition of the oil embargo and in the military coordination between Cairo and Damascus had revived pan-Arab sentiment among the West Bank elite and populace.

front's program. Not only Israel's opposition to PNF tactics and goals, but PLO threats undermined the front. Initially, both the PLO and the PNF were inclined to explore diplomatic options and to coordinate their activities with those of the Arab countries. A PNF statement of early January 1974, for instance, pointed to complete coordination with the PLO.[30] The PNF's political pragmatism reinforced the position of the emerging moderate stream in the PLO. The front was instrumental in generating popular support and political legitimacy for the PLO in the occupied territories and among the Arab countries.

And the PLO in the summer of 1973 had endorsed the formation of the PNF.[31] In an interview with the Egyptian weekly, *Ruz al-Yusif*, on April 8, 1974, Arafat spoke highly of the front's resistance to Israel's occupation and asserted that the PNF was an integral part of the Palestinian "revolution." In early 1974, the PLO's executive committee at the request of a PNF delegation accepted eight of the front's deported members into the Palestine National Council.[32] That acceptance recognized the PNF's desire that at its next two sessions the Palestine National Council endorse the idea of forming an independent Palestinian state in the occupied territories.

THE PLO'S OPPOSITION.   But the honeymoon was short-lived, as a struggle for power and political control developed between the PLO and the PNF. The struggle revolved around whether the PNF was a political extension of the PLO in the occupied territories or a rival institution. The front's physical location inside the territories presented a considerable challenge to the PLO's long-term leadership, as Palestinian allegiance and loyalty to the PLO might be challenged. The problem was compounded by the PLO's efforts to consolidate its leadership and expand its power base and popularity in the occupied territories.

The PLO's executive committee faced the question of whether PLO activities in the occupied territories should be filtered exclusively through the PNF or through other channels as well. How large would the various political groups that made up the front be, and what political weight would each of them have? Would the

30. "Landmarks on the Road."
31. Interview with Yasir Arafat in *Filistin al-Thawrah*, August 1, 1973.
32. Dakkak, "Back to Square One," pp. 76, 97n.

PNF be governed by the same regulations and rules of consensus-building that controlled the PLO's operations? And should the PLO limit the PNF's initiative and autonomy?

The communists' preeminence within the PNF—their control of its activities and their quest for more independence and assertiveness—heightened the PLO's fear that the front could evolve into an independent power center. The PLO's executive committee worried that the communists would use the PNF to advance their interests at the expense of Palestinian nationalist objectives. The PLO's anxieties were not unfounded. After all, it was the communists who had formulated the PNF's political program and were in charge of its publications and policy statements. The communists also claimed to have control over 60 percent of the front's rank and file. In addition, communist-front organizations such as labor unions and student councils played a leading role in the PNF's activities.

Under communist influence, the PNF began to demand that West Bank political preferences and interests have a direct bearing on the formulation of PLO policies. And the PNF demanded a more effective role for West Bank Palestinians in PLO councils as well as the incorporation of a communist representative in the PLO's executive committee.[33] The PNF further requested that it be the only political link between the occupied territories and the PLO and the only channel of West Bank views and interests.

The constellation of suspicions and perceived challenges to the PLO's executive committee caused it to limit the autonomy and degree of initiative of the PNF and to constrain the PNF's policy-making powers. In 1975 the Palestine Central Council (an intermediate political organ between the executive committee and the Palestine National Council) requested that the PNF confine its activities to issuing pro-PLO statements. And the PLO's executive committee requested that the PNF's literature be prepared outside the occupied territories, with the PNF responsible only for its distribution in the West Bank and Gaza Strip. Thus the PLO came to view the PNF as no more than an organ in the occupied territories for implementing the resolutions and directives of the PLO's political councils.

33. Ibid., pp. 78, 90–91.

COLLAPSE OF THE PNF.   Inside the PNF, Fatah leaders accused the communists of trying to establish an alternative leadership in the occupied territories. They held that because of communist control, the PNF did not represent the prevailing social and political forces in the West Bank and Gaza. Eventually, they charged the communists with responsibility for the downfall of the PNF.[34]

The communists, for their part, accused the PLO's right wing, Fatah, of causing the collapse of the PNF. They alleged that the PLO had become interested in the occupied territories only after its diplomatic gains in the mid-1970s. It had then tried to strengthen its power by sowing seeds of dissension and conflict in the ranks of the PNF. And because of the "conservative nature" of its right wing, the PLO had aligned itself with pro-Jordanian traditional politicians and had worked to contain both leftists and communists by encouraging the formation of an alliance among West Bank moderate mayors.[35]

The communists saw the PLO executive committee's reluctance to endorse the front's political programs and the media blackout on PNF activities as evidence of the PLO's hostility to the PNF. The hostility, they believed, arose from fear that the PNF could become a rival institution in the occupied territories. But, the communists pointed out, it was the front's activists who in 1974 had pushed hard for the designation of the PLO as the sole legitimate representative of the Palestinian people. And they argued that, contrary to Fatah's charges, the PNF was a comprehensive organization that incorporated various political and social forces in its ranks, including communists—something the PLO's executive committee did not do.

The communists attributed the rise of the right wing in the PLO to Fatah's increasing reliance on conservative Arab regimes for its financial and political survival. The result was the transformation of the PLO into a representative of the status quo. And

34. For the arguments and counterarguments concerning the collapse of the PNF, see "Symposium: Issues of National Struggle in the West Bank and Gaza Strip" (in Arabic), moderated by Bilal al–Hassan, *Shuun Filistiniya*, September 1981, pp. 45–77, which presents the views of representatives of Fatah, the Popular Front, the Democratic Front for the Liberation of Palestine, and the Palestine Communist Organization. See also Dakkak, "Back to Square One," pp. 76–80, 90–91.

35. "The Rise and Evolution of the Palestinian Revolution and the Mission of Resistance during the Transitional Phase" (in Arabic) (pamphlet, 1981).

the PLO's rift with Syria in the Lebanese civil war in the mid-1970s had pushed the organization further into the "Arab reactionary and Western imperialist camp."

The PLO's slippage into the "imperialist camp" was seen as dangerous because the PNF opposed any political solution to the Palestinian question that might result from Western mediation. It preferred that any non-Arab initiative be a joint venture between the West and the Soviet Union. Thus, in its final communiqué, issued on March 3, 1977, the PNF expressed utmost concern over the mounting "hostility" of Palestinian and Arab "reactionaries" to the Soviet Union and leftist forces in the occupied territories.[36]

Another contributor to the PNF's collapse in 1977 was the loss of the sense of optimism and confidence that had been generated by the 1973 October war. The Geneva Peace Conference had not evolved into a viable tool for solving the Palestinian question—the conference had never gone beyond its first session. Nor had the PNF's hopes for a comprehensive settlement of the Arab-Israeli conflict through collective Arab action materialized—Egypt was moving rapidly in the direction of reaching a separate, unilateral political arrangement with Israel, while Syria, the PLO's staunchest ally, was moving against the Palestinians in the Lebanese civil war. The weakening of the PLO's effectiveness and the demoralization of the West Bank urban elite were blows to the front's existence.

But a central factor in the collapse of the PNF was the continuing loyalty of the political forces in the front to their external custodians. Rather than giving primary allegiance to the front, the PNF's four principal components—the communists, the followers of Fatah, the Democratic Front, and the Baath party—were consistently faithful to their political patrons within the Palestinian nationalist movement.

Israel's opposition and restriction of the PNF's political activities dealt a heavy blow to the PNF's overall effectiveness, vitality, and leadership. Despite the fact that the PNF's political program did not call for the destruction of the Jewish state or the pursuit of military struggle to realize Palestinian national rights but advocated a political solution, the Israeli military authorities regarded PNF activists and followers as radicals and the front's activities as a

36. Dakkak, "Back to Square One," pp. 77–78.

threat to "security" and "public order." On December 10, 1973, the Israeli government deported eight prominent PNF leaders (the mayor of Al-Birah, three communists, three professionals, and one member of the Islamic Supreme Council). The harassment of PNF members in 1974 included the arrest of more than one hundred and fifty members in May and over three hundred by July. On November 4, four PNF leaders were deported for their role in drafting the petition asking the Arab Summit Conference in Rabat to proclaim the PLO as the sole legitimate representative of the Palestinian people and on November 21, five more were deported.[37]

Had the PNF been permitted to operate freely, it might have become a forceful representative of the interests of West Bank Palestinians. The front enjoyed widespread popularity and political legitimacy in the occupied territories. It encompassed varying political opinions and social forces, and its agenda reflected the political needs and wishes of the West Bank Palestinians. The comparatively realistic and pragmatic terms of its political program were aimed at a quick end to Israel's military occupation through diplomatic means.

Throughout its existence, from 1973 to 1977, the Palestine National Front operated as a pressure group urging PLO leaders to adapt their goals and tactics to the exigencies of the post–1973 October war era. Front leaders were keen on communicating West Bank political interests and demands to the PLO and on incorporating those interests in PLO policies. The PNF's advocacy of diplomacy over any military option to realize Palestinian interests and its goal of establishing a West Bank–Gaza state were precursors of the PLO's eventual diplomatic flexibility. The PNF served as a lobby that prompted the PLO to regard the occupied territories as one of its primary constituencies.

The political demise of the PNF was associated with a diminution of political activity in the occupied territories. The decline in political activity in part reflected the deteriorating power position of the PLO following the outbreak of the Lebanese civil war of 1975–76 and Syria's intervention in that war against the Palestin-

37. Lesch, *Political Perceptions*, pp. 56, 58, 60. For a narrative account of the suppression of West Bank nationalists, see Felecia Langer, *Those Are My Brothers* (in Arabic), trans. Esam Abasi (Jerusalem: Salah al-Din, 1976), pp. 31–38.

ians. After the municipal elections in April 1976, the mayors, with their popular mandate and pro-PLO orientation, assumed center stage in West Bank politics.

Politicization of the Municipalities

Israel's decision to retain the structure of the municipalities and to allow elections to take place in 1972 and 1976 gave high political visibility to holders of municipal office. In the absence of rival political institutions, municipal office became the highest political post in the West Bank. Municipal council members, and particularly mayors, assumed new political roles, articulating the interests of their townsmen and presenting these interests before the military government.

The traditional municipal responsibilities (supervision of financial affairs, city planning, providing services for the citizens) were superseded by more pressing claims. Securing visitors' permits for relatives from Jordan and the Arab countries, speeding up the processing of requests for family reunions, and interceding on behalf of the families of political prisoners and owners of confiscated land became the local politicians' principal duties. The mayors, singly and collectively, issued statements denouncing Israel's excessive policies in the occupied territories and called on the local populace to demonstrate and strike.[38] As Western governments and even Israelis increasingly looked on the mayors as representatives of West Bank interests in any peace talks, the political significance of the municipalities grew.

THE 1976 ELECTIONS.   The decision of the Israeli government in the fall of 1975 to conduct the municipal elections on time, in the spring of 1976, is perplexing. It was a period of increased diplomatic gains for the PLO as well as growing Palestinian nationalist sentiment and support for the PLO's objectives. The Israeli

38. Osama Shahwan, *Municipal Services in the West Bank* (in Arabic) (Jerusalem: Abu Arafeh Agency, 1980); Maoz, *Palestinian Leadership*, pp. 119–26; Muhammad Nazzal al-Armouti, *The Citizen's Guide* (in Arabic) (Amman: Jordanian Government Publication, 1955); Emile A. Nakhleh, *The West Bank and Gaza: Toward the Making of a Palestinian State* (Washington, D.C.: American Enterprise Institute, 1979), pp. 9–15.

decision was not, however, haphazard or accidental. Israeli poli-
cymakers may have intended to reduce the momentum generated
by the PLO's political gains. The confirmation by the Arab countries
of the PLO as the exclusive representative of the Palestinians and
the granting to it of observer status at the United Nations General
Assembly were alarming developments for Israel. Such unwelcome
events could possibly be neutralized by promoting an indigenous
and authentic Palestinian leadership. Disturbed by the prospect of
an international peace conference in which the PLO would be a
participant, Israel may have authorized the elections to deflect
attention from the PLO. In 1975 Israel's defense minister, Shimon
Peres, proposed a widened range of responsibilities for West Bank
municipalities and limits on the military government's intervention
in their civil affairs. This was to be the precursor of autonomous
regions in the West Bank and Gaza Strip.[39]

By the mid-1970s, West Bank proponents of Palestinian autonomy had lost much of the limited power they had once enjoyed.
Thus the Israeli government, for the success of its civil administration scheme, had to cultivate the cooperation of members of
the new nationalist elite. The 1976 municipal elections could help
to do that.

To show the liberal nature of Israel's rule over the West Bank,
the Israeli Labor government may have felt compelled to allow
elections to take place in 1976. When the Israeli government
amended Jordan's municipal law of 1955 to allow women and
propertyless men to vote, the number of eligible voters rose from
31,746 in 1972 to 88,462 in 1976.[40]

Still another explanation for the authorization of the 1976
elections could have been the hope expressed by some Israeli
officials that new municipal leaders would confine themselves to
administrative activities. This objective was particularly important
since the post–1973 October war period had witnessed the emergence of a new pro-PLO nationalist leadership. New leaders in 1976
might help in calming the local populace following the popular
uprising that had erupted in the fall of 1975.

---

39. Lesch, *Political Perceptions*, pp. 65–66; Maoz, *Palestinian Leadership*, pp. 122,
134.

40. Maoz, *Palestinian Leadership*, pp. 133–36; Lesch, *Political Perceptions*, pp. 71–
74.

The PLO's attitude toward municipal elections was a change from its opposition in 1972. Indeed, the leadership of the mainstream PLO tacitly consented to candidates participating in the elections. The mounting wave of strikes and demonstrations and the new elite's strong pro-PLO and Palestinian nationalist sentiments may have convinced PLO leaders that the elections would bring pro-PLO figures into office. They certainly seem to have been confident that rival politicians would not be elected. On the contrary, the elections would enable a defeat of the conservative pro-Jordanian incumbents, a move that would erode Jordan's political influence among West Bank Palestinians and politicians.

Not all of the PLO's factions took a conciliatory attitude toward the 1976 elections. The Popular Front for the Liberation of Palestine, the Popular Front–General Command, the Popular Struggle Front, and the Arab Liberation Front, all opposed the elections and urged potential candidates and voters not to participate.[41] The rejectionists' arguments for a boycott were identical to those they had produced in 1972.[42] The rejectionists were critical of the communists and other members of the Palestine National Front for their willingness to go along with the elections.

Jordan's attitude toward the 1976 municipal elections was one of ambivalence—understandably so at a time when the political influence of its followers was at a low ebb, while support for the PLO was on the rise. The Jordanian government attacked Israel's amendment of the municipal law as a violation of international law;[43] the amendment, of course, allowing propertyless men and women to vote in the elections, would not serve the interests of the traditional politicians. Faced with the inevitability of holding the elections, Jordan first tried to promote the idea of having uncontested elections, thus keeping the incumbents in office. Having failed to do that, the Jordanian government resumed its financial aid to the municipalities in order to support the election campaign of its followers.

41. On these rejectionist factions, see Helena Cobban, *The Palestinian Liberation Organisation: People, Power and Politics* (Cambridge University Press, 1984), pp. 139–67.

42. For further reaction to the 1976 elections, see *Filistin al-Thawrah*, April 25, 1976; for rejectionists' arguments, see *Al-Hadaf*, April 17 and May 8, 1976.

43. *Jerusalem Post*, April 9, 1976.

In contrast to the hesitation and apathy with which the West Bank urban elite had received the 1972 elections, in 1976 they exhibited a firm resolve both to contest and to win the elections. Opposition to the elections was mostly confined to followers of the Popular Front and pro-Jordanian politicians. The latter group favored the retention of the incumbents, as they appeared to have the most to lose if elections were to be held.

VICTORY FOR THE NEW URBAN ELITE.   Thus in 1976 a majority of the West Bank urban elite were openly in favor of the elections. They called for the formation of nationalist blocs to contest the elections and urged citizens to vote. As several mayors pointed out later, the PLO had given advance approval to their decision to run.[44] They were not encroaching on the PLO's role of representing Palestinian interests but aiding in the consolidation of PLO political gains in the occupied territories and in stepping up resistance to Israel's military occupation. As the mayor of Anabta, Wahid al-Hamdallah, remarked: "We participated in the elections so as not to give the opportunity for the nonnationalist elements to take over the municipalities. I do not believe in giving priority to the pavement of streets over the problems of my nation."[45]

This politicization of the 1976 municipal elections accounted for the fact that 577 candidates, compared to 337 in 1972, contested the 205 municipal seats. With few exceptions—notably the mayor of Bethlehem, Elias Freij—the 1976 elections constituted a major victory for members of the new nationalist elite. Roughly 75 percent—153—of the seats were won by new members, and 14 of the 24 mayoral positions.[46]

The elections consequently marked the climax of the political ascendancy of the new elite and the ideological reorientation of the West Bank populace. The new council members publicly professed their loyalty to the PLO and advocated the formation of an independent West Bank–Gaza Palestinian state. Support for Jordan was rarely uttered in public after this time. The pro-Jordanian traditional elite, with its political influence at a record

44. Interviews with the author in December 1982.
45. Interview, December 12, 1982.
46. Maoz, *Palestinian Leadership,* p. 136.

low, began to identify with the PLO and to regard the PLO as its sole legitimate representative.

The victory of the new nationalist elite came as a great disappointment to those Israelis who had hoped that the new mayors would act independently. For despite their overwhelming mandate, the mayors emphatically asserted that the PLO alone should perform the role of speaking for the West Bank.[47] The victory of the new politicians therefore reinforced the PLO's role of representing Palestinian national interests and simultaneously promoted the West Bank and Gaza Strip to the position of one of the PLO's major constituencies.

The elections did even more, for they indicated that the politically powerful were lawyers, engineers, doctors, pharmacists, teachers, workers, and farmers, not just businessmen and landowners. And the majority of municipal council members elected in 1976 were much younger and better educated than those elected in 1972— 10 percent were below the age of thirty, 57 percent between the ages of thirty and fifty. Twenty-eight percent of those elected had a university education, and over 25 percent a high school education, whereas the comparable figures for the 1972 elections were 10 percent and 25 percent, respectively, and in 1972, 65 percent of the council members elected had not had a high school education. Finally, 40 percent of those elected in 1976 were white-collar workers in various professions while 40 percent were businessmen and merchants and 20 percent farmers and landowners.[48]

What distinguished the municipal council members elected in 1976, particularly at the level of mayor, from traditional West Bank politicians was their strong attachment to Palestinian nationalism and the PLO, as well as their educational achievements. The mayors came from the same well-to-do and socially prominent families in their towns that had always provided leadership.[49]

47. Such views were emphasized by the mayors immediately after their election, in interviews in both Israeli and West Bank Arabic dailies.

48. Maoz, *Palestinian Leadership*, pp. 135–37.

49. Karim Khalaf of Ramallah was a lawyer, Bassam al-Shaka of Nablus held a bachelor's degree, Fahd al-Qawasmah of Hebron was an agronomist, Ibrahim al-Tawil of Al-Birah was a pharmacist, and Muhammad Milhim of Halhoul also had a university education. See Yehuda Litani, "Leadership in the West Bank and Gaza," *Jerusalem Quarterly*, no. 14 (Winter 1980).

THE MAYORS AS LEADERS.   With the demise of the PNF, the role
of the new mayors was significantly enhanced. Their strength was
based not only on their popular mandate but the recognition of
their legality by Israel, Jordan, the PLO, and many members of
the international community.

Encouraged by their wide-based support, the new mayors did
not conceal their nationalist sentiments and support for the PLO.
Their approach, however, was confined to passive resistance and
protest. None of them advocated the use of violence against the
Jewish state. Rather, they issued political statements and sent
petitions to both Arab and Western countries, as well as to the
United Nations' secretary general, to protest Israel's practices in
the occupied territories and to promote Palestinian national interests and the PLO's representation of those interests. For example,
in September 1976, mayors of leading West Bank towns sent a
memorandum to the Arab League protesting Syria's intervention
in the Lebanese civil war against the PLO and Jordan's support of
Syria's role. On January 31, 1977, the mayors forwarded a petition
to the U.S. secretary of state, Cyrus Vance, calling not only for a
quick end to Israel's military occupation but for the formation of
a West Bank–Gaza Palestinian state. A month later, the twenty-
four mayors jointly appealed to the thirteenth session of the
Palestine National Council to authorize the PLO to participate in
an international peace conference and to endorse the formation
of a West Bank–Gaza Palestinian state.[50]

Despite their involvement in politics, however, the mayors
repeatedly asserted that they would not assume any role in
representing the interests of West Bank Palestinians. That was the
exclusive preserve of the PLO. Their task was to mobilize the local
populace behind the PLO and to bring an end to Israel's occupation
as soon as possible.

At the local level, the mayors frequently issued statements
condemning Israel's restriction on freedom of the press, closure
of universities and schools, demolition of houses, deportation,
construction of settlements, and land expropriation, and the Jewish
encroachment on Islamic holy places in Hebron and Jerusalem.
In August 1976, for instance, the mayor of Nablus declared a

50. Lesch, *Political Perceptions*, pp. 79–87.

strike to protest Israel's imposition of the value-added tax on West Bank businesses and several other major West Bank towns followed suit. The mayors also successfully protested Israel's declared intention of deporting the mayor of Nablus in the fall of 1979 and the actual deportation of the mayors of Hebron and Halhoul in May 1980.[51]

The mayors went beyond their own protests, sending messages and petitions to local groups inciting them to initiate strikes, demonstrations, and sit-ins. These moves were aimed both at Israel's excessive policies and at undesirable Arab and international diplomatic initiatives. In these activities, the mayors closely coordinated their moves with the representatives of professional associations, labor unions, student councils, and women's organizations. They used West Bank Arabic newspapers, particularly *Al-Fajr, Al-Shaab,* and *Al-Talia,* to publicize and circulate their political ideas and statements. And to gain international recognition and support for Palestinians' position, the mayors made themselves accessible to the foreign press and newsmen and visited Arab and Western capitals.

Like the PNF, the mayors succeeded in having the occupied territories recognized as one of the PLO's main constituencies and served as a channel for West Bank preferences and demands to the organization. Both Jordan and the PLO made the mayors responsible for distributing economic aid among West Bank towns and villages, a role that provided them with political influence among their followers. Often the mayors performed a mediating role, reconciling opposing nationalist groups and institutions, particularly at the student level.

The National Guidance Committee

The 1974–76 period marked the zenith of Palestinian nationalism among the West Bank urban elite and populace alike. The two years following the 1976 municipal elections were relatively quiet. Yet two distinct lines of political thought became discernible

51. Rafik Halabi, *The West Bank Story,* trans. Ina Friedman (Harcourt Brace Jovanovich, 1982), pp. 109–66; Lesch, *Political Perceptions,* pp. 19–20, 80; Maoz, *Palestinian Leadership,* pp. 140–75.

among the West Bank urban elite and in particular among the mayors.

One group of West Bank mayors was dedicated to avoiding a confrontation in their dealings with Israel. These pragmatists included Fahd al-Qawasmah of Hebron, Hilmi Hanoun of Tulkarm, and the pro-Jordanians Elias Freij from Bethlehem and Rashad al-Shawwa from Gaza. All four appreciated the value of maintaining close ties with the Jordanian regime and they did not oppose United States involvement in the resolution of the Palestine question. On the contrary, they underlined the vital role the U.S. government could play in finding a credible solution to the Arab-Israeli conflict. These mayors welcomed President Carter's spring 1977 reference to the right of the Palestinians to a homeland and viewed it as an encouraging sign. Moreover, the president's remarks encouraged some of the politicians to meet with American diplomatic emissaries to the region.

In keeping with their pragmatic posture, the mayors did not initially oppose President Anwar Sadat's trip to Jerusalem in November 1977. The mayors of Bethlehem, Gaza, and Hebron, as well as several prominent politicians from Nablus, praised the Egyptian president's courage and vision. Burhan al-Jabari of Hebron and others led small delegations to Cairo to express their support for Sadat's diplomatic initiative.[52]

A second group of mayors consisted of a coalition of leftists led by Karim Khalaf of Ramallah and Bassam al-Shaka of Nablus that was supported by followers of the Popular Front, the Democratic Front, the Baath party, and the communists. They projected a hard-line position on the major issues related to the Palestinian question. They were unwilling to cooperate with the military authorities because they were committed to generating political support for the PLO, wanted to resist Israel's military occupation, intended to obstruct American-sponsored diplomatic initiatives, and sought to arrest Jordan's influence in the occupied territories. They refused to meet with American envoys to the region and denounced those West Bank politicians who did. This hard-line group described President Carter's reference to a Palestinian

52. Halabi, *West Bank Story*, pp. 178–80; Lesch, *Political Perceptions*, pp. 91–92.

homeland as insincere and deceptive; they were convinced that the U.S. government was unable or unwilling to play an objective role in the resolution of the Palestinian problem.

Similarly, this group of mayors criticized Fatah's leaders both for initiating a limited reconciliation with the Jordanian government in early 1977 and for forming a joint Jordanian-PLO economic committee two years later. Fatah's growing economic and political reliance on Saudi Arabia also disturbed them. From the beginning, these politically inflexible leaders opposed Sadat's political initiative, describing it as untimely and ill planned, since it failed to coordinate with both the PLO and Syria.[53]

The clear divergence in the political stands of the pragmatic and hard-line camps became blurred by the late 1970s. A constellation of political developments between 1977 and 1979 ended the period of relative calm and political inactivity, creating an environment where the two groups began to share similar views. At this time the National Guidance Committee was formed, and with it politics came back to life.

The National Guidance Committee (NGC) was essentially a West Bank response to the policies of the Likud government. The coming to power of the Likud-led coalition in 1977 marked a change in Israel's official outlook toward the West Bank and Gaza Strip. The territories were no longer seen as occupied but as liberated and inseparable parts of the historic Land of Israel. The Israeli prime minister, Menachem Begin, sought to materialize his ideological and religious stands through land expropriation and intensification of Jewish settlements in the West Bank's hinterlands. Israel's policies narrowed the differences between pragmatic and hard-line politicians in the West Bank and deepened their anti-Israeli sentiments.

The signing of the Camp David Accords in September 1978 furnished the NGC with the immediate task of orchestrating the West Bank's opposition to the accords. An overwhelming majority of the urban elite viewed the conclusion of the accords as a denial of their national rights and a sellout by Egypt of the Palestinian

53. Dakkak, "Back to Square One," p. 83. See also Lesch, *Political Perceptions,* pp. 91–95.

cause. The opposition of Jordanians and the PLO to the accords helped to create an anti–Camp David consensus among Palestinians in the occupied territories.

Political activists joined the committee to check Jordan's efforts to revive its influence in the West Bank. In 1978 the Jordanian government opened passport offices in a number of towns. It then became the PLO's partner in distributing the financial assistance to West Bank institutions and politicians that had been allocated by the Arab Summit Conference in Baghdad. West Bank militants saw those moves and the evolving dialogue between Fatah and the Jordanian government as jeopardizing the 1974 resolution at the Rabat conference that had designated the PLO as the sole legitimate representative of the Palestinian people.[54]

The spark that led to the formation of the National Guidance Committee was a large political rally convened in Jerusalem on October 1, 1978, to discuss the signing of the Camp David Accords. With the notable exception of the pro-Jordanian mayors of Bethlehem and Gaza, the rally was attended by most West Bank mayors and representatives of professional associations, labor unions, women's organizations, and youth movements. Conferees recommended the formation of a committee to orchestrate West Bank opposition to the accords. On November 4, when the National Guidance Committee was formed, members decided to conduct their activities in the open and confine them to the political realm, away from violence.[55]

The National Guidance Committee was not designed to reflect the political weight of various PLO factions. Its composition did not reflect strict ideological interests and platforms save the opposition of members to the Camp David Accords and their support of the PLO. Twenty-three members of the committee represented

54. The National Guidance Committee and the ill-fated attempt to revive the PNF in 1979 were embarked on by West Bank leftists in part to institutionalize their interests against those of Fatah and Jordan. It was the political preeminence of the hard-line politicians in the NGC that accounted for Fatah's initial ambivalence and Jordan's boycott of the committee.

55. Discussion of the National Guidance Committee is based principally on my interviews with NGC members and other West Bank politicians in December 1981, July, August, and December 1982, and January 1983. For views of the mayors of Hebron, Ramallah, Nablus, Tulkarm, Bethlehem, and others, see *International Herald Tribune*, March 13, 1979; *Maariv*, March 12, 1979; *Davar*, March 14, 1979.

organized corporate and geographic interests.[56] Ten of the members displayed political leanings toward the PLO's mainstream Fatah, four were ardent supporters of the PLO's rejectionist camp, and four were communists. Only four members exhibited pro-Jordanian tendencies.

In 1979 there was an attempt to increase Jordan's influence within the NGC. It was suggested that Mayors Freij of Bethlehem and al-Shawwa of Gaza and the former governor of Jerusalem, Anwar al-Khatib, join the committee—a move rejected by the NGC. Because the Jordanian government disapproved of the committee's composition, it did not deal with the NGC as a collective body but did cooperate with several of its members individually. Pro-Jordanian politicians criticized the NGC and its work and accused it of dividing West Bank Palestinians. To improve their own precarious position, they established contacts with PLO leaders, including a meeting between Arafat and the mayors of Bethlehem and Gaza and the prominent politician from Nablus, Hikmat al-Masri.

Although the NGC was a large organization, its power was exercised by an inner committee of six.[57] Communists attempted to create local committees in different West Bank towns but had only partial success, in contrast to towns like Ramallah and Bethlehem where they had a strong presence and were well organized.

Several of the hard-line leaders in the NGC complained that many members were unwilling to engage actively in its operations. Some wanted to ensure the flow of financial assistance from Jordan.

---

56. The National Guidance Committee included eight mayors: al-Shaka of Nablus, Hanoun of Tulkarm, al-Hamdallah of Anabta, Khalaf of Ramallah, al-Tawil of Al-Birah, al-Sati of Jericho, al-Qawasmah of Hebron, and Milhim of Halhoul; three journalists: Mamoun al-Sayid, editor of *Al-Fajr*, Akram Haniyah of *Al-Shaab*, and Bashir al-Barghuthi of *Al-Talia*; women represented by Samiha Khalil; Dr. Amin al-Dajani representing welfare societies; representatives of the student movement, chosen annually but always including the president of the Bir Zeit University student council; Adil Ghanim representing the labor unions; Ikrima Sabri representing the Islamic Supreme Council; Dr. Haidar Abd al-Shafi and the lawyer Zuhair al-Rayis representing the Gaza Strip; Ali al-Taziz and Said Ala al-Din representing the business community; and representing professional associations, Ibrahim Dakkak of the engineers' union, Jiryis Khouri of the lawyers' union, and Azmi al-Shuaibi from Al-Birah of the dentists' union.

57. Among the more active were the mayors of Nablus, Ramallah, Al-Birah, Halhoul, and Hebron.

Others, like the representatives of welfare societies, were keen on preserving a good working relationship with the Israeli authorities in order to facilitate the rendering of humanitarian services to the local population.[58]

Because so many members of the NGC were token supporters, the inner committee was able to issue statements, send petitions, and call for strikes and demonstrations in the name of the National Guidance Committee. The inner committee was instrumental in convening four large popular rallies in the fall of 1978 to protest the signing of the Camp David Accords and Israel's policies in the occupied territories.[59] It saw to it that West Bank institutions, municipalities, worker and youth movements, and the PLO took part in the protests.

National Guidance Committee members jointly and singly worked for rejection of the accords on a number of grounds. The accords, they maintained, failed to provide for the Palestinians' national rights of self-determination and statehood or to address the issues of the PLO's representation of Palestinian interests, the future of Israeli settlements, and the status of East Jerusalem. The accords' treatment of the West Bank and Gaza Strip as a separate issue from the rest of the Palestinian question was unacceptable to West Bank politicians and leaders. They were particularly angered by the proposal that Egypt, Jordan, Israel, and the United States be empowered to determine the future of the occupied territories and that the choice of Palestinian representatives be confined to residents of the West Bank and Gaza Strip, thus excluding outside Palestinians.

Members of the committee believed that the autonomy plan proposed by the Camp David Accords would only legitimize and perpetuate Israel's control over the West Bank and Gaza Strip.

58. Interview with NGC member, December 22, 1981.
59. The NGC declared a strike on March 11, 1979, to protest President Carter's visit to Israel, and in early January 1980 it called on leaders in the occupied territories to boycott Sol Linowitz, the U.S. diplomatic envoy to the region. On February 25, 1980, it called on West Bank Palestinians to go on strike to protest the exchange of ambassadors between Israel and Egypt. It issued statements protesting construction of settlements, land expropriation, closure of universities and schools, and other Israeli practices. Al-Fajr, January 19 and February 2, 1980, February 28, 1982; Al-Shaab, November 23, 1979, January 16, February 25, and March 18, 1980.

Their conclusion was understandable. Israel's prime minister, Menachem Begin, had asserted that his government would claim the right of sovereignty over the West Bank and Gaza Strip following the five-year transitional stage, and his definition of autonomy did not include Palestinian control of land and water resources. Begin confined the autonomy to the right of the Palestinians to administer civilian affairs. The Camp David Accords' allocation of a role for Jordan in the resolution of the Palestinian question also angered committee members; an overwhelming majority opposed it.[60]

DISSENSION IN THE NGC.   The NGC managed to provide effective leadership for West Bank Palestinians until the spring of 1980. From then until it was outlawed in March of 1982, its capacity to provide viable institutional leadership to the local populace was severely curtailed. The multiplicity of political groups and opinions within the NGC made it virtually impossible for the committee to project a united stand and effective leadership on anything other than opposition to Israel.

Behind the facade of national unity, the hard-line politicians, followers of Fatah, and pro-Jordanian politicians vied for control of the committee. Their struggle for power weakened the overall effectiveness of the NGC. Each group believed that the committee was being used by its rivals to advance their influence at the expense of the other political forces.

Leftist politicians, particularly the communists, complained that the committee served as a political alliance for the pro-Fatah mayors and Jordan's followers, whose aim was to contain the political influence of the leftist forces. The leftists accused the moderates of being reluctant to pursue a confrontational approach in their dealings with the Israeli military government and charged them with being primarily concerned with promoting their own business interests, preserving close contacts with Jordan, and maintaining a workable relationship with Israel.[61] The communists

60. For a comprehensive study of the West Bank reaction to the Camp David Accords, see Lesch, *Political Perceptions*, pp. 4–23; Halabi, *West Bank Story*, pp. 122–30; Maoz, *Palestinian Leadership*, p. 177. For Begin's administration plan, see *Jerusalem Post*, December 29, 1977.

61. Interviews with NGC members, December 22, 1981, August 9, 1982.

contended that the moderate leaders were opposed to the formation of local national guidance committees because the committees might diminish their influence in their towns. In the communists' opinion the presence of moderate politicians within the NGC was preventing the committee from taking a more militant posture toward Israeli military authorities.

Leftist criticism of Fatah's followers was primarily motivated by considerations of power, for Fatah followers were beginning to make headway in controlling student councils and labor unions and in forming mass organizations (especially labor unions) independent from communist control. The left also criticized Fatah leaders for initiating a dialogue with the Jordanian government and for creating the Joint Jordanian-Palestinian Economic Committee. At the instigation of leftist politicians, the NGC sent a memorandum to the PLO's executive committee expressing its reservation over Jordan's participation in the joint committee.[62] The leftists also warned Fatah leaders not to encourage their supporters in the West Bank and Gaza to meet with American diplomats. Indeed, it was leftist leaders' pressure that led moderate members of the NGC and pro-Jordanian politicians to refrain from meeting with U.S. diplomats.

Leftist politicians also accused Fatah leaders of strengthening the position of conservative politicians by providing them with financial assistance. They complained that while Fatah was generous in its treatment of conservative politicians, requests for financial aid made by leftist mayors and politicians were delayed and in some cases refused.

Hard-line politicians did not have a monopoly on criticism. The leftists' leadership of the National Guidance Committee was disturbing to the PLO's mainstream and its followers. Identification of West Bank leftists with the PLO's rejectionist camp gave greater political weight and legitimacy to those factions not only within the PLO but among West Bank–Gaza Palestinians. A coalition of this sort confronted Fatah with a serious rival in the PLO's political councils and could undermine its efforts to widen its power base and legitimacy in the occupied territories. Moreover, as the hard-

---

62. *Al-Watan,* April and June 1979; *Al-Talia,* May 17, August 16, and December 3, 1979.

line leaders gained strength in the National Guidance Committee, they began to assert greater independence and autonomy.

The PLO's executive committee, in a variety of ways, tried to contain the influence of the left.[63] Fatah leaders encouraged the formation of a coalition of moderate mayors who disagreed with the leftists' suggestion that the West Bank mayors collectively resign in protest to Israel's intention of deporting Mayor Bassam al-Shaka of Nablus. Fatah's reluctance to sanction collective resignations was prompted by a desire to maintain its political position among the majority of West Bank mayors.[64] Moreover, with Jordan's support Fatah succeeded in having Anwar Nusseibeh appointed chairman of the board of the East Jerusalem Electric Company rather than Karim Khalaf, the candidate of the hard-line politicians. Similarly, PLO leaders did not share the anxiety and hostility of West Bank leftists to Jordan's opening of passport offices in West Bank towns.[65]

Leaders of the hard-line camp also failed to stop Fatah followers being assigned a majority of seats in the newly created Council on Higher Education in the West Bank. In response to leftist charges that the PLO had embarked on a rapprochement with Jordan, Fatah and its supporters in the occupied territories argued that the PLO's only aim was to ensure that King Hussein's government would not accept the Camp David Accords. Fatah leaders sought to cultivate the support of key pro-Jordanian politicians, arranging Arafat's meeting with the political leaders of Bethlehem, Gaza, and Nablus. And Fatah used the Joint Jordanian-Palestinian Economic Committee to extend generous assistance to the Hebron municipality, whose mayor was Fatah's main pillar within the National Guidance Committee.

REACTIVATION OF THE PNF. The struggle between Fatah and the hard-line politicians reached a climax over an attempt to reactivate the Palestine National Front. An eight-member committee representing the Popular Front, the Democratic Front, the Baath party, and the communists in 1979 undertook the task of reactivating the PNF and writing its political program. The leftists

63. Halabi, *West Bank Story*, pp. 120–21.
64. *Filistin al-Thawrah*, November 19 and December 10, 1979.
65. *Al-Talia*, August 3, 1980; Dakkak, "Back to Square One," p. 87.

wished to revive the front because they strongly disagreed with Arafat's growing tendency toward political moderation and were dissatisfied with the performance of the National Guidance Committee.[66] They favored establishment of a clandestine political organization that would take a militant stand against the Camp David Accords and increase resistance to Israel's military occupation. One of the hard-line leaders noted the "urgent need to develop more effective techniques than the ones used by the National Guidance Committee in order to neutralize the impact of these alarming political developments [the Camp David Accords and the signing of the Israeli-Egyptian peace treaty]."[67]

Proponents of the PNF indicated that the National Guidance Committee was not a substitute for but an instrument of the PNF and that the NGC program should be shaped by that of the PNF.[68] The PNF of 1979, like the PNF formed in 1973, included a limited number of Fatah followers. Again the communists played a prominent role in drafting the political program, but their positions were more militant in 1979 than in 1973. The 1973 PNF had had no representation from the Popular Front, but two Popular Front followers were members of the eight-member preparatory committee in 1979. In sharp contrast to the first PNF, the 1979 front projected a more militant posture than the PLO in the political programs it endorsed and in a memorandum it sent to the PLO's executive committee.

The PNF's political program firmly opposed the Camp David Accords and the autonomy plan. It was equally opposed to Egypt's unilateral peace treaty with Israel and to King Hussein's plan for a United Arab Kingdom. All of these plans, the PNF held, shared the objectives of "liquidating the Palestinian question," restoring Jordan's influence in the occupied territories, stripping the PLO of its right to represent Palestinian interests, and weakening a West Bank–Gaza indigenous leadership.[69]

The program asserted that the reemergence of the PNF would

66. "The Rise and the Evolution of the Palestinian Revolution and the Dictates of the Struggle in the Present Phase" (in Arabic), *Al-Mustaqbal*, November 1979; *Al-Hadaf*, October 19, 1979.

67. Interview with NGC member, December 12, 1982.

68. Interviews with NGC members, July 30 and December 12, 1982.

69. *Al-Hadaf*, October 19, 1979.

provide a framework for the restoration of Palestinian national unity in the occupied territories that would obstruct the implementation of "liquidationist" solutions. Its reemergence would ensure adherence to those particular Arab and United Nations resolutions that acknowledged Palestinian rights of national self-determination, statehood, and attachment to the PLO. The PNF program also called on all Palestinians to desist from opening any dialogue with the United States or meeting with its representatives to the region.

Leaders of the PNF argued that the PLO's relations with other Arab countries should be based on those countries' respect for Palestinian national interests and their support of the PLO, without discrimination against particular factions. Syria, Iraq, and the PLO should be urged to establish a united front to obstruct the implementation of the autonomy plan, and PLO leaders should be asked to solidify their ties with the national liberation movements in third world and socialist countries.

To set the PNF's relationship with the PLO on a proper path, PNF leaders sent a memorandum to the PLO's executive committee that defined their position on relations with the PLO and on the PLO's relations with Jordan. The PNF leaders requested that their organization be the PLO's sole political instrument in the occupied territories and that the PLO cease dealing with all other organizations, institutions, and persons in the West Bank and Gaza Strip. The PLO's cessation of "suspicious contacts" would restore national unity to the occupied territories and preserve the PLO's political credibility and legitimacy. The PNF leaders demanded that the PLO deal directly with the front, without intermediaries, and that the PLO executive committee regularly inform the PNF of adjustments in its political program and its dealings with Arab countries and members of the international community.

In return, the front would abide by the PLO's political program and defend the organization's status as exclusive representative for the Palestinian people. The leaders promised to routinely provide the PLO's executive committee with reports on political developments in the occupied territories and the needs of the local populace.

The PNF's leaders called on their counterparts in the PLO's executive committee to correct their relationship with the Jordanian regime. The leaders were absolutely opposed to the Joint Economic Committee, which gave Jordan partnership, power sharing, and participation in economic decisionmaking. They considered the PLO's acceptance of Jordan's partnership a political concession that enabled the Jordanian government to dominate the committee and use its financial resources to rebuild its influence in the occupied territories. Front leaders demanded that Jordan's role be confined to coordination. They insisted that Jordan publicly reiterate its commitment to the 1974 Arab League resolution designating the PLO as the sole representative of the Palestinian people. And they requested that Fatah's power monopoly of the Joint Economic Committee come to an end, and that all PLO factions and Palestinian political forces be represented inside the committee.

Front leaders also criticized the PLO for agreeing to link West Bank institutions and organizations, including the departments of health, social welfare, agriculture, and education, with their counterparts in the East Bank. They demanded that the PLO rescind the agreement since it would make West Bank institutions subservient and vulnerable to Jordan's pressures.

As a sign of protest, PNF leaders boycotted the Joint Jordanian-Palestinian Economic Committee. Mayors Khalaf of Ramallah and al-Shaka of Nablus and several others made private contact with countries in the Persian Gulf and North Africa to raise funds for their municipalities. In its memorandum, the PNF stated that once the membership of the joint committee was changed and Jordan's role reduced, the PNF would not only cooperate with the PLO but use its economic plans for the development of the occupied territories.

REJECTION OF THE HARD-LINE POSITION. Fatah leaders, not surprisingly, rejected the PNF's political program. Reactivation of the PNF would only give political backing to the rejectionist faction in the PLO and widen its power base and political legitimacy in the occupied territories. Fatah leaders, preoccupied with building power centers and creating mass organizations for themselves, were not interested in sustaining the emergence of a rival institution or channeling activities and operations inside the occupied territories through noncomformist intermediaries.

Under Fatah influence, the PLO's executive committee concluded that the PNF's political program contradicted that of the PLO and reflected the political stance of hard-line factions. The executive committee insisted that only its own political program should prevail in the occupied territories.[70]

The struggle for power between the PLO and the hard-line politicians never centered on the goals or the leadership of the PLO. Leftist leaders' commitment to the PLO as the sole legitimate representative for the Palestinian people was unwavering. Their dissent reflected larger political differences within the Palestinian nationalist movement—between those willing to explore the diplomatic option and those who insisted on pursuing military struggle with Israel before resorting to the political option, or between those who believed that cooperating with Jordan improved the prospects for terminating Israel's military occupation and those who continued to distrust the Jordanian regime and refused to depart from the goal of establishing an independent Palestinian state.

While debate over the attempt to revive the PNF was going on, the Israeli military government discovered that the plan existed. The plan was aborted when the military government threatened politicians working to reactivate the PNF with deportation and imprisonment should they fail to halt their activities.[71]

Israel's Policy toward the New Elite

Israel's policy toward the West Bank political elite after the 1976 municipal elections determined, to a considerable extent, the elite's involvement in politics. Two competing approaches within Israel's political and military apparatuses affected the degree of the urban elite's engagement in politics.

One approach was somewhat tolerant of political activity in the West Bank. The main proponents of this "liberal" approach were

70. See the views of Majid Abu Sharar, a Fatah central committee member, in "Symposium: Issues of National Struggle"; Samih Samarah, "The West Bank and the Debate of the Inside and the Outside" (in Arabic), *Shuun Filistiniya*, December 1980, pp. 3–9; *Al-Hadaf*, March 13, 1981.

71. *Jerusalem Post*, October 11, 1979; *Maariv*, October 14, 1979; *Al-Quds*, October 12, 1979; *Al-Fajr*, October 13, 1979.

Israel's defense ministers Shimon Peres of the Labor party, from 1974 to May 1977, and Ezer Weizman of the Likud coalition, from 1977 to 1980. Both hoped that the West Bank's new elite, particularly the mayors, would evolve into independent political leaders, outside PLO control. The signing of the Camp David Accords in the fall of 1978 made the presence of an indigenous leadership urgent. Most Israelis viewed the PLO as an unacceptable partner, while Jordan would not negotiate under the accords without Palestinian participation. Weizman decided to allow the National Guidance Committee to operate to encourage its members to become Israel's partners in the talks on autonomy.

At the initiation of this permissive approach, West Bank municipalities and institutions were allowed to receive outside financial aid from Arab and Palestinian sources. And West Bank mayors were not discouraged from traveling to Arab countries to solicit economic aid for their towns. Moreover, the Israeli government did not prevent the National Guidance Committee, despite its pro-PLO political stands, from convening a number of popular rallies in the West Bank and Gaza Strip in October and November of 1978 to express its attitude toward the Camp David Accords.[72]

Yet, at the same time that Weizman was trying to foster a viable local leadership from among the new West Bank political elite, another group was working to limit the mayors' powers by creating a rural-based leadership. That group came from military government circles and was led by Menahem Milson, a professor of Arabic literature at the Hebrew University who had been an advisor to the military government on Arab affairs from 1976 to 1978 and would later (1981–82) serve as West Bank civilian governor. Milson argued that the mayors were incapable of providing an independent leadership for the occupied territories because of their subservience to the PLO. He proposed that an alternative leadership be created from the conservative politicians in the towns and rural areas and that the local population be encouraged to seek favors from them.[73]

72. Maoz, *Palestinian Leadership*, pp. 180–81, 194; Lesch, *Political Perceptions*, p. 13.
73. Menahem Milson, "How to Make Peace with the Palestinians," *Commentary*, May 1981, pp. 25–35; Cobban, *Palestinian Liberation Organisation*, pp. 176–77; Maoz, *Palestinian Leadership*, pp. 198–203.

Advocates of Milson's approach proposed to apply pressure on the mayors by limiting municipal budgets, delaying or disapproving municipal development projects, and limiting the flow of financial aid to West Bank municipalities and institutions from abroad. Between 1977 and 1978 the proponents of this approach had several mayors ousted from office on various charges, including the mayors of Yatta, Qabatya, and Beit Jala in the regions of Hebron, Nablus, and Bethlehem, respectively.

The relatively permissive phase of Israel's policy had run its course by the early 1980s and an iron-fist approach had taken over by the summer of 1981. The resignations from the cabinet of Moshe Dayan in October 1979 and Ezer Weizman in May 1980 marked an important turning point; both had helped to restrain the Likud's policy in the West Bank and Gaza Strip. Also by 1980 the momentum generated by Sadat's trip to Jerusalem was waning. The second Likud government took power in the summer of 1981, with Menachem Begin as prime minister, Ariel Sharon as defense minister, Yitzhak Shamir as foreign minister, and Raphael Eitan as the army's chief of staff, all unsympathetic to the permissive approach. The rise of the Gush Emunim settlement movement accelerated the collapse of that approach.

LIMITING LOCAL AUTHORITY.   The effort to limit the authority of the West Bank nationalist leadership began with the deportation of the mayors of Hebron and Halhoul on May 2, 1980, in retaliation for a PLO-inspired attack on Jewish settlers in Hebron, in which six Jews were killed and seventeen others wounded. Three days later, Israeli television announced that the government was endorsing a number of measures restricting freedom of action for members of the National Guidance Committee. On June 2, Israeli settlers tried to assassinate three mayors and succeeded in maiming the mayors of Ramallah and Nablus.[74] In early August, seven of the more active members of the NGC were placed under town arrest. The two mayors in the group were banned from making political statements, attending political rallies, or leaving their towns without advance approval from the military government, and the telephone lines of all seven NGC members were discon-

74. Maoz, *Palestinian Leadership*, p. 193.

nected. The second Begin government tightened restrictions on the West Bank even further.[75]

After Sharon was named minister of defense, municipalities were not allowed to receive financial assistance from abroad, and the amount of money that individuals could bring into the territories from Jordan was reduced to a trickle—500 Jordanian dinars per trip. Such measures were meant to obstruct investment in the economic infrastructure of the West Bank. At the same time, the military government withheld the approval of municipal development projects. Several mayors complained that the restrictions were aimed at eroding their political legitimacy and credibility and making them appear unable to render services to their constituents.

Begin's second government saw the National Guidance Committee as a threat to Israel's security. Its members were held responsible for much of the political turmoil and violence in the West Bank and Gaza Strip. In early March of 1982 the Israeli government outlawed the NGC, and within a few months had ousted eight mayors, including those of Ramallah, Al-Birah, Nablus, Hebron, and Jenin, as well as the moderate pro-Jordanian mayor of Gaza.

The reluctance of the mayors to meet with Menahem Milson, head of the civil administration, was used as an excuse to oust them from office. The mayors justified their refusal on the grounds that their towns were under military occupation and that they should only meet with the military government. Though the civil administration was run by military officers and was under the Defense Ministry, the mayors feared that by dealing with it they would open the way to the imposition of autonomy.

The outlawing of the National Guidance Committee and the removal of the mayors were a severe blow to the West Bank leadership and particularly the hard-line camp. The decrease in the leftists' political weight was apparent in their failure to induce the mayors still in office to resign in protest against Israel's restrictive measures. The leftists contended that collective resignation would

75. Those placed under town arrest were mayors al-Tawil of Al-Birah and al-Hamdallah of Anabta and journalists Haniyah, al-Sayid, and al-Barghuthi, as well as Ibrahim Dakkak, chairman of the engineers' union and secretary of the NGC, and Samiha Khalil, head of the Family Welfare Society in Al-Birah. See Maoz, *Palestinian Leadership*, pp. 195–99.

lead to civil disobedience and escalate tension in the occupied territories. But the mayors were only willing to suspend municipal services for a short time, claiming it was more prudent to continue rendering services to the citizens than to allow Israeli military officers to take charge of their towns. The remaining mayors were in fact moderate and pro-Jordanian and thus reluctant to support their leftist rivals. Their position was bolstered by the stand that the Palestine Central Council took in March 1982 in favor of suspending municipal services rather than collective resignation.[76]

MILITARY ACTION.   Israel's restrictive policy was wide-ranging. The military government closed West Bank universities for several months in 1981 and 1982, increased the censorship of the West Bank Arabic press, banned the circulation of daily newspapers, and placed several West Bank towns under siege for several weeks in the spring of 1982. Under Milson's guidance, military authorities sought to engineer an indigenous leadership in the West Bank's rural areas by setting up six village leagues in the West Bank's main districts.[77]

The village leagues were intended to provide local leaders with whom Israel could negotiate the details of an autonomy agreement. The decision to allow the leagues to have their headquarters in the main towns in their districts was aimed at containing the political influence of the urban elite.[78] Israel's civil administration authority appointed local collaborators to head the leagues in smaller West Bank towns. But Israeli military officers were appointed to the main towns of Ramallah, Al-Birah, Nablus, and Hebron where local politicians refused appointment.

Begin's second government crowned its restrictive policy by intensifying Jewish settlements in the West Bank hinterland. The settlements were put near population centers to ensure that the West Bank and Gaza Strip would not be relinquished or partitioned. This pattern of settlement supported the Likud's ideological belief

76. *Al-Hurriya*, March 29 and April 5, 1982.
77. These leagues appeared in the districts of Hebron, Bethlehem, Ramallah, Nablus, Tulkarm, and Jenin. See Maoz, *Palestinian Leadership*, pp. 199–200.
78. See *Jerusalem Post*, March 19, 1982; Salim Tamari, "In League with Zion: Israel's Search for a Native Pillar," *Journal of Palestine Studies*, vol. 12 (Summer 1983), p. 52.

that the West Bank and Gaza Strip were an integral part of "Eretz Israel." As the culmination of its iron-fist approach, the Likud waged all-out war against the PLO's military infrastructure in southern Lebanon and its political headquarters in Beirut in the summer of 1982.[79]

The imbalance in the political influence of Jordan, the PLO, and Israel in the West Bank grew steadily in the early 1980s. The Likud government's coercive techniques undermined the position of leftist politicians, while the dismantling of the PLO's military bases and political headquarters in Lebanon inflicted losses on the new nationalist, pro-PLO elite. In contrast, Jordan's diplomatic stature was enhanced markedly following the 1982 Lebanon war.

With the shift in power and changes that were taking place in the West Bank and throughout the Middle East, two opposing trends emerged in the West Bank. Among the masses, and particularly young people, an Islamic revival was catching on, while among the urban elite a sense of political realism and pragmatism became discernible (the two trends are investigated in chapters 7 and 8). Both communists and students had a part in undermining the traditional elite's influence and played active roles in politically mobilizing the West Bank mass public. Yet differences between them prevailed. The communists attempted to develop a viable political leadership in the West Bank, while the student movement looked to the PLO for leadership and eventually was manipulated by rival PLO political forces. The students became the strongest pro-PLO force in the occupied territories.

79. For a detailed treatment of Israel's invasion of Lebanon in 1982 and the subsequent expulsion of the PLO's troops from that country, see Emile F. Sahliyeh, *The PLO after the Lebanon War* (Westview, 1986).

CHAPTER FIVE

The Communists' Quest for Leadership

🔳 🔳 🔳

ONE OF THE influential and politically visible groups in the West Bank throughout the 1970s was the communists. Yet the history of the West Bank communists in the years following the 1967 June war offers still another example of the constraints and difficulties that any elite group would encounter in seeking an assertive political position. For a time the communists appeared to be developing the basis for an assertive leadership, working in conjunction with the Palestine National Front and the National Guidance Committee and demanding a participatory role in the policymaking apparatus of the Palestine Liberation Organization (PLO). Through their control of mass organizations, the communists managed to derail the traditional elite from their power position and to broaden the base of West Bank politics.

The communists' party structure, discipline, and ideological indoctrination and their possession of both a core of leaders and rank-and-file followers inside the West Bank provided them with seemingly excellent qualifications to develop a viable indigenous leadership. Yet despite these assets and their willingness to assert themselves politically, the communists never manged to establish a wide base of popular support and legitimacy.

Outside the West Bank the communists encountered opposition from Jordan, Israel, and the PLO in their quest for leadership. Domestically, they ran into a conservative, religiously oriented populace unwilling to allow them a leading autonomous position.

Because of their interest in seceding from the Jordanian Communist party (JCP), the communists embraced the concept of Palestinian nationalism, thus identifying themselves with the PLO. But major differences separated the West Bank communists from the Palestinian leaders outside the occupied territories. Eventually, the communist efforts to mobilize the masses and create internal organizations led to a showdown with the PLO.

Precursors of the Palestine Communist Party

Although an independent Palestine Communist party came into existence in February 1982, the history of communism in Palestine goes back to the early twentieth century.[1] In 1919 a socialist party, consisting of both Jews and Arabs, was established in Palestine. Two years later it disintegrated, but a majority of the communists regrouped as the Palestine Communist party (PCP), which by 1924 had been recognized as the official Comintern section for Palestine. Throughout its existence from 1921 to 1943, the PCP remained an underground organization of Arabs and Jews opposed by both the British mandate government and the world Zionist movement.

Incompatibility between the objectives of Arab nationalism and of Zionism caused conflict in the PCP from the beginning. Jewish immigration to Palestine between the world wars intensified the differences, and in 1943 the party broke into two wings. The Arab wing took the name National Liberation League. The Jewish wing, which had many Arabs in its ranks, later came to be known as the Israeli Communist party.

In 1944, the National Liberation League adopted a political program at its first congress in Haifa. It elected Fuad Nassar, a leading Palestinian communist, secretary general—a post he held for nearly three decades.[2] The conferees rejected the Zionists' exclusivist ideology that envisioned a resolution of the Jewish problem at the expense of the national rights of Arabs living inside Palestine. In the league's opinion, the rights and interests of both

1. See Musa Budeiri, *The Palestine Communist Party, 1919–1948: Arab and Jew in the Struggle for Internationalism* (London: Ithaca Press, 1979), especially pp. 5–7; Maher al-Sharif, *Communism and the Arab National Question in Palestine, 1919–1948: The Nationalist and the Classist in the Resistance Liberation Revolution against Imperialism and Zionism* (in Arabic) (Beirut: Palestine Liberation Organization Research Center, 1981), pp. 55–83; Samih Samarah, *The Communist Activity in Palestine: Class and People Opposing Colonialism* (in Arabic) (Beirut: Dar al-Farabi, 1979), pp. 21–81.

2. For a history of the league, see Budeiri, *Palestine Communist Party*, pp. 153–263; Samarah, *Communist Activity*, pp. 229–310. For a detailed exposition of Fuad Nassar's political views, see Bashir al-Barghuthi, *Man and the Issue* (in Arabic) (Jerusalem: Salah al-Din, 1977).

Jews and Arabs could best be served through formation of a secular democratic state in Palestine.

The league's leaders had to alter that position after the United Nations General Assembly, on November 29, 1947, passed Resolution 181 calling for the establishment of two states in Palestine. Many of the league's central committee members initially opposed the partition resolution, but at the insistence of the league's secretary general, a majority ultimately accepted it. Several articles in *Al-Muqawama al-Shabiya*, the official organ of the league, also endorsed the formation of two separate states in Palestine.

The establishment of Israel in 1948 dealt another serious blow to the league. It divided members living in Israel proper from those living in what came to be known as the West Bank of Jordan. The West Bank members, including the secretary general, sustained the league until 1951, staunchly defending the league's stand in favor of an autonomous state. Thus they opposed the West Bank's incorporation into Jordan and insisted that an independent Palestinian state be created in the areas designated by the partition resolution. While the league suffered from the creation of the state of Israel, it could not support the decision of several Arab countries to send armies to check the new nation's establishment. League members contended that the true motive behind sending Arab troops was to facilitate Jordan's annexation of the West Bank and prevent the creation of a Palestinian state.[3]

The league fell apart, however, because of a basic ideological shift among its own members. The league's central committee moved away from advocating a Palestinian state to accepting Jordan's annexation of the West Bank. The result was that, after the unification of the two banks of the Jordan River in 1950, the National Liberation League was dissolved. In 1951 the Jordanian Communist party (JCP) took the league's place.[4]

With the appearance of the JCP, West Bank communists abandoned their demands for an independent Palestinian state in favor

3. Amnon Cohen, *Political Parties in the West Bank under the Jordanian Regime, 1949–1967* (Cornell University Press, 1982), pp. 27–28.

4. Shaul Mishal, *West Bank/East Bank: The Palestinians in Jordan, 1949–1967* (Yale University Press, 1978), pp. 19–20; Amnon Cohen, "The Jordanian Communist Party in the West Bank, 1950–1960," in Michael Confino and Shimon Shamir, eds., *The U.S.S.R. and the Middle East* (Jerusalem: Israel Universities Press, 1973), p. 420; al-Barghuthi, *Man and the Issue*.

of consolidating ties between Palestinians and Jordanians. Even before the league's dissolution, its central committee had called on the West Bank populace to participate in Jordan's August 1951 parliamentary elections. From then until the early 1970s the communists were committed to the unity of the two banks of the Jordan.

Instead of attending to the needs of the working class, the JCP sought to mobilize the intelligentsia—teachers, journalists, professionals, and students. Its activities were concentrated in Nablus, Ramallah, Jerusalem, and Bethlehem, in the central area of the West Bank. The party lacked support in rural areas, though it was active in West Bank refugee camps.[5]

In 1951, the Jordanian government declared the JCP illegal. This was not surprising, as it had outlawed the National Liberation League in 1949. In spite of persecution, however, the new party introduced slogans such as "emancipating Jordan from Western imperialism" and demanded the granting of civil liberties to the individual, especially the freedoms of the press, speech, and association. In the mid-1950s, along with the Baathists and Nasserites, the communists were major instigators of a wave of demonstrations and strikes in Jordan. After an abortive coup in 1957, however, many communists were arrested and the party's activities were consequently curtailed.

While the JCP remained underground from 1951 to 1967, two trends in party thought were developing. One group, led by Fahmi al-Salfiti, acting secretary general of the party, favored a policy of accommodation with the Jordanian government. That group spoke of positive developments in Jordan's foreign policy. As a sign of his support for the government, al-Salfiti denounced the wave of demonstrations and strikes that broke out in the wake of a 1966 Israeli attack on Al-Sammu village in the Hebron area. The other group, led by Fuad Nassar, the exiled secretary general, was more militant and uncompromising in its stance toward Jordan. The followers of Nassar did not detect any change in Jordan's pro-Western foreign policy.[6]

After the outbreak of the 1967 June war the al-Salfiti group

5. Cohen, *Political Parties*, pp. 29–41.
6. Bashir al-Barghuthi, *A Persistent Fighter against Opportunism* (in Arabic) (Jerusalem: Salah al-Din, 1977).

called on King Hussein to lead "the struggle" to end the Israeli occupation of the West Bank. It also accepted United Nations Security Council Resolution 242 calling for a peaceful settlement of the Arab-Israeli conflict. Under the influence of al-Salfiti, the JCP's political bureau discouraged the communists from engaging in "armed struggle" against Israel. In contrast, Nassar's followers sided with Palestinian commando groups and in 1969 formed Al-Ansar, a military unit that could take part in the "war of liberation." They also denounced al-Salfiti's endorsement of Resolution 242 and criticized him for his failure to side with the PLO in the 1970 Jordanian-Palestinian civil war.

Breaking Away from the JCP

With the outbreak of the 1967 war, West Bank communists lost their leaders, for the occupation not only separated them from JCP headquarters in the East Bank but made direct contact with East Bank communists more difficult. The late 1960s thus marked another low point in the communists' political influence and organization. Growing ideological differences within the JCP created problems for West Bank communists. And the rising popularity of the Palestinian resistance movement following the defeat of the Arab armies in 1967 further alienated those communists living in the West Bank. Thus, shortly after the war, West Bank communists faced three urgent tasks: to reestablish ties with their comrades in the East Bank, to rebuild communist cells at home, and to encourage Palestinians to remain in the West Bank and Gaza Strip.

Early on, several West Bank communists who were attracted by the PLO's strategy of armed struggle engaged in military operations against Israel. However, much of the military influence disappeared when two leading communist activists, Arabi Musa Awwad and Sulaiman Rashid al-Najjab, were deported in 1973 and 1975, respectively. The policy of political struggle then gained strength under the direction of Bashir al-Barghuthi, a Ramallah journalist. During the initial years of occupation, local communists advocated the return of the West Bank to Jordanian sovereignty.

This pro-Jordan communist posture was not surprising, for West Bank communists were accustomed to working through the

JCP. As an integral part of the Jordanian party, they held themselves bound to an official policy that endorsed the West Bank's return to Jordan. Moreover, the Soviet Union's official party line not only accepted Resolution 242 but called on Israel to withdraw from the occupied territories, thereby restoring the West Bank to Jordan. For West Bank communists, maintaining close ties with the Jordanian political opposition seemed essential, especially after the 1970 civil war. Besides, the labor movement had not matured enough to support the establishment of a West Bank communist party. Nor was there any effective political rival to the Jordanian government or alternate source for political allegiance in the West Bank. The PLO had not yet discovered any political significance in the occupied territories.

Given these circumstances, it was logical that the communists would maintain their leaning toward Jordan. Lawyers and engineers, labor union leaders, Christians and Muslims issued statements condemning Israel's annexation of Jerusalem and asserted instead that the West Bank was an inseparable part of Jordan. And the Higher Committee for National Guidance, which had communist representatives, called for the West Bank's return to Jordanian sovereignty and opposed the formation of a Palestinian state.[7]

IDENTIFICATION WITH THE PLO.   Yet in 1973, the communists shifted their position and launched a campaign for the formation of an independent Palestinian state in the West Bank and Gaza Strip and for the recognition of the PLO as the sole legitimate representative of the Palestinian people. The shift of position arose from a desire to be independent from the Jordanian Communist party. Political developments outside the occupied territories also prompted the communists to redefine their position. The separation of the West Bank from Jordan and the prolongation of Israel's military occupation had by the early 1970s prompted a new Palestinian nationalist leadership in the occupied territories to call for the establishment of an independent Palestinian state and to support the PLO. Communists aligned themselves with this group and in the summer of 1973 played a leading role in the formation

7. The Higher Committee had been formed after the 1967 war to lead the resistance against Israel's military occupation.

of the Palestine National Front with its aim of resisting Israel's military occupation, opposing any attempt to return the occupied territories to Jordanian sovereignty, and establishing an independent Palestinian state.

The increasing identification of West Bank Palestinians with the PLO was paralleled by a decline in the political influence of pro-Jordanian forces. To some extent, Israel's opposition to the emergence of pro-Jordanian leaders had brought on the demise of Jordanian influence, but Jordan's reluctance to participate in the 1973 October war had degraded its claims for leadership and recovery of the West Bank.

The political gains and the increasing political legitimacy of the PLO in the Palestinian community and Arab world reinforced the communists' resolve to press for autonomy. The shift in their position to a pro-Palestinian nationalist posture followed a gradual change of the Soviet party line, as Moscow endorsed the formation of an independent Palestinian state in the West Bank and Gaza Strip and recognized the PLO as the legitimate spokesman for the Palestinian people.

Israel's position also supported the communists' interests, for Israel appeared tolerant of their existence—probably from a desire to limit the influence of pro-Jordanian supporters. The Israeli government's concern not to antagonize the Soviet Union also softened its position toward West Bank communists. Israel may have tolerated the West Bank communists because Rakah, the Israeli communist party, had a large Arab constituency. And the communists' advocacy of political struggle was more acceptable than the military struggle that pro-PLO followers contended was the only viable means for liberating Palestine.

The political reorientation of the West Bank communists can be seen as simply an endorsement of a solution they had remained committed to since the 1940s—an independent Palestinian state. On the other hand, the high visibility of the Palestinian question and the PLO's advocacy of a separate Palestinian identity might have compelled the communists to reconcile their ideological Marxist stands with the tenets of Palestinian nationalism. That sort of shift would parallel their previous ideological adjustments, especially their acceptance of the integration of the West Bank with Jordan.

Moreover, support of Palestinian nationalism gave the communists a way to mobilize mass support in the occupied territories before the PLO could fill the vacuum left by the pro-Jordanians. This drive for autonomy became more urgent when the Palestine National Council endorsed the formation of a national authority in the occupied territories at the 1974 Cairo meeting. The bitter power struggle that ensued within West Bank institutions and mass organizations pitted communists against PLO followers, particularly the supporters of Fatah.

THE NEED FOR SEPARATE IDENTITY. In their demand for greater autonomy from the Jordanian Communist party, West Bank communists argued that they needed control over day-to-day decisionmaking so that they could develop strategies and tactics for resisting Israeli practices in the occupied territories, particularly the expropriation of land. They had to formulate policies for handling the problems of occupation that were quite different from the problems confronting the Communist party in Jordan. Part of their mission was to promote Palestinian steadfastness,[8] and an autonomous status would enable them to unify their ranks with their comrades in the Gaza Strip. The West Bank communists also discerned a growing tendency among JCP central committee members—including the acting secretary general, Fahmi al-Salfiti, and his successor, Faiq Warrad—to accommodate the Jordanian regime.

The Jordanian Communist party, however, opposed the West Bank communists' attempts to establish an autonomous organization. The JCP central committee insisted that such a quest would undermine the viability of the Jordanian party. They further contended that communists on the two banks of the river had been united since 1951 and had common goals. More important, they stressed, West Bank institutions, trade unions, professional associations, and municipalities had close links with their counterparts in East Jordan. In addition, the Jordanian communists believed that the Palestinians' dispersal among several Arab countries would impede the formation of an autonomous communist organization in Palestine.

8. Yaqoub Zaiyaddien, *The Beginnings* (in Arabic) (Jerusalem: Salah al-Din, 1981); Naim al-Ashhab, "The Battle in Search of National Existence," *Problems of Peace and Socialism* (in Arabic) (Moscow), April 1981.

The 1970 civil war between Jordan and Palestinian commando groups convinced the Jordanian communist leadership that party unity must be maintained and the Jordanian nationalist movement strengthened. Similarly, the JCP's unflagging commitment to restoring Jordan's sovereignty over the West Bank, and possibly pressure from the government in Amman, discouraged the party from granting autonomy to the West Bank communists.

THE PALESTINE COMMUNIST PARTY.   Despite the wishes of the Jordanian communists, the West Bank communists established the Palestine Communist Organization in 1975. West Bank communists chose not to break completely with the Jordanian party, however, and maintained their representation in its central committee. In fact, the manifesto proclaiming the founding of the Palestine Communist Organization (PCO) stated that it was a branch of the Jordanian Communist party in the occupied territories. But the new organization appears not to have been subordinate to the Communist party in Jordan. It formed its own steering committee to supervise activities in the occupied territories.

The West Bank communists contacted their counterparts in the Gaza Strip to unify their ranks.[9] But few responded positively, most being apprehensive about the relationship between West Bank communists and the Jordanian Communist party. They demanded formation of an independent party as a prerequisite for unification. The PCO thus served as a prelude to the full-fledged Palestine Communist party, organized in February 1982. Palestinians in Lebanon and Syria formed separate communist organizations in 1980.

In August 1981, the steering committee of the PCO submitted a memorandum to the JCP demanding establishment of a full-fledged Palestine Communist party.[10] Simultaneously, it appealed

9. Members of the National Liberation League in the Gaza Strip cultivated contacts with the Egyptian Communist party when the Gaza Strip was placed under Egyptian jurisdiction after the establishment of Israel. With the dissolution of the Egyptian Communist party in the mid-1960s, the Gaza communists had no political organization.

10. "For the Sake of an Independent Palestine Communist Party and for the Sake of Promoting the Struggle of the Two Brotherly Peoples of Jordan and Palestine" (in Arabic) (pamphlet, August 1981). See also al-Ashhab, "Battle"; Al-Watan (organ of the Palestine Communist party), February 10, 1982.

to a number of Arab and international communist parties to endorse its demand. The committee argued that a separate party would unite Palestinians inside and outside the occupied territories and help establish an independent Palestinian state. Both the accelerated growth of Palestinian nationalism and the PLO's increasing political gains necessitated the creation of an independent party, whereas a continuing partnership with the JCP would not aid the West Bank communists' quest for autonomy. The West Bank communists believed that their integration into the JCP in 1951 resulted from Jordan's annexation of the West Bank.

They contended that their quest for autonomy was consistent with the prevailing trend of each Arab country having its own national liberation movement. An independent West Bank party could formulate its own programs and strategies, mobilize the masses, and enlist support for the Palestinian cause. It would unite communists in the West Bank and Gaza and help propagate communism among Palestinians. All of these things the JCP was incapable of doing because of its location in the East Bank of Jordan. It could not serve Jordanians and Palestinians simultaneously because conditions in the West and East Banks were too dissimilar.

Using Marxist-Leninist arguments, the West Bank communists noted that new socioeconomic conditions had transformed many peasant farmers into a labor force of industrial and construction workers in Israel. A communist party was needed to advance the struggle of the proletariat.

When Faiq Warrad, who had been named secretary general of the JCP, criticized those PLO factions that advocated the liberation of all of Palestine (which he believed was an impossible task),[11] West Bank communists criticized his statements to avoid being outmaneuvered by their pro-PLO rivals. But after the Camp David Accords were signed in September 1978, the political influence of the pro-PLO factions, particularly Fatah, increased noticeably. Their rising fortunes came at the expense of the communists, especially those in the student movement.

It was then that West Bank communists pressed more strongly for their independence. But the Jordanian Communist party

11. *Al-Shaab*, May 15, 1981.

continued to oppose a growing consensus among Arab communist parties in support of the West Bank communists.

The Jordanian communists stressed a "worldwide" rather than a national class struggle. They believed that a Palestinian communist party could come into existence only after the establishment of a Palestinian state and that it would be exceedingly difficult to form a united party because Palestinians were scattered through several countries. A majority of Palestinians held Jordanian citizenship and many lived in Jordan and operated in the Jordanian Communist party, marking a unity between West and East Bank populations that should be preserved.

Palestinian communists in Lebanon also opposed the independence of the West Bank communists. Under Arabi Musa Awwad, they established the Palestine Communist Organization of Lebanon (PCOL) in 1980 as a branch of the JCP. They supported Warrad's stand against the creation of an independent Palestinian communist party. In the PCOL publication *Al-Muqawama al-Shabiya*, they argued that the proposed party was incapable of mobilizing Palestinians in the occupied territories against Israel because it failed to promote military struggle. They criticized the party's political program for excluding the PLO's "strategic" goal of creating a "secular democratic state in all of Palestine" and for emphasizing formation of a West Bank–Gaza state. The proposed party's program neither highlighted the PLO's role in spreading Palestinian nationalism nor acknowledged the presence of the PLO's Marxist-Leninist organizations. And it failed to address the nature of relationships between Palestinians living inside and outside the occupied territories. The PCOL's leaders complained also that they had not been included in the debates on the formation of a Palestinian communist party.

In spite of all the opposition, the PCO steering committee announced the formation of a full-fledged, independent Palestine Communist party (PCP) in the occupied territories on February 10, 1982.[12] Various Arab and international communist parties recognized its legitimacy, including those of Syria, Egypt, Iraq, South Yemen, and the Soviet Union. Even the PCOL eventually extended its recognition and joined the newly formed party (in

12. *Al-Watan*, February 10, 1982.

part because the new party opposed Arafat's dialogue with Jordan and Egypt and his interest in cultivating American support to pursue a solution to the Palestinian question).[13] The PCP also won political backing from the Palestine Communist Organization in Syria.

The Communist-Nationalist Rivalry

The independent Palestine Communist party was never able to secure the dominant and exclusive power position it sought on the West Bank. Rather, the communists in both their activities and their political views were often in conflict with the PLO. The PLO supporters attributed the conflict to the communists' insistence on fusing Palestinian nationalism with international communism. In their view, the communist attitude toward the Palestinian question was determined by considerations of class struggle. The PLO followers were staunch nationalists who believed that the communists' overriding goal was not so much to realize Palestinian national rights as to advance international communism. Such a dual loyalty, they contended, threatened both the national unity and identity of Palestinians and their pan-Arab orientation.[14]

Communists and nationalists differed over the nature of political objectives and the means of attaining goals. The ultimate goal of communists was the establishment of international communism, the creation of a Palestinian state an interim objective. The overall objective of nationalists, on the other hand, was the establishment of a Palestinian state. The communists advocated a Palestinian state comprising the West Bank and Gaza; nationalists insisted on the formation of a Palestinian state in all of Palestine. Occasionally, their differences were bridged, as when the Palestine National Council (in 1977 at its thirteenth session) endorsed the concept of an independent state in the occupied territories. But after the 1982 Lebanon war, Arafat's dialogue with King Hussein on the issue of

13. Ibid., May 15, 1982.
14. On the controversy between the communists and the nationalists, see Munir Shafiq, *A Reply to the Errors of al-Azem* (in Arabic) (Beirut: Palestine Liberation Organization Research Center, 1983); *Red Papers and Critical Notes* (in Arabic) (pamphlet, Jerusalem, 1981); Muhammad Musa Manasrah, *An Open Letter to Beirut* (in Arabic) (pamphlet, January 1981). This section is also based on my conversations with advocates of the conflicting groups.

a PLO confederation with Jordan led to an acrimonious debate in the West Bank over the future of the occupied territories. Many nationalists accepted the confederation plan; the communists remained vehemently opposed to it.

Another point of contention was the perception of the role of the Israeli Communist party. Followers of the communist movement believed that the Israeli Communist party would someday be capable of assuming political authority in Israel. The nationalists were not convinced of that, nor could they accept the communist assertion that the Israeli working class was sympathetic both to a Palestinian national right of self-determination and to the formation of an independent Palestinian state.

The nationalists also rejected the communists' demand that they be given a seat on the PLO's executive committee.[15] The communists complained that, although they had joined the Palestine National Council in 1968, PLO institutions did not yet reflect the political weight of the Palestinian "working class." The Popular and Democratic fronts supported the communists' request for inclusion on the executive committee, but Fatah rejected it. Fatah argued that the communists had consistently underestimated the relevance and significance of the strategy of armed struggle. Yet Fatah clearly feared a redistribution of seats that would enhance the communists' prestige and widen their political influence in the occupied territories.

The strategy of military struggle was itself an issue of great contention. While communists focused on diplomacy, nationalists continued to uphold the relevance of armed struggle despite the shattering effects of the Lebanon war. The nationalists believed that military struggle conferred political legitimacy and respectability on the PLO at the local, regional, and international levels.

The PLO and its factions were convinced that military struggle was the main instrument for liberating Palestine and that political activism in the West Bank and Gaza Strip could undermine that objective. Initially, the PLO showed no interest in the political development of the region, which discouraged the rise of West Bank leaders who might challenge the PLO's exclusive representation of Palestinian interests.

15. *Al-Watan*, February 10, 1982.

By the mid-1970s, however, the PLO had shifted its views. The Palestine National Council at its sessions in 1973, 1974, and 1977 adopted resolutions noting the political significance of the West Bank and Gaza Strip. This shift reflected the rising influence of the Fatah faction following the 1973 October war. And the Arab countries' turn toward diplomacy as a viable means of solving the Arab-Israeli conflict[16] strengthened Fatah's advocacy of an independent state in the West Bank and Gaza Strip as a way of settling the Palestinian problem.

With changing political perceptions in the PLO, the West Bank and Gaza Strip began to assume a pivotal role as the site of a future Palestinian state. Those PLO leaders who were trying to secure a wide base of civilian support for themselves in the occupied territories treated it with a sense of urgency.

Not surprisingly, these political moves were disquieting to the communists. For despite their long-standing position favoring a political settlement, the communists were wary of Fatah's interest. They accused Fatah leaders of seeking a solution to the Palestinian question through both Western mediation and collaboration with "reactionary Arab regimes." Through the Palestine National Front (PNF) they warned against dealing with "imperialists" and urged Palestinians to boycott the missions of American diplomatic envoys to the Middle East.

The PNF's criticism of Fatah and the communists' control of the PNF's publications and policy statements alarmed the PLO's moderate leadership. Fatah quickly diminished its activities in the front and in 1979 objected to communist attempts to revive the PNF.

Both the PLO and the communists had an exaggerated view of communist influence in the Palestine National Front, as the 1976 municipal elections made clear. The communists won only about 15 percent of the contested municipal seats despite an active campaign. The PLO's growing influence thereafter in the municipalities prompted the communists in late 1979 to call for the West Bank mayors' resignations to protest Israel's intention of deporting the mayor of Nablus.

16. This was evident from troop disengagement agreements concluded between Syria and Israel in May 1974 and between Egypt and Israel in 1974 and 1975. In addition, there was the Israeli-Egyptian peace treaty in March 1979.

The communists believed that the PLO's interest in the occupied territories was purely selfish. They asserted that the PLO's political activism was aimed at ending communist influence rather than serving Palestinian interests and resisting Israel's military occupation. Moreover, they contended that rather than promoting unity by attracting new followers to mass organizations and penetrating groups under "reactionary influence," PLO followers were seeking control over organizations and institutions that the communists had been fostering since the 1967 June war. They accused Fatah of ignoring the fact that the communists had taken a lead in mobilizing labor unions and youth movements. They had been the first to recognize the centrality of the occupied territories in the struggle with Israel, and the various PLO factions had only recently recognized the significance of the communists' long-held views.

The effort to rally support among Palestinians had become a gauge of the degree of political involvement of each PLO faction in the West Bank and Gaza Strip. Indeed, the communists held Fatah responsible for the outbreak of divisions within the Palestinian nationalist movement and the weakening of Palestinian national unity and steadfastness.[17]

The main battleground for the bitter struggle between communists and nationalists was the labor unions and student and youth movements. The communists insisted they were the natural custodians for such movements and should organize and represent them, a contention the followers of Fatah bitterly challenged. With the nationalists contending that the PLO alone should represent the interests of the Palestinian working class, the West Bank union movement split into two wings.

The breakup was triggered by a communist attempt to amend by-laws of the Ramallah and Al-Birah labor unions to extend tenure in their executive committees from one to two years. The idea was to give the committees enough time to plan for coordinating their unions' elections with union elections throughout the West Bank. But the Ramallah unions refused and split up. Splits in the unions of other towns followed, culminating in the breakup of the General Federation of Labor Unions.

17. Salim Hikmat, "Problems of National Unity within the Occupied Territories" (in Arabic), *Al-Katib*, February 1982.

Fatah followers argued that annual elections would make the unions' executive committees more responsive to the interests of workers. They felt that a two-year tenure would perpetuate communist control over the labor union movement and preclude any defeat in the elections. The nationalists accused the communists of keeping the size of unions limited to preserve their privileged positions and hegemony and of transforming these organizations into exclusive social and cultural clubs rather than using them to serve the interests of workers.[18]

In response to communist activism in the voluntary work program, Fatah followers formed the youth committees, Lijan al-Shabibah, whose members they encouraged to contest the communists' traditional hegemony in the student councils of Bir Zeit University and other West Bank colleges.

Communist Activities in the West Bank

Except for a short period before 1973 when they were engaged in occasional military operations against Israel, West Bank communists concentrated on the political mobilization of Palestinians in the occupied territories. They were thus a powerful force in the West Bank throughout the 1970s.

The communists were—and still are—more concentrated in towns than in villages, though their influence varied from region to region. Ramallah, Jerusalem, Bethlehem, and Nablus in the central region served as centers of communist activism, as they were more urbanized, cosmopolitan, and secular in their political organization than towns in the north and south. With both Christians and Muslims in their ranks, the communists in these towns were a religiously heterogeneous group. In contrast, communist influence was limited in northern and southern towns where traditional village life was conservative and Islam assumed an important political role.

Rural areas too had a conservative religious orientation and

18. Interview (in Arabic) with Adil Ghanim, secretary general of the pro-communist General Federation of Labor Unions, and Shahadeh Minawi, secretary general of the pro-Fatah General Federation of Labor Unions, in *Al-Shira*, December 1982; Mustafa Jaffal, *The Palestinian Working Class and the Labor Union Movements in the West Bank and the Gaza Strip* (Beirut: Dar al-Jamahir, 1980).

strong traditional values. However, Palestinians in refugee camps—
especially the young—were attracted to the Palestine Communist
party because of poor housing and health conditions and inade-
quate social services in the camps. The fact that many camp
dwellers worked in agriculture, construction, and industry made
the camps a natural milieu for communist activity. And the party's
offer of scholarships for study in the Soviet Union and Eastern
European countries attracted the youth.

The leading role that the communists played in the Palestine
National Front is evident in the assertion that communists or
communist sympathizers made up 60 percent of the front's power
base in the mid-1970s. The PNF not only had the declared aim of
resisting Israel's military occupation but opposed King Hussein's
plan to restore Jordan's sovereignty over the West Bank by a
federation of the occupied territories with the East Bank. To
advance those aims—and communist influence—the PNF proclaimed itself an arm of the PLO in the occupied territories and
recognized the PLO as the sole legitimate representative of the
Palestinian people. The crackdown by Israeli military authorities
in the mid-1970s and the feuding between followers of Fatah and
the communists led to the PNF's decline.[19]

The communists attempted also to dominate municipal government. In the 1976 municipal elections, however, the prestige,
wealth, family links, kinship, and pro-PLO allegiances of the local
politicians limited communist gains. Craftsmen, shopkeepers, merchants, salesmen, professionals, and land and property owners
were unorthodox targets for the communists. Their strength was
at the popular level, in the labor-union movement, professional
associations, women's organizations, and student and youth movements.

THE LABOR UNIONS.   Viewing themselves as the natural protec-
tors of the Palestinian working class, the communists focused their
efforts on unions. In 1969 they reactivated the West Bank General
Federation of Labor Unions, which in the mid-1970s broke away
from its Jordanian-based headquarters and allied itself with the

19. *Al-Ittihad* (published by the Israeli Communist party in Jerusalem), October
5 and 17, 1974.

PLO.[20] By summer 1981, when the federation broke up, it included thirty unions with a membership of 7,000 workers, roughly 5.4 percent of the 130,000-strong West Bank work force.[21] The communists controlled twelve of the unions, which were concentrated in the Ramallah, Bethlehem, and Nablus regions, and shared power in the remainder.[22]

The communists failed to broaden union membership beyond 5.4 percent of the work force in part because workers doubted that the unions could serve and promote their interests; the General Federation did not have enough power either to satisfy their needs or resolve their problems. The 35,000 to 40,000 Palestinians working inside Israel did not join because the unions had no authority to defend their interests against Israeli employers. And the tradition of limiting union membership to certain vocations and geographic regions restricted recruitment—besides, critics charged that communist leaders wanted to ensure their privileged positions in the unions and avoid competition from other pro-PLO factions.[23]

The Jordanian labor law of 1960 was a further hindrance to the labor-union movement. It prevented government employees and members of the bureaucracy from joining unions and gave the Ministry of Labor responsibilities that infringed on those of the unions. The ministry, for instance, could open employment offices to help workers find jobs, and it was encouraged to issue certificates of vocational training and undertake vocational-training programs. Instead of letting unions implement the labor law, the government gave the task to its employees.[24]

Israeli military authorities opposed amending the Jordanian labor regulations in a way that would encourage expansion of unions. They allowed the unions to operate but restricted their recruitment potential and political activities. The military govern-

20. "A History of the Palestinian Labor Union Movement" (in Arabic), *Al-Baiyader al-Siyassi* (1982); Jaffal, *Palestinian Working Class*; Dais Abu Kishk, *The National Reawakening of the Palestinian Trade Union Movement in the Occupied Territories* (in Arabic) (Beirut: Manshurat Al-Wihdah, 1981).

21. Jaffal, *Palestinian Working Class*.

22. Manasrah, *Open Letter*.

23. Jaffal, *Palestinian Working Class*.

24. Mahmoud Abd al-Fattah, "The Labor Union Movement amid the National and Class Struggle" (in Arabic), *Al-Katib*, November 1982.

ment did not allow the General Federation, established after the 1967 June war, to supervise the employment offices that helped workers find jobs in Israel. And it rejected the federation's request that income taxes and deductions for health insurance and social security (from the wages of workers employed in Israel) be transferred to the unions' West Bank headquarters. These funds— 30 percent of workers' total earnings—would have been invested in health and social services.[25]

Israeli military authorities frequently imposed town arrest on union leaders, closed union offices, and refused to permit publication of workers' newspapers.[26] In February 1980, the West Bank military governor issued Military Order 825 (amending Article 83 of the 1960 Jordanian labor law), which attempted to limit the unions' political power by giving the military government the right to interfere in labor-union elections. It excluded from membership in the executive committees those workers who had been found guilty of an offense. And the military government could require candidates to submit their names thirty days before a union election, which gave the authorities time to examine the candidates' records.

The communists attributed workers' limited support of unions to a lack of class consciousness among those from a conservative rural background who continued to maintain strong links to their villages. They also contended that Israel's military occupation and repressive measures caused national concerns to overpower class struggle and consciousness. Labor union leaders thus engaged in political activities rather than attending to the needs of the working class.[27]

Union protests, however, hardly went beyond the issuing of statements condemning Israel's coercive practices in the occupied territories. Appeals to Palestinians working inside Israel to go on strike were rarely heeded, probably because of a lack of confidence in the unions' ability to promote their interests and to offer financial assistance to their families if workers were imprisoned or lost their

25. *Al-Talia*, January 20, 1983.
26. Workers' unions did issue occasional papers such as *Sawt al-Ummal* published by the Ramallah labor unions, *Al-Ittihad* by the Jerusalem electric company workers' union, and *Ittihaduna* by the General Federation for the West Bank labor unions in Nablus.
27. Ghassan Harb, *The Labor Unions in the West Bank and Their Role in Promoting Steadfastness* (in Arabic) (Jerusalem: Arabic Thought Forum, 1981).

jobs. The discord from feuding between the supporters of Fatah and the communists eventually led to the breakup of the labor-union movement.

THE VOLUNTARY WORK PROGRAM.   The voluntary work program, initiated by Bir Zeit University students in 1972, provided yet another route to political leadership. By 1980, the program was so large that it required a central committee to coordinate the activities of 37 branches with 1,200 members in the occupied territories.[28] Two years later, 6,500 volunteers belonged to 96 local committees. And the communists contended that all but 6 of the 192 delegates attending the general congress of the voluntary work committees in 1982 had Marxist affiliations.[29]

Members of the voluntary work program were drawn primarily from West Bank universities, training programs, and high schools. Women participated in programs in the Ramallah, Jerusalem, and Bethlehem regions but not in the northern and southern sections of the West Bank.

Though the program's original aim was to mobilize mass support for the communists, its activities were geared to economic development, including reclamation of 6,000 dunums of uncultivable land.[30] Between 1980 and 1982, voluntary workers planted 34,000 olive and fig trees, investing a total of 76,000 working hours in West Bank–Gaza towns, villages, and refugee camps. Their work was aimed at making it difficult for Israelis to expropriate land in the West Bank. And it helped to meet the dire need for workers in the agricultural sector in the West Bank to replace those who had taken jobs inside Israel. Moreover, the absence of a national government that could implement public projects made the volunteer programs a necessity.

The increasing significance of the work was reflected in the requirement that, before graduation, each Bir Zeit University student work 120 hours in community development. Picking olives became an annual tradition, and art exhibitions and folk festivals developed into program activities.

28. *Al-Katib,* February 1981.
29. *Al-Talia,* August 12, 1982.
30. A dunum is one-fourth of an acre.

STUDENT AND OTHER SPECIAL GROUPS.   Because many students were attracted to Marxism-Leninism, especially at the university and college level, the communists and other Marxist-Leninist groups were able to dominate the student councils for many years, especially during the 1970s. This was particularly true at Bir Zeit and Bethlehem universities. Eventually, however, Fatah supporters pushed the communists into the background.

With the erosion of their political influence on university and college campuses, the communists turned their attention to the high schools. In 1975 they had reactivated the Jordanian Student Union as the Palestine Student Union. This union was active among students in high schools, vocational training centers, colleges, and universities, and from time to time published a newspaper, *Kifah al-Talabah*.[31] In 1981 the communists formed committees of secondary school students to mobilize youth support.

The communists tried to mobilize West Bank women but found their societies and organizations resistant to communist penetration. Women's activities were mainly confined to philanthropic, welfare, and social services and attracted primarily the middle class, where Marxist ideas had little appeal. To mobilize women from lower-income groups, the communists established committees for working women in towns, villages, and refugee camps in the central part of the West Bank. However, competition from other PLO groups and the conservative nature of Palestinian society hindered recruitment of women.

The communists also established youth clubs and sponsored lectures on health, arts, and politics. They had their own newspapers and magazines to communicate communist ideas among the West Bank intelligentsia and youth. The underground *Al-Watan* was their official organ and they occasionally published other newspapers for both students and workers. Between 1972 and 1976, the leading Arabic daily, *Al-Fajr*, had a communist editor-in-chief, Bashir al-Barghuthi. And in 1976 the communists began publishing *Al-Talia*, a weekly Arabic newspaper that developed a high circulation among the West Bank intelligentsia and students. Finally, in 1980 the communists began issuing a monthly literary and political magazine, *Al-Katib*.

31. *Al-Katib*, December 1980.

The Communists' Political Stance

The manifesto that announced the Palestine Communist party's establishment described the party as an organization for the Palestinian "toiling masses" inside and outside the occupied territories. It declared that the party's aim was to unite the Palestinian ranks by creating an alliance of workers, peasants, intelligentsia, students, youth, professionals, and petite bourgeoisie. The party would work to promote Palestinian steadfastness, as well as to resist Israel's military occupation and other "imperialist" plans to dominate the region.

West Bank communists perceived the outside world as composed of an enemy camp of imperialists, Zionists, Arab reactionaries, and Palestinian reactionaries and a friendly camp of third-world national liberation movements, communist parties, progressive and socialist movements, and socialist countries led by the Soviet Union.[32] They urged the PLO to solidify its ties with the friendly camp and warned against establishing close links with the West or conservative Arab regimes. They mobilized Palestinian and Arab workers to help in efforts of progressive Arab regimes to resist the enemy camp. And, following the lead of the Soviet Union, they called for reactivation of the Front of Steadfastness and Confrontation States.[33]

The West Bank communists also formulated detailed positions on immediate and urgent problems confronting the Palestinian people. In spite of their confirmed allegiance to the PLO, and recognition of it as the sole legitimate representative of the Palestinian people, the communists advocated creation of an independent Palestinian state in the West Bank and Gaza Strip. They called on the PLO to recognize Israel and endorse the doctrine of peaceful coexistence between Israelis and Palestinians. They urged PLO factions to modify the Palestine national charter by omitting articles that called for dismantling Israel's political, military, social, and economic infrastructure. Preservation of those

32. This description is drawn from *Al-Watan,* February 10 and May 15, 1982, and *Annual Report of the Palestine Communist Organization, 1979* (in Arabic).

33. The front, launched after the signing of the Camp David Accords in 1978, aimed at checking Sadat's policy of reconciliation with Israel; it consisted of Syria, Libya, Algeria, South Yemen, and the PLO.

articles, they argued, would enable Israel to mobilize world opinion behind its "expansionist" policy in the region.

The communists' position on the formation of a West Bank–Gaza state and recognition of Israel contrasted sharply with the PLO's repeated assertions—particularly among hard-line groups—of the right of refugees to return to their homes and the formation of a secular state in Palestine. Over the years the communists appeared more pragmatic than the PLO. Indeed, they contended that a West Bank–Gaza Palestinian state would help end adverse living conditions not only for the Palestinians in the occupied territories but for Palestinian refugees outside the occupied territories. Such a state would deny Jordan the opportunity of restoring its sovereignty over the West Bank.

The communists' position regarding the resolution of the Palestinian question was in line with Soviet views on the Arab-Israeli conflict, especially the 1980 Brezhnev plan which called for settlement of the Palestinian problem through recognition of Israel, formation of an independent Palestinian state, and the convening of an international peace conference sponsored by the United Nations. The peace conference, West Bank communists suggested, should be attended by both Israel and the PLO, as well as the five permanent members of the UN Security Council.[34] To ensure the safety and security of all states in the region, the communists proposed that international guarantees be offered. Moreover, they suggested that the problem of Palestinian refugees be settled through compensation, repatriation, and resettlement in existing Jewish settlements in the West Bank and Gaza Strip.

Only by implementing the Brezhnev plan, *Al-Watan* stated in its issue of February 10, 1982, could lasting peace in the region and a just settlement of the Palestinian problem be ensured. In line with their insistence on convening a UN-sponsored peace conference, West Bank communists took a tough line toward the Camp David Accords and worked closely with PLO followers in orchestrating opposition to the accords. (The communists' opposition was partly due to the exclusion of the Soviet Union from the conception and implementation of the Camp David agreements.)[35]

34. *Al-Watan*, February 10, 1982.
35. Bashir al-Barghuthi, *Against Camp David* (in Arabic) (Jerusalem: Salah al-Din, 1979).

The communists' advocacy of an international peace conference was entirely consistent with their preference for a diplomatic and political solution over the military option. With few exceptions, they had avoided military operations against Israel, believing that a strategy of armed struggle was an inappropriate tool to end occupation. For them, the military option was the highest form of resistance, an instrument of permanent revolution. They believed that an armed struggle should be based on the principle of popular warfare and that, if it were to succeed, progressive Arab regimes would have to be readily available to provide protection for the fighters. The PLO's sporadic military operations, they believed, could hardly be considered an "armed struggle." They resented the use of terrorism by several PLO radical groups and the launching of military operations against civilian targets. West Bank communists viewed such activities as "signs of despair," both useless and harmful to the Palestinian cause.[36]

Following the formation of the Palestine Communist party, however, the communists began to consider "all forms of resistance" to achieve Palestinian national rights.[37] To allow Palestinian communist groups outside the West Bank to pursue whatever tactics were appropriate, the PCP manifesto had to be broad. Thus Palestinians outside the occupied territories could pursue armed struggle while local communists continued with political struggle.

Changing circumstances, however, were to affect all parties concerned. In the wake of Israel's invasion of Lebanon in the summer of 1982 and mounting military attacks against the Israeli army by Lebanese and Palestinian militias, PCP leaders sought to take advantage of the rising popularity of military options. Having so long advocated diplomacy, the communists were concerned that they not be construed as lagging in the armed struggle. In addition, the PCP had urged the PLO to increase its military operations— perhaps to embarrass Arafat, who was attempting to conclude a diplomatic accord with Jordan. One of the members of the Palestine Communist party's central committee, Naim al-Ashhab, argued that the Israeli army's lack of familiarity with Lebanese terrain and topography made it vulnerable to Palestinian and Lebanese resis-

36. Interview with communist activists, December 4, 1982.
37. *Al-Watan*, February 10, 1982.

tance attacks and that vast quantities of weapons and trained Palestinian cadres were available for the attacks.[38] Escalating military operations and mounting casualties would prompt the Israeli public to exert pressure on its government to withdraw troops from Lebanon.

In all of this there was no indication that the communists themselves engaged in military operations inside the West Bank. The shift in their political stand arose from their displeasure over Arafat's diplomatic moves following his evacuation from Beirut. They were upset by his talks with King Hussein on the issue of creating a confederation between the West Bank and the East Bank of Jordan, and with his quest for Western recognition of the PLO as well as his search for a Western-sponsored political solution to the Palestinian problem.

Further, West Bank communists were opposed both to the Reagan initiative of September 1982 and Arafat's readiness to endorse American solutions to the Palestinian problem. They warned that the PLO's continuing drift into the "imperialist camp" would lead to the breakup of Palestinian national unity. A confederation between the occupied territories and Jordan, they pointed out, would negate Palestinian national rights, violate Arab summit resolutions and Palestinian consensus, and divest the PLO of its status as the sole legitimate representative of the Palestinian people.[39] The communists also condemned Arafat's reconciliation with Egypt in December 1983. And they denounced both the convening of the Palestine National Council in Amman in November 1984 and the February 1985 signing of the Arafat-Hussein Agreement to coordinate diplomatic action. (The agreement envisaged a solution to the Palestinian-Israeli problem based on an exchange of territory for peace, formation of a joint Jordanian-Palestinian delegation, and the confederation of the West Bank–Gaza Palestinian state with Jordan.)

The communists' opposition to the Arafat-Hussein dialogue

38. *Al-Katib*, March 1984.

39. On November 4, 1982, *Al-Talia* published a memorandum signed by representatives of the leftist forces in the occupied territories, including labor unions, professional associations, youth and women's organizations, in which the signatories rejected the confederation plan as well as the Reagan initiative of September 1982.

reflected their fear that the linkage between the occupied territories and Jordan would throw their separate identity in doubt. They were suspicious that the JCP would attempt to reinstate its control over their followers, especially because 70 percent of Jordanian Communist party members were of Palestinian origin.[40] Moreover, they needed to register their discontent that the Arafat-Hussein diplomatic moves had excluded the Soviet Union from the political game. The communists were pleased with the collapse of the Arafat-Hussein dialogue in February 1986.

The communists had strong opinions on the split within Fatah and the rift with Syria and adopted a neutral stance similar to that of both the Popular and Democratic fronts. They urged warring factions within Fatah to stop fighting and resolve their differences through democratic and peaceful means.[41] In addition, they called on Arafat to reform the PLO and appealed to antagonistic factions within the organization to adhere to the resolutions adopted at the sixteenth session of the Palestine National Council in February 1983 and to endorse the reconciliation provisions of the Aden-Algiers Agreement of June 1984.

The communists played down the seriousness of disagreements between Fatah and the Syrian regime and instead urged them to reconcile their differences.[42] They also reminded the PLO leaders of the strategic centrality of Syria to the PLO and argued that Syria was the only remaining Arab confrontation state.

The Future of the Communists

The communists are likely to continue to derive support from the forces that have traditionally been attracted to Marxism—students, the West Bank intelligentsia, and labor unions. In addition, they can be expected to maintain the backing of hard-line PLO groups and their followers in the occupied territories, as long as both share a hostility to Fatah's diplomatic moves. The com-

40. The JCP central committee had never been willing to grant separate identity to the communists in the occupied territories.

41. *Al-Katib*, December 1983. For views of the Popular and Democratic fronts, see Emile F. Sahliyeh, *The PLO after the Lebanon War* (Westview, 1986), pp. 161–63.

42. *Al-Talia*, March 10, August 25, and July 21, 1983.

munists will continue to enjoy financial and cultural assistance from the Soviet Union, including scholarships for students to study in the Soviet Union and Eastern European countries.

But the communists' political influence in the West Bank has been decreasing since the late 1970s. They have encountered concerted attempts by Fatah to reduce their political influence among the people and within political institutions. Not only has Fatah succeeded in limiting communist influence on university campuses, but it has created parallel institutions in the labor union movement and voluntary work programs. The rivalry between Fatah and the communists for control of West Bank institutions has often overshadowed their mutual commitment to resisting Israel's military occupation. Indeed, the struggle continues despite Israel's campaign against all facets of Palestinian nationalism in the occupied territories and abroad. A temporary halt in such competition occurred during the 1987–88 uprising.

Support from PLO hard-line groups has also become tenuous and unstable. Political coordination between the communists and other Marxist groups has mainly been based on their shared opposition to Arafat's diplomatic moves, particularly his dealings with Jordan. The hard-line groups have always opposed the communists' demand to revise the PLO's charter to allow for the formation of a West Bank–Gaza Palestinian state alongside Israel. And because they derive their ideas from Marxism, the PLO's radical groups believe that they are as well qualified as the PCP to lead and represent the interests of the Palestinian work force.

Not only has the communists' political influence been challenged by nationalists at the mass level, but their influence among the West Bank political elite has been limited. The religiosity and conservatism of West Bank Palestinians have not provided a congenial atmosphere for the propagation of Marxist ideas. Nor has the class nature of Palestinian society been conducive to communism, despite the intellectual attractiveness of Marxism to some middle-class Palestinians. The society has neither an industrial working class nor a radicalized peasantry that would feel attracted to communism, and urban Palestinians have middle-class aspirations and a national, rather than class, political orientation. Thus, socioeconomic conditions in the West Bank have worked against the communists.

Their influence has also suffered setbacks from the growing strength of Islam. Advocates of Islam have harbored intense hostility toward the communists, whom they consider their bitter adversary. Moreover, the communists face opposition from the pro-Jordanian conservative political elite who favor the occupied territories' association with the East Bank rather than the formation of an independent Palestinian state. Over the years, communist influence has been truncated by the Israeli military authorities' deportation, town arrest, and jailing of communist leaders and sympathizers.

By the early 1980s the communists' struggle for control of West Bank politics appeared to have been lost to the pro-PLO nationalist forces. From a dominating position during the 1970s, the communists had dropped to a position of competing against two other political forces for control of the occupied territories. These forces were the nationalists and the followers of the Islamic movement; communist losses to them were most obvious in the student movement.

CHAPTER SIX

The Radicalization of the Student Movement

卐 卐 卐

URING MOST of the 1970s the Palestine Liberation Organization (PLO), the most widely accepted repository of leadership among the Palestinians, provided a point of reference and a source of political identification for West Bank students. As the PLO's most ardent and staunchest supporters, students worked to increase the legitimacy of the PLO and to expand its power base. The politicization of the students was accompanied by the broadening of the arena of participatory politics and the drop in the elite's control over politics.

Secular ideologies—Palestinian nationalism and Marxism-Leninism—dominated student thought until the latter years of the decade when political affiliation to Islam became salient among the youth. By the late 1970s, the student movement had become an arena for political struggle among the followers of the secular ideologies and the proponents of Islam. Rival student groups supporting the various PLO factions and their indigenous clients and constituents contended for local political power. Student blocs used their connections with outside groups to turn the political contest in their favor. They also linked themselves with elite groups in the West Bank who shared their political preferences and external ideological affiliations. Students played a crucial role in deciding the outcome of the political struggle among the rival elite groups and between Jordan and the PLO.

The student movement also actively resisted Israeli military occupation of the West Bank. Indeed, the prolongation of Israel's occupation, as well as the deep sense of grievance and deprivation accompanying it, radicalized the student movement and transformed it into a formidable political force.

Early Student Organizations

Before the 1967 June war, two student organizations had been active among West Bank high school students. The General Federation of the Students of Palestine, founded in 1959 and with headquarters in Beirut, was an assembly of smaller student organizations that had been established in the early 1950s in Cairo, Alexandria, Damascus, and Beirut. The largest and most important of these, the Union of Palestinian Students in Cairo, had been founded in 1952; its chairman was Yasir Arafat, an engineering student at Cairo University.[1] In the early 1960s, the General Federation came under the influence of the Arab Nationalist movement led by George Habash, a former medical student at the American University of Beirut. After the PLO's formation in 1964, the General Federation became one of its constituents and was assigned a number of seats in the Palestine National Council.

The influence of the General Federation, however, was marginal among West Bank high school students, as student politics were dominated by the Jordanian Student Union (JSU). The JSU had been established in 1954 as an offshoot of the Jordanian Communist party, with high schools and teacher-training colleges as the backbone of the organization. The JSU was forced to operate underground following the outlawing of the Jordanian Communist party and its front organizations in the 1950s. The JSU was responsible for a wave of demonstrations and strikes that swept through Jordan in the mid-1950s and 1960s. After the Israelis attacked Al-Sammu (a village in the Hebron district) in 1966, in retaliation for a land-mine killing of a number of soldiers, large student demonstrations broke out protesting the Jordanian government's policy of disarming the Palestinians. The Jordanian government subsequently prohibited the Jordanian Communist party and its front organizations, forcing the Jordanian Student Union to operate underground. The Palestinian resistance movement, with its advocacy of armed struggle to liberate Palestine, was a source of inspiration and moral support for the JSU, and during the 1966 demonstrations, students openly professed their support for the Palestinian commando groups.

1. *A Short History of the Palestinian Student Movement* (in Arabic) (pamphlet, 1980).

Aside from such occasional outbursts, the student movement remained subdued. It was unable to formulate a well-defined, effective, and mature political orientation, in part because of the rivalry among political groups—the Baathists, the Arab Nationalist movement, the Muslim Brotherhood, the communists—competing for students' allegiance. In addition, opponents of Jordan's defense and foreign policies used the student movement to protest the regime's actions.

Neither the General Federation of the Students of Palestine nor the Jordanian Student Union was able to provide effective and strong leadership for the student movement. Thus, until 1967, students' activities were sporadic, event-oriented, and reactive only to major political developments.

The situation was completely reversed following Israel's occupation of the West Bank after the 1967 war. The student movement grasped the opportunity to appropriate a leading role in West Bank politics. The change was not immediate but rather developed over the first decade of occupation.[2]

For a number of months after the war, schools were closed. Many student activists fled the West Bank in fear of being arrested by the Israeli army. But despite their fears, high school students took to the streets to protest Israel's military occupation, its introduction of changes in curricula, and the appointment of an Israeli officer to head the West Bank educational system.

After the reopening of the schools in early 1968, the General Federation of the Students of Palestine resumed activities. As part of the Arab Nationalist movement, the General Federation was controlled by the Popular Front for the Liberation of Palestine. The Popular Front's slogans of armed struggle and the Israeli army's losses in manpower and equipment at the Al-Karameh battle in March 1968 in Jordan encouraged some students in the General Federation to engage in military operations against the Israelis.[3] But that activism ended after the severe crackdown on

2. The discussion in this section is based on my conversations in 1982 with activists in the student movement during the late 1960s and early 1970s.

3. In March 1968 the Israeli army engaged the Palestinian commandos in Al-Karameh village in the East Bank in retaliation for the latter's attack on Israeli targets. The Israelis incurred relatively heavy losses in equipment and manpower. This clash, coming on the heels of an Arab defeat in the 1967 June war, boosted

local resistance in late 1969 and the imprisonment of several Palestinian student activists.

The competing Jordanian Student Union also resumed its activity among students soon after the war. By the mid-1970s, it held an unrivaled position of leadership among West Bank students. The General Federation questioned the legitimacy of the JSU as leader, particularly because communists were preserving their political allegiance to Jordan.[4] The Jordanian Student Union often responded to demonstrations and strikes organized by the General Federation with rival demonstrations.

The communists accused followers of the General Federation of lacking political clarity and of engaging in useless acts. The debilitating effects of the civil war in Jordan in 1970 and the obliteration of the PLO's military infrastructure, they contended, had vindicated their argument that military struggle not based on fully mobilized and politicized masses would fail. Leaders of the JSU confined their activities to the political realm and sought to mobilize and politicize the student body, ostensibly delaying student participation in military struggle to a later stage. By refraining from military operations, JSU followers were able to avoid Israel's military crackdown in 1969.

Thus the Jordanian Student Union had unchallenged control of West Bank student politics. Fatah's takeover of the General Federation in the late 1960s did not pose a serious challenge to communist influence among West Bank students because the occupied territories did not figure prominently in the calculations of Fatah's leaders. Fatah's objectives—liberating all of Palestine rather than establishing a West Bank–Gaza state—gave the communists practically a free hand among the West Bank populace, including the student body. And the Jordanian Student Union had a powerful instrument in the scholarships extended by the Jordanian Communist party to West Bank students to study abroad. They provided the JSU with leverage in recruiting students to its ranks.

---

the morale of the Palestinian fighters and the Jordanian army. The event is commemorated annually.

4. The communists' allegiance to Jordan was evident from the fact that until 1975 the name Jordanian Student Union was preserved despite the fact that all student members were Palestinian.

Student activism was low in the three years following the 1970 civil war in Jordan. However, the gloomy political atmosphere inside and outside the occupied territories disappeared after the 1973 October war. Morale began rising with the emergence of the PLO as leader of the Palestinians.

In the fall of 1974 West Bank students waged large-scale demonstrations in support of the PLO. A year later they launched massive demonstrations to protest Israeli Defense Minister Shimon Peres's plan to introduce a civilian administration in the West Bank. In the spring of 1976 hundreds of students took to the streets and a number were killed protesting Israel's confiscation of Arab property in Galilee.[5]

With the 1975 establishment of the Palestine Communist Organization, the Jordanian Student Union was renamed the Palestine Student Union (PSU). This was consistent with the communists' quest for autonomy from the Jordanian Communist party. After the change, the PSU published an occasional newspaper, *Kifah al-Talabah*. It also became a member of the parent General Federation of the Students of Palestine.

The establishment of autonomous communist institutions on the West Bank coincided with the appearance of student activism at the university and college level. Several universities were opened, student bodies expanded, and student councils and student committees formed, which eclipsed the political activism of secondary schools. Moreover, the introduction of the political views of the different PLO factions undermined the communist hegemony over the student movement. Indeed, university student councils assumed such a strong political role that in 1980 the communists suspended the activities of the Palestine Student Union, only one year after they had issued a political program for the union.

By the mid-1980s, university students were no longer the leading activists in the student movement. Youth from the middle and high school levels frequently initiated violent demonstrations and strikes. The decrease in economic opportunities following the oil slump of 1982–83 contributed to student unrest. The increasing political involvement of the youth opened new opportunities for

5. Ann Mosely Lesch, *Political Perceptions of the Palestinians on the West Bank and the Gaza Strip*, Special Study 3 (Washington, D.C.: Middle East Institute, 1980), pp. 60, 65–71.

the communists, pro-PLO factions, and Islamic groups to strengthen their foothold in the region.

The Rise of Political Activism

One factor in the rise of the student movement to a position of power and influence in West Bank politics has been the students' willingness to strike and demonstrate against Israel's control mechanisms.[6] Many of the demonstrators had been born around the time of the 1967 war and had few hopes or dreams for the future if the West Bank and Gaza Strip remained indefinitely under Israel's control. The long and eventful history of the Palestinian problem provided the students with occasions to commemorate and celebrate through protest. Annually they marked the issuing of the Balfour Declaration in 1917, the United Nations Partition Resolution of 1947, the establishment of Israel in 1948, the June war of 1967, the signing of the Camp David Accords in 1978, Land Day, and Prisoners Day. The Palestinian-Arab conflicts, the 1970 Jordanian-Palestinian civil war, the 1976 civil war in Lebanon, Syria's overt support of the dissident movement within Fatah in 1983, and frequent Syrian-inspired attacks by Lebanese groups on Palestinian refugee camps after the 1982 Lebanon war provided further incitement. Students also worked diligently against any political initiative that compromised Palestinian national rights. They vehemently opposed plans such as the Reagan initiative, the Camp David Accords, and King Hussein's proposal for a federation of the West Bank and Gaza with Jordan that they believed contravened basic Palestinian political rights.

Shared grievances and deprivations were not the only motives for student involvement in politics. Student activism was also a natural outcome of the rapid growth of Palestinian nationalism in the aftermath of the 1967 June war. The students' identification with the values and goals of Palestinian nationalism disposed them to take part in political protest. The political gains of the PLO at

6. These include land expropriation, construction of Jewish settlements, demolition of houses, deportations, town arrests, imprisonment of local politicians and leaders, dissolution of municipal councils, closure of academic institutions, and continuous violations of Palestinian human and political rights.

both the Arab and the international level during the mid-1970s were a further stimulus to student politicization and mobilization.

LOYALTY TO THE PLO.   The PLO and its factions manipulated the student movement to generate support for themselves in the occupied territories. They provided students with money, legitimacy, ideology, and the organizational and structural frameworks for their activities. The variety of student blocs formed to represent varying points of view of PLO factions and the flow of resources from outside actors expanded the student movement and ensured continued student participation in political activities.

The 1973 October war convinced PLO leaders that the West Bank and Gaza were the only realistic site for a Palestinian state. They became increasingly attentive to political developments in the territories and worked to broaden their base of support among both the elite and the masses. Thus while encouraging students to demonstrate against occupation, the PLO was primarily interested in their loyalty and allegiance. Student celebration of the founding of each PLO faction was intended to underline loyalty to the PLO.

In the late 1970s Palestinian prisoners released from Israeli jails who enrolled in universities provided effective leadership for the student movement. These highly politicized student leaders manipulated their Palestinian connections to advance the interests of their particular blocs. In addition to the outside support that these leaders attracted, the student movement benefited from a tolerant West Bank society that acquiesced to the students' rising political role.

The new West Bank political elite were equally adept at manipulating student factions to serve their interests. Among the groups that used the student movement as a vehicle to gain influence and legitimacy were the Palestine National Front, the National Guidance Committee, and the Palestine Communist party. To accommodate the interests and growing power of students, the National Guidance Committee even assigned a seat for a student representative.

To consolidate their political gains, the students created special committees to coordinate their political stance and activities with those of West Bank leaders. The students limited their cooperation, however, to strong supporters of the PLO, excluding members of the pro-Jordanian elite. In fact, pro-Jordanian politicians were frequently targets of student political campaigns. The climax of the students' political coordination with PLO factions was the fall 1978 rallies they convened to protest the signing of the Camp David Accords. A year later, they joined pro-PLO mayors in protest against the military government's intention of deporting the mayor of Nablus.

HIGHER EDUCATION AS A WAY OF LIFE.   The academic milieu of the late 1970s contributed significantly to the students' politicization. With the growing number of students seeking a college education, new universities were opened at Al-Najah, Bir Zeit, and Bethlehem, and a new college at Hebron, with a combined student body of 7,500 by the early 1980s. Also, in 1980 three technical junior colleges in Hebron and Jerusalem, a four-year nursing school in Ramallah, and two junior colleges of Islamic theology were added to the five junior colleges and teacher-training centers already in operation.[7]

Following the establishment of Israel in 1948 and its occupation of the West Bank in 1967, higher education for the overwhelming majority of West Bank Palestinians became a vehicle for self-preservation, social mobility, political identity, and an improved standard of living.[8] The Israeli military government's periodic restrictions on travel permits and on the transfer of money for students studying abroad led to the establishment of colleges in the West Bank. Also, the increase in incomes of villagers and refugee camp dwellers who worked inside Israel and remittances from abroad enabled larger numbers of families to educate their children. Low tuition in universities and colleges and a wealth of scholarships made higher education accessible to many.[9]

As students from conservative rural and poor families entered

7. Munir Ahmad Awad, *Higher Education in the West Bank and the Gaza Strip: Its Development and Foundation* (in Arabic) (Al-Najah University, Markaz al-Dirasat al-Rifiyah, 1983).

8. Muhammad Hallaj, "Mission of Palestinian Higher Education," in Emile A. Nakhleh, ed., *A Palestinian Agenda for the West Bank and Gaza* (Washington, D.C.: American Enterprise Institute, 1980), pp. 58–63; Sarah Graham-Brown, "Impact on the Social Structure of Palestinian Society," in Naseer H. Aruri, ed., *Occupation: Israel over Palestine* (Belmont, Mass.: Association of Arab-American University Graduates, 1983), p. 245.

9. Munir Fasheh, "Impact on Education," in Aruri, *Occupation*, pp. 308–11.

universities, they introduced a religious orientation in student life that helped to accelerate an Islamic resurgence. Another group of students, particularly those from refugee camps, was drawn into Marxist-Leninist political thinking. University campuses gave all students an opportunity to participate in politics and provided a forum where activists and student councils could articulate political demands, issue statements, and convene popular rallies, demonstrations, and strikes. Student councils provided the leadership needed to mobilize students, and in 1980 they set up special committees to organize student bodies against Israel's occupation.

Students' frequent involvement in the political process prompted them to engage in more and more risky activities, which reinforced their politicization. The student blocs they formed encouraged them to translate their strong beliefs and ideological stands into actions. University life was so infused by political activity that reluctant students often felt compelled to participate in protests to avoid the criticism of their fellow students.

Uninvolved in economic life and without the personal constraints of marriage and family responsibilities, students were free to be politically active. In fact, their engagement in political activities markedly diminished after their graduation. The political inefficacy of trade unions and professional associations in resisting Israel's military occupation gave the student movement dynamism and a sense of mission and purpose.

STUDENTS' SENSE OF MISSION. University life generated an awareness in students of their national identity and a sense of solidarity and cooperation. It also promoted confidence and a romanticism about their society and the problems facing the Arab world.[10] The intense atmosphere in which they lived, and the complex problems they encountered, led students to believe that their political protests would leave a deep imprint on political events and would advance Palestinian national interests.

10. Ahmed Murad, *The Youth Revolt* (in Arabic) (Jerusalem: Al-Sharq Cooperative Press, 1977); Walid Salem, *The Student Movement: Theoretical Dimensions and Patterns of Participation* (in Arabic) (Jerusalem: Al-Sharq Cooperative Press, 1983); Iyad al-Barghuthi, "The Social Political Dynamics of the Intelligentsia and the Students in the Arab Countries" (in Arabic), *Al–Katib,* July 1983; Bassam al-Salhi, "The Nature of the Student Movement" (in Arabic), *Al-Katib,* August 1983.

West Bank students envisioned themselves not only as part of the intelligentsia but also as part of a larger secular nationalist or religious political movement with ready-made precepts to help untangle complex social and political problems. Some believed that an Islamic cultural reawakening held the key to the future; others saw themselves as part of an Arab and third-world national liberation movement struggling against "imperialism, Zionism, and reactionary Arab regimes." At the local level, both the secular nationalists and the religious camps considered themselves the vanguard of their society, reflecting and articulating its political preferences and spearheading its resistance to Israel's military occupation.

Student activists also saw themselves as the principal agents for social and political modernization. Their primary aims were to preserve Palestinian national and cultural identity and to solidify ties among West Bank towns, villages, and refugee camps. To achieve these objectives they launched and participated in voluntary work programs—reclaiming land, planting trees, paving roads, picking crops, and visiting families of prisoners or families whose children were killed by the Israeli army during the demonstrations. To promote national self-preservation, they sponsored art shows, poetry contests, local industry exhibitions, and dancing groups.

To educate outsiders about the Palestinian problem, student councils invited journalists to their campuses, met with foreign delegations, and arranged lectures, tours of the West Bank, and meetings with local politicians. The student council of Bir Zeit University sponsored summer camps for foreign students and launched an exchange program with students of foreign universities. The goal of these contacts was to enlist foreign student support for Palestinian national rights and academic freedom for West Bank universities. Some student councils established contact with peace groups and the academic community in Israel, though the usefulness and wisdom of such links were widely questioned.

Students' defense of their corporate interests extended to the academic field and the quality of student life. Student councils insisted on student representation on university committees charged with planning and policymaking. Students frequently held strikes to oppose changes in university regulations and rules that they considered harmful to their interests. Acting in the name of the student body, student councils succeeded in winning concrete benefits from university administrations, including health insurance, subsidies for food and books, and reductions of tuition fees. They established committees to raise funds inside and outside the occupied territories to provide scholarships for needy students. Other committees worked to promote social and cultural life on university campuses.

Students frequently used street demonstrations and strikes to protest Israel's military practices and to demonstrate student support for the PLO. Their demonstrations often served as a stimulus for popular uprisings. Many of their demonstrations were organized and well planned to commemorate political events and to protest new political developments. To avoid unwarranted provocation of the Israeli army and haphazard or untimely demonstrations, special committees were established. They coordinated the political views and forms of protest throughout the university and high school community. The committees had a broad representation to ensure cooperation and compliance with their resolutions (secondary school students were much less open to discipline than university and college students). They kept regular contact with West Bank leaders to coordinate political moves, such as issuing of statements and declarations or calls for strikes.

In the late 1970s, students turned to confrontation with Israeli authorities. Because their activities often led to the closing of their institutions, they devised new tactics and forms of protest, using press conferences and foreign visitors as a conduit for publicizing their views.

By the mid-1980s a new aspect of student activism began to unfold as middle and high school students became increasingly involved in political protests. The activities of those youths were spontaneous. As a consequence of their participation in West Bank politics, there was a sixfold increase in the number of violent demonstrations and strikes. The youths' political activism reached its climax in the uprising that broke out on December 9, 1987, and continued into 1988.

Political Blocs in the Student Movement

By 1980 the student movement had become the arena for a power struggle among nationalists, Marxists, and followers of the Islamic movement. Marxists had led in organizing West Bank students after the 1967 June war, but by the early 1980s, the communists' long hegemony had ended and supporters of Fatah provided the student movement with a strong and effective nationalist leadership. The supporters of Islam were even then making impressive gains among students—in 1981, eight of the ten educational institutions above the high school level came under Islamists' control.

Three student blocs—the Progressive Student Union (procommunist), the Progressive Student Action Front (pro-Popular Front), and Student Unity (pro-Democratic Front for the Liberation of Palestine)—were active Marxist groups. All three were supporters of the PLO, an allegiance that sometimes brought them into alliance with one another and with the Student Youth movement (a pro-Fatah bloc). Those four were staunchly in league against a fifth, the Islamic Student bloc.

The Islamic bloc surfaced among university and college students in the late 1970s and dominated a majority of student councils by 1981. The rise of this bloc was a response to the formation of the Islamic Republic of Iran, the emergence of several Islamic revivalist groups in the region, and the growth in the number of West Bank students from conservative and rural backgrounds. These students became a viable political force in most academic institutions between 1979 and 1982. The tension between the Islamic bloc and pro-PLO student groups was so great that it occasionally erupted in physical conflict.

COALITIONS AGAINST THE ISLAMIC BLOC.   While the Islamic students were less hostile to the Student Youth movement than to the communists and other Marxists, all four of the pro-PLO student blocs were dedicated to containing the rising Islamic "menace." Thus the four blocs that normally were in competition for power occasionally formed coalitions. Between 1979 and 1983 they formed national unity blocs to denounce the Islamic movement and enhance their chances of winning student elections. In a large popular rally at Bir Zeit University on February 12, 1982, representatives of the four blocs characterized the Islamic movement as a "reactionary movement," "destructive," and "a stooge" in the hands of the Muslim Brotherhood, which over the years had maintained "suspicious" relationships with the West and "Arab reactionary regimes."[11] Some argued that the Islamic student movement flourished only because of the weakness of the nationalist movement, that religion was a disguise to conceal the "real motives" of Islamic students.

While Islam's rising influence was a primary motive for the formation of the pro-PLO blocs, they had common ideological denominators that drew them together. All four supported the PLO as the sole legitimate representative of the Palestinian nationalist movement. They were committed to the establishment of a Palestinian state, and they consistently engaged in activities geared to resist Israel's military occupation. They also shared a firm belief that the West, Israel, and the conservative Arab regimes were the "real enemies" of the Palestinians, while only Arab nationalists, the third world, and the socialist camp were their "true friends." The preservation of academic freedom and opposition to Israel's Military Order 854 tightening control over university life were also areas of common concern to them.[12]

The mood of reconciliation that appeared within the PLO before and during Israel's invasion of Lebanon in the summer of 1982 also encouraged unity among the pro-PLO student blocs. The PLO factions urged their student followers to coordinate their activities to arrest the expansion of Islam. The four student blocs unanimously denounced Israel's Lebanon war and participated in a wave of demonstrations and strikes to protest Israel's military policies. Only the Student Action Front expressed any reservations about the PLO's 1982 decision to withdraw from Beirut.

Students also embraced the resolutions of the sixteenth session of the Palestine National Council of February 1983, rejecting the Reagan initiative and reconfirming the Palestinian right to have an independent state and to be represented by the PLO. They appealed to PLO factions to uphold the resolutions.[13] They were convinced that the Reagan initiative, the Camp David Accords, and King Hussein's plan for confederating the occupied territories

11. A student document from Bir Zeit University (in Arabic), February 12, 1982.

12. Naseer H. Aruri, "Universities under Occupation: Another Front in the War against Palestine," in Aruri, *Occupation*, pp. 325–36.

13. For a detailed treatment of the Palestine National Council resolutions, see Emile F. Sahliyeh, *The PLO after the Lebanon War* (Westview, 1986), pp. 108–11.

with Jordan would impede attainment of the Palestinian national rights of self-determination and statehood. The students singled out the Camp David Accords and the Reagan initiative because they excluded the PLO from the political game.

In the national unity blocs, student council seats were distributed in accordance with the numerical and political weight of each of the four pro-PLO blocs within the student body at large. For example, in the 1981 student council elections at Bir Zeit University, three seats were allocated for representatives of the pro-Fatah Student Youth movement, two each for the pro–Popular-Front Student Action Front and the procommunist Student Union bloc, and one each to the pro–Democratic-Front Student Unity bloc and the independents. The distribution of seats varied both from one university to another and from one year to the next. When the quadruple alliance at Bir Zeit broke up in 1983, for instance, the Youth movement and the Student Action Front formed an alliance, as did the Student Union and the Student Unity blocs. At Al-Najah University and Hebron College in 1984, disagreement on the distribution of council seats upset the coalition. And at Bethlehem University, the four pro-PLO student groups never united because there was no urgent need to do so since the Islamic student movement was not strong. With its establishment in the late 1970s, the Bethlehem University student council was dominated by the Student Action Front and aligned with the Student Union bloc, the Student Unity bloc, and independents.

The national unity blocs also had a rule against monopoly of student councils and expected all four blocs to participate in the student congresses' decisionmaking process. (The congresses, wider in membership than the councils, formulate the election platform, submit a list of candidates to contest council elections, and lay down the guiding principles of the operation of the student council.) National unity blocs were not to encroach on the right of individual blocs to operate freely among their own followers and propagate their ideas to enlist support among students. In activities such as the celebration of a PLO faction's annual day, advance authorization from the student council was required. And in the event the four student blocs failed to win elections in institutions, an alternative committee could be created as a sign of their nonrecognition of the legitimacy of an Islamic-dominated student council. Such committees were established at Al-Najah University and Hebron College.

THE MARXIST BLOCS AND THE PLO. Political coalitions were possible only as long as the members agreed on the rules governing their relationships. Similarly, the coalitions often depended on alliances among the patron PLO factions of the student groups. Thus, the sharpening of differences between PLO moderates and hard-line supporters over issues such as the Reagan initiative, dialogue with Jordan, confederation of Jordan and the occupied territories, and relations with Syria and Egypt, all had a divisive impact on the unity of the student movement. The three Marxist student blocs exhibited a congruity of political attitudes that allowed them to form bilateral and trilateral alliances when the larger coalition failed. The Student Action Front was more critical of Arafat's policies and tactics and less compromising with the nationalist positions of the Student Youth movement than were the Student Union and Student Unity blocs.

All three Marxist blocs attributed the political cleavages in the PLO to Arafat's diplomatic moves, including his close coordination with Jordan and his attempt to open a dialogue with the United States. In their opinion, Arafat's diplomatic moves not only departed from the Palestinian national consensus but from the basic tenets of the Palestine National Charter and various resolutions of the Palestine National Council. Consequently, Arafat's visit to Cairo in December 1983, in violation of resolutions of the Palestine National Council, was denounced by the three leftist student blocs because of Egypt's peace treaty with Israel.[14] They argued that reconciliation with Egypt would serve only the interests of the West, Israel, and conservative Arab regimes. Instead, because the government of Hafiz Asad was opposed to the Camp David Accords and the Reagan initiative, they proposed consolidating ties with Syria. The Student Union bloc and Student Action Front attacked Arafat's style of leadership, calling it authoritarian and antidemocratic. They held Arafat and his colleagues responsible for the split within Fatah. In their view, Arafat's military appointments in the spring of 1983 and his replacement of "nationalist officers"

14. On Arafat's visit, see ibid., pp. 178–84.

with men of "dubious loyalties and poor military records" had sparked the mutiny within Fatah.[15] Yet even though they supported the mutineers' demands, the three Marxist organizations opposed any recourse to military force to settle differences among Palestinians.

The communist-dominated Student Union bloc urged West Bank students—no matter what their political persuasion—to hold public rallies to put pressure on the PLO factions to reconcile their differences. Following Arafat's trip to Egypt, the Student Union bloc refrained from advocating his resignation, favoring instead the democratization of the PLO's policymaking apparatus. It also supported the Palestine Communist party's demands for a reorganization of the PLO's executive committee through the inclusion of a representative from among the communists.[16]

In announcing the political program of the General Federation of High School Students in 1983, the Student Union bloc denounced the PLO's tendency toward moderation, as reflected in Arafat's diplomatic alliances with Egypt and Jordan. The program sharply criticized King Hussein's federation plan and Arafat's alleged violation of the political communiqué of the sixteenth session of the Palestine National Council. The Union bloc also rejected any plan leading to the liberation of the occupied territories under the sponsorship of Jordan, Egypt, or the United States. It urged Fatah leaders to stay within the Palestinian national consensus and work for reconciliation within the PLO.[17]

15. On the split, see ibid., pp. 139–75.

16. The Student Union bloc, which through the 1970s was the leading political force in the student movement, lost power as the PLO's influence among students grew. The gradual decline in communist control of the movement culminated in losses in student council elections at Bir Zeit, Al-Najah, and Bethlehem universities in 1982. The communists had already moved to widen their base of support among secondary school students and in 1981 with the pro–Democratic-Front Student Unity bloc had cosponsored the formation of committees for high school students, ostensibly to ensure their effective participation in resisting Israel's military occupation and to help them overcome problems related to their classrooms, examinations, and the quality of their education. In 1983, the Union bloc formed the General Federation of High School Students. The Action Front and the Youth movement then established committees among high school students, as they were determined not to allow the communists to monopolize the secondary schools. In 1984, the communists reactivated the Palestine Student Union, which had been suspended four years earlier.

17. The political program of the General Federation of High School Students (in Arabic), 1983.

After Arafat's visit to Egypt, the Student Action Front was less compromising toward Fatah followers in the occupied territories than before. Its objection to any dialogue with Jordan was categorical. Likewise, in response to Arafat's meeting with representatives of Israeli peace groups, the Action Front demanded that such contacts be confined to the "progressive and democratic non-Zionist Jewish forces."[18] Following its patron the Popular Front, the Action Front professed a strong pro-Syrian posture and argued that the real aim of U.S. diplomacy in the Middle East was to weaken Syria and ultimately bring it into the pro-Western camp. Therefore a Palestinian-Syrian "strategic partnership" should be formed to frustrate the American plan and reinforce Syria's resolve to resist the Reagan initiative, the Camp David Accords, the normalization of ties between Egypt and Israel, and Jordan's ambition to recover the occupied territories.[19]

The Student Unity bloc, which modeled its views on those of the Democratic Front, did not fully agree with the Student Action Front's assessment of Arafat's leadership and policies. And even though the Unity bloc acknowledged that the demands of Fatah mutineers for the democratization of the PLO were valid, it criticized their use of military force against Arafat. Student Unity cautioned that the alignment of Fatah rebels with the Popular Front–General Command, Al-Saiqa, and Syria and Libya would lead to the domination of the Fatah movement by these forces. From the Unity bloc's perspective, a relationship with Syria would remain strong so long as the Syrian regime was opposed to the Camp David Accords and stayed committed to the realization of Palestinian national rights to self-determination and statehood.

Student Unity literature revealed a sensitivity to the preservation of the PLO's autonomy and its concern not to place the organization under Syrian guardianship.[20] Repeated attacks on the Palestinian refugee camps in Lebanon in 1985 and 1986 by the pro-Syrian

18. Statement of the Progressive Student Action Front (in Arabic), April 1983.

19. The influence of the Action Front was marginal in West Bank academic institutions, with the exception of Bethlehem University. Hence the Action Front's interest in aligning itself with the Union and Unity blocs.

20. The Unity bloc, which appeared on the student scene in the mid-1970s, had no more influence among students than the Democratic Front, its patron, had in the PLO and the Palestinian nationalist movement abroad. The Unity bloc often aligned itself with larger groups to secure a seat on student councils. After 1983, it drew closer to the pro-Fatah Student Youth movement.

Amal Shia militia substantiated the Student Unity bloc's suspicion of the Syrian regime. Indeed, the bloc sharply denounced both Syrians and the Shia group. And despite continuing differences with the Student Youth movement over Arafat's dialogue with Jordan and Egypt and his quest for a dialogue with the United States, the Student Unity bloc aligned itself with the Youth movement in student council elections at Bir Zeit in 1984–85 and in other West Bank academic institutions.

THE PRO-FATAH BLOC. The Student Youth movement, which in the early 1980s was the main pro-PLO political force, took its positions from those of Fatah.[21] Echoing the complaints of PLO leaders both on the crisis within Fatah and the relationship with Syria, the Youth movement held the Asad regime primarily responsible for the outbreak of the mutiny. It charged that, by supporting the mutineers, Syria intended to cover up its failure to offer military assistance to the PLO during the siege of West Beirut and meant to create an alternative PLO that would be subservient to Syrian interests. That behavior was not surprising since it was consistent with the Asad regime's long-standing hostility toward Palestinians.[22] In sharp contrast to the Student Action Front and Student Union bloc, the Youth movement denied that the mutiny in Fatah was a Palestinian affair caused by individualism and unilateral decisionmaking at the expense of collective leadership. The Youth movement rejected such arguments as superfluous and insisted that the split was engineered by radical Arab regimes, particularly Syria.

The Youth movement also criticized the Marxist student blocs

21. The Student Youth movement was the last group to be introduced to the student political scene. Once the leaders of Fatah accepted the goal of establishing an independent state in the West Bank and Gaza Strip, the Youth movement became the most active and largest single political force among West Bank students in the 1980s. The simplicity of Fatah's political thinking and its concentration on narrow Palestinian nationalist goals vis-à-vis the more complex Marxist-Leninist theories in part accounted for the Youth movement's appeal among students. The flexibility of Fatah's political thinking allowed the Youth movement to incorporate a variety of political opinions, ranging from Marxist elements to nationalist and Islamic views. Many of the former prisoners who enrolled in the universities in the late 1970s and early 1980s joined the Youth movement. Fatah's scholarships were an important source of influence for the Youth movement.

22. *Al-Shabibah* (Student Youth movement publication), July and October 1983.

for not denouncing the Syrian president's role in the Fatah mutiny and for the eviction of the last remaining pro-Arafat PLO troops from northern Lebanon in late 1983. Further, the Youth movement could not comprehend the Student Action Front and Student Union bloc issuing statements denouncing Arafat's leadership and policies. Indeed, the organization reconfirmed its full confidence in Arafat's leadership and defended his policies, including the rapprochement with both Egypt and Jordan.[23]

BREAKUP OF THE PRO-PLO COALITIONS.   Divisions in the student movement were so deep seated that the four student blocs' concerted stand vis-à-vis the Islamic movement and the political problems confronting the PLO could not endure. Nor could the blocs agree on the timing of popular rallies, the issuing of joint political statements, or the celebration of national festivals. On January 23, 1984, however, thirty-three student councils and student committees did meet on the Bir Zeit University campus to protest King Hussein's move to reconvene the parliament.[24] But unity was short lived; a battle between moderates and hard-line followers within the PLO broke out over questions of convening the seventeenth session of the Palestine National Council in Amman in November 1984 and the signing of a diplomatic accord between King Hussein and Arafat in February 1985. Tension and friction between the two student political camps extended from the main universities and colleges to high schools, youth clubs, and other youth organizations in towns, villages, and refugee camps of the West Bank and Gaza Strip. The outbreak of violent feuds between the rival camps culminated in the killing of a high school student from the Youth movement by leftists, and a fight among students of Bir Zeit University in late May 1985 that ended in damage to the university premises. Tension, however, among the different student blocs diminished following the reconciliation among the PLO's differing factions in April of 1987. The youth uprising that erupted later that year further closed the ranks of the student movement.

23. Ibid., January 1984.
24. On Jordan's action, see Sahliyeh, *PLO after the Lebanon War*, pp. 184–89.

The Future of the Student Movement

Because students have been willing to take risks in their political activism, the student movement has assumed a dominant political role in the West Bank. Since the late 1970s, it has defined the parameters of political behavior of the West Bank urban elite. In their statements and actions, local politicians—particularly casual PLO supporters and pro-Jordanian politicians—have had to take possible student reactions into account. Student political activities have overshadowed those of trade unions, professional associations, women's groups, and other West Bank organizations.

The political power of the student movement significantly expanded in the wake of the frequent participation of the youth in the demonstrations and strikes since the mid-1980s. The uprising that began in December 1987 reinforced the students' belief in their ability to influence the unfolding of political events.

Over the years the student movement operated as an effective barrier against the formation of an indigenous political elite and as such contributed to the process of promoting an external ideological and political leadership for West Bank Palestinians. As a powerful tool of the PLO, the student movement enabled the organization to consolidate its legitimacy and power base against its archrival, Jordan. The student population has remained the most active force in resisting Israel's military occupation. Through their connections with different PLO factions, various student groups have reinforced their power within the movement and against outside rivals.

The viability and overall strength of the student movement in the future, however, will depend on a host of considerations. Prolongation of Israel's occupation of the West Bank will provide a strong motive for activism, not only among university students but among the youth. An intense ideological identification with PLO goals and values will encourage political participation.

The structural framework for student leadership—student councils, committees, and blocs in the universities and colleges—is well entrenched and will ensure student involvement in politics. Moreover, the ability of student leaders to mobilize resources and create structural networks will also influence student participation in various forms of political protest. The concentration of students will facilitate the recruitment of new activists and demonstrators.

Their experiences in high school may encourage many students to throw themselves into politics as soon as they enroll in the universities. The flow of money, legitimacy, and organizational and ideological support from external Palestinian or Arab sources will affect the strength, size, and scope of the student movement.

Society's support for and tolerance of student political activities and the cooperation that labor unions, women's and professional associations, and local elite groups have offered will undoubtedly continue to encourage students' politicization. And the absence of work, family, and marriage responsibilities will facilitate the mobilization, recruitment, and organization of students.

Israel so far has failed to diminish the intensity of student political activism, despite the variety of techniques it has used to break the students' morale and nationalist spirit.[25] Despite the Israeli military administration's use of increasingly harsh techniques—such as shooting to kill rather than firing in the air—the degree and frequency of student political protest have not diminished. These techniques have not dissuaded neutral students from becoming politically active. And despite the mounting casualties and injuries among the Palestinians in the occupied territories during the 1987–88 uprising, society's tolerance of student political activities has not waned. Students' resolve to oppose the occupation and their choice of tactics and strategies for doing so depend in part on relative success in past encounters.

The PLO as ideological reference point of course has a direct bearing on students' political performance. Identification with PLO values will continue to provide strong motives to act. The degree

25. The Israeli army has consistently been sent to break up student demonstrations and disrupt rallies, and since the mid-1970s has frequently used live ammunition to do so. Soldiers have invaded student residences at night and arrested scores of students without warning. To dampen students' political activities, selected universities and schools have been closed each year for two months or more. Israeli army units have set up checkpoints on roads leading to West Bank campuses for several days and sometimes weeks, disrupting studies and class attendance. Student council members have been placed under town or house arrest for several months. Students convicted of throwing stones at Israeli military vehicles or erecting roadblocks are often given jail sentences of one to two years. The identity cards of many students are confiscated during demonstrations, rallies, and strikes. The army often rounds up students shortly before their final exams, thus denying them the opportunity to complete their academic year. Jewish settlers have also harassed West Bank students. See Aruri, "Universities under Occupation," pp. 319–36; Olga Kapeliouk, "The Palestinian Universities under Occupation," *Arab Studies Quarterly*, vol. 7 (Spring/Summer 1985), pp. 88–91.

of involvement will ebb and flow with the availability of PLO resources for the student movement. As the PLO factions compete to advance their legitimacy and their clients' interests, the resources extended to the student movement will determine which student blocs and local elite groups are most powerful.

As Fatah has become the primary political force in the PLO, the influence of the Student Youth movement has grown. Fatah's financial assistance has significantly contributed to the growth and political weight of the Student Youth movement. Relations between the two have not been free from tension, however, nor the flow of influence one-sided.

The same holds true of other ties between the student movement and PLO factions. The adjustment of the PLO's diplomatic posture and its switching of alliances have sometimes been met with student dismay and disapproval. Often student blocs have adopted more militant positions than their PLO custodians. Student groups have manipulated their connections to advance their own goals and affect the behavior of other groups. Students have used bargaining, persuasion, political protest, and occasionally violence to impress rival student groups and their outside patrons. The Youth movement, for example, has often adopted more extremist views than those of Fatah.

The expansion of participatory politics in the 1980s to include the high school students made many of the traditional players less relevant to local West Bank politics. The politicization of the youth further undermined the political authority and legitmacy of the local elite and reduced the West Bank–Gaza Palestinians' reliance on outside forces. In particular, the 1987–88 uprising increased the difficulties the PLO and Jordan face in controlling the course of political developments in the occupied territories.

Since the late 1970s, the problems confronting the secular student movement have not been confined to dissension among rival supporters of the PLO or Israel's restrictive measures. The resurgence of Islam among West Bank youth has posed a serious challenge to the proponents of secular ideologies.

CHAPTER SEVEN

Islam as an Alternative

⚑ ⚑ ⚑

B Y THE END of the 1970s, secular nationalism had failed to provide acceptable answers for the Palestinian problem. Some West Bankers, particularly the youth, began to search for a new source of political identification. Many found in Islam an alternative reference point. An Islamic political movement, its followers believed, offered a new perspective, which would mobilize the support of the Muslim world. They argued that Islam, if tried, would provide solutions to the problems confronting Palestinians and Arabs.

Israeli challenges and threats to the physical, political, and cultural life of Palestinians in the occupied territories made a religious point of reference appealing, for Islam served as a force for ethnic identity, attachment to the land, and cultural purity of Palestinians. Neither Israel nor Jordan attempted to forestall the rising Islamic movement since it helped to contain the popularity of Palestinian nationalism and the Palestine Liberation Organization (PLO).

Islamic Groups under Jordanian Rule

This was not the first emergence of an Islamic movement in Palestine in modern times. Islamic uprisings that occurred between the two world wars protested British practices and Jewish immigration into Palestine. The uprisings were not purely religious, for political, economic, and social factors contributed to popular unrest in Palestine.

In the 1930s an Islamic uprising, mainly of rural people, was led by Iz al-Din al-Qassam in northern Palestine. The aim of al-Qassam's movement was to reawaken the Muslim masses and lead them in a jihad, a holy war, against Great Britain and Jewish immigration. The movement did not achieve any of these goals as it came to an end shortly after al-Qassam's death in 1936.

In the mid-1940s the Muslim Brotherhood in Egypt sent a number of its followers to Palestine to preach its ideas and establish branches of the movement. By the end of 1946, branches had been set up in Jerusalem, Nablus, Tulkarm, Haifa, Jaffa, and numerous other towns. A branch was established in Hebron in 1949 and several other towns in the early 1950s. During the 1948 Arab-Israeli war, the Muslim Brotherhood movement in Egypt dispatched volunteers to fight alongside the Arab Salvation armies to prevent the establishment of a Jewish state.[1]

Fearful of provoking the Jordanian regime, the Muslim Brotherhood refrained from establishing itself as a political party and in early 1953 applied to Jordan's Ministry of the Interior to be licensed as an association. Its support of the regime and slight involvement in political activities accounted for King Hussein's government's sanctioning of the Brotherhood. Leaders of the Brotherhood who supported the regime contested the parliamentary elections of the 1950s and 1960s and won a handful of seats in each election.

An Islamic party, Al-Tahrir (Liberation party), was launched in the early 1950s by a Palestinian religious jurist, Ahmad Taqi al-Din al-Nabhani.[2] Because of the party's program of *inqilabiya*—overthrow of the existing political, economic, and social order—the Jordanian government rejected al-Nabhani's request to form a political party. The party's platform contradicted the Jordanian constitution by calling for the election of a ruler and by asserting that religion rather than nationalism was the foundation of the society. As a result, the party's operations between 1950 and 1967 were clandestine. Like the Muslim Brotherhood, Al-Tahrir drew support from towns in northern and southern areas of the West Bank; its following, however, was not as extensive as that of the Muslim Brotherhood.

Between 1948 and 1967 the Islamic political movement was weak. This was not surprising as the Islamic movement, particularly

1. Amnon Cohen, *Political Parties in the West Bank under the Jordanian Regime, 1949–1967* (Cornell University Press, 1982), pp. 144–47.
2. Sadiq Amin, *The Islamic Call: Legitimate Religious Duty and Human Need* (in Arabic) (n.p., 1981), p. 92.

the Muslim Brotherhood, was suppressed by President Gamal Abd al-Nasser in Egypt and the Baath party in Syria. The political climate in the Arab world was not conducive to a pan-Islamic movement, for the dominant issues were hostility to the West, anticolonialist sentiment, assertion of national independence, and achievement of social justice and economic modernization. Pan-Arabism, socialism, and a commitment to the liberation of all of Palestine were the foremost political interests of most Arab regimes. Both President Nasser of Egypt and the Baath party in Syria (the two rivals for pan-Arab leadership) sought to discredit the Muslim Brotherhood in the eyes of the Arab masses. For West Bank Palestinians, the Brotherhood's support of the Jordanian monarch further discredited it.

The Rise of the Islamic Movement

The 1967 June war marked the beginning of the demise of the pan-Arab approach to the Palestinian question and provided a breeding ground for the reemergence of an Islamic movement. The political vacuum after the defeat of the Arab armies was filled, however, by the Palestinian resistance movement, which grew rapidly within and outside the occupied territories after the June war. The PLO's political ascendancy by the mid-1970s consolidated sentiments of Palestinian nationalism. The strength of Palestinian nationalism and the widespread backing of its proponents kept the Islamic movement dormant. Neither the Muslim Brotherhood nor Al-Tahrir enjoyed a mass following.

Changing local and regional conditions in the late 1970s encouraged a rise of interest in Islam, particularly among young people. Pan-Arabism, Palestinian nationalism, and Marxism had all failed to end Israel's occupation of the West Bank. Neither Arab, Palestinian, nor international initiatives to end the Israeli occupation of the West Bank and Gaza Strip had borne fruit. Not only had the Arab armies failed to liberate Palestine, but the 1973 October war, Arab diplomatic efforts, and oil wealth had not produced any tangible political gains for Palestinians. The PLO itself had begun to soften its commitment to military struggle and to seek Western-sponsored diplomatic settlement plans for the Palestinian question.

The PLO's adjustment of its long-term objective—the goal of liberating all of Palestine—to the narrower objective of establishing a West Bank–Gaza state, and then to the concept of confederation with Jordan, was confusing and disappointing for many of the youth in the occupied territories. For adherents of the Islamic movement, the shift in PLO tactics and strategies did not yield positive results. On the contrary, from their perspective after two decades Palestinian nationalism was losing its glamour and appeal. Islam, by contrast, appeared to provide well-defined answers and a clear vision for the future.

Bitter divisions in the Arab world and the split in the ranks of the PLO following the Lebanon war increased the frustration of some Palestinians and compounded the crisis of secular nationalism. Some Palestinians came to believe that neither Arab and Palestinian nationalism nor Western, Soviet, or other international approaches to the Palestinian question could end the Israeli occupation and restore Palestinian rights. Only Islam, and an Islamic interpretation of the Arab-Israeli dispute, could provide a solution to the Palestinian question. The Islamic revolution in Iran in 1979, the assassination of Egyptian president Anwar Sadat by an Islamic group, and the guerrilla attacks of the Islamic militia in southern Lebanon against the Israeli army (creating an impression of having driven the Israelis out of a place they intended to leave) all provided momentum for the spread of Islamic ideas in the occupied territories. The perceived success of Islam in those three instances suggested that only through religion could political change and an end to Israel's military occupation be brought about.

Mounting Israeli threats to Palestinian group identity, cultural purity, and the integrity of their land also prompted Palestinians to invoke their Islamic traditions. Particularly the generation of Palestinians who had grown up under conditions of military occupation had no hopes or dreams. Subjugated to an alien culture and a government that was determined to take away their land, they saw Islam as a source of hope, discipline, and mission and a means to ensure their survival and cultural purity. Islam's followers believed that exposure to Judeo-Christian culture and civilization contributed to the erosion of the Islamic value system and was responsible for the decline of Muslim social and political institutions.

The Islamic movement in the occupied territories was also a response to the rise of the Likud bloc in Israel. Prime Minister

Menachem Begin and other Likud leaders considered the West Bank and Gaza an integral part of the biblical Land of Israel and asserted that Jews had an inalienable right to settle anywhere there. The invocation of such arguments to control the territories, frequent attacks by Jewish extremists on Islamic holy shrines in Jerusalem and Hebron, and the emergence of Jewish fundamentalist groups such as the Gush Emunim movement and the Kach movement of Rabbi Meir Kahane drove Palestinians to Islam.[3] With construction of Jewish settlements by Gush Emunim followers increasing and Palestinian and Arab nationalism in crisis, many Palestinians seized on Islam as the most viable vehicle to counter rising Jewish extremism inside Israel.

Israel's 1982 war against the PLO in Lebanon and the accompanying bombardment of Palestinian and Lebanese civilian centers, coupled with American support of Israeli war objectives and the massacres at the Palestinian refugee camps of Sabra and Shatila by Christian Lebanese allies of Israel, were perceived as a joint Judeo-Christian conspiracy against Islam.[4] Undoubtedly the military successes of the Islamic resistance movement in southern Lebanon reinforced the conviction of the movement's followers in the West Bank and Gaza that Islam was capable of resolving the Palestinian question. The Islamic revolution in Iran and the successful guerrilla war waged by the Shiites in Lebanon produced a nostalgia for Islam's golden age. Many Muslims believed that the reconstruction of an Islamic state and the restoration of an Islamic cultural identity were the key to a glorious Islamic future.

The Islamic revival was helped by the fact that the Arab-Islamic culture did not separate politics and religion. It provided a congenial atmosphere for the revitalization of religious ideas. Similarly, Islam was an essential component of Arab nationalism as well as a source of personal identity; thus it too reinforced the revitalization of religious ideas in the political realm. In addition, Arab leaders used religious symbols to enlist popular support and widen political legitimacy.

The interplay of politics, religion, and ethnicity, and the manip-

3. Ehud Sprinzak, "Kach and Meir Kahane: The Emergence of Jewish Quasi-Fascism," *Patterns of Prejudice*, vol. 19, nos. 3 and 4 (1985); Walter Reich, "The Kahane Controversy," *Moment*, vol. 10 (January–February 1985), pp. 15–24.

4. Such views were expressed in *Al-Nur al-Ilahi, Al-Talia al-Islamiya, Al-Sahwah, Al-Muntalaq,* and *Al-Nida.*

ulation of religious symbols, facilitated Islam's resurgence in the West Bank and Gaza. Socioeconomic conditions were conducive to the spread of the Islamic movement. For instance, the conservative, religious nature of Palestinian society and the fact that over half of the Palestinians lived in rural areas, coupled with a large concentration of refugees in the Gaza Strip, provided fertile soil for Islam's resurgence.

A survey of one hundred fifty Muslim students in colleges and junior colleges in the West Bank and the Gaza Strip in 1982 revealed that a majority (54 percent) came from families where Islamic prayers, fasting, and conservative attire were observed by all the family.[5] Twelve percent were from families where the father alone observed Islam, and 16 percent from families where only the mother fully observed Islamic practices. Fourteen percent indicated that only brothers and sisters in the family observed Islam, and 4 percent that they came from families where Islam was not practiced. A majority of those interviewed in the survey came from large, poor families—66 percent from families of six children or more, 26 percent from families of three to five children, and only 8 percent from families of fewer than three children. A majority of the students lived in either refugee camps or rural areas. The father's occupation of 54 percent of the students was laborer (mostly in construction), of 30 percent farmer, and of 16 percent service worker.

Political developments in the West Bank and the Gaza Strip also contributed to the growth of the Islamic movement. In the late 1970s when West Bank communists were in control of the main youth movements, trade unions, and other mass organizations, pro-Fatah forces aligned themselves with the followers of Islam to win student council elections. This alliance at Bir Zeit and Al-Najah universities gave the Islamic movement political credibility.

The movement probably profited also from the support and encouragement of Israel and Jordan. While no tangible evidence exists to prove such a proposition, the rise of the Islamic movement certainly served the interests of both states by checking the PLO's influence in the West Bank and Gaza Strip. In contrast to its

5. The survey of Muslim students, selected randomly, was conducted under my supervision at Bir Zeit University.

restrictive measures against pro-PLO groups, the Israeli government was quite tolerant of the rise and activism of the Islamic youth movement. Moreover, Israeli military authorities chose not to interfere during Islamic provocations and incitement of Palestinian nationalist forces. For example, when Islamic fundamentalists attacked the premises of the Palestinian Red Crescent Committee in Gaza in January 1980, the Israeli army "did not intervene until the last stage of the rioting."[6] Similarly, Islamic magazines, newspapers, and books were allowed to circulate freely in the West Bank and Gaza Strip even though Islamic literature contained strong anti-Israel propaganda.

The Israeli government probably tolerated the growing Islamic movement because tension between secularists and followers of Islam, and between Muslims and Christians, facilitated its rule over the occupied territories. The Islamic movement was a countervailing force to pro-PLO groups in the West Bank. An Islamic movement hostile to the PLO's secular orientation and opposed to the formation of a nationalist, secular Palestinian state complemented Israel's policy of striking against all facets of Palestinian nationalism.

Jordan too had a stake in weakening the influence of the PLO in the occupied territories, particularly because by the mid-1970s the power base of pro-Jordanian politicians had eroded. When various associations, institutions, and other mass organizations came under the domination of pro-PLO and communist groups, the Jordanian government extended political and financial backing to Islamic activists.[7] Until the mid-1980s, it was tolerant of the Muslim Brotherhood's activities in Jordan, as evidenced by the Brotherhood's winning two seats in the 1984 parliamentary election. Saudi Arabia also financed a number of Islamic institutions in the occupied territories, such as the Islamic Center in the Gaza Strip, which houses a number of nurseries and Islamic schools.

The trend toward increased literacy among West Bank–Gaza Palestinians also helped to spread Islam. The availability of Islamic

6. Chairman of the Palestinian Red Crescent Committee in Gaza, quoted in Shalom Cohen, "Khomeinism in Gaza," *New Outlook*, vol. 23 (March 1980), p. 7.

7. Jordan publicly financed the Department for Islamic Religious Endowments in Jerusalem, which was in charge of various mosques, properties, and clergy in the West Bank, and subsidized existing Islamic colleges.

literature and the establishment of Islamic religious schools and colleges in Jerusalem, Gaza, and Hebron after 1978 accelerated the rise of the Islamic political movement in the occupied territories.

Signs of an Islamic Reawakening

The trend toward Islam was apparent in social and educational institutions and associations, and in politics. It was common to find students of Islamic religious colleges visiting neighboring villages or preaching during Friday prayers on the glories of the first Islamic state as well as a return to Islam.

An obvious manifestation of the Islamic movement was the number of women donning traditional Islamic attire, *hijab*, and of men growing beards. These symbols of commitment to Islam served as signs of brotherhood, fraternity, and identity among members of the movement. They also asserted the presence of Muslims on the local political scene and thus presented a challenge to leftist political forces.

In the 1982 survey of Muslim students, all one hundred fifty declared that they strictly observed Islamic practices, including fasting and praying. Of the fifty female students interviewed, 78 percent indicated that they always wore the *hijab*, 22 percent that they did so from time to time. All members of the sample group asserted that no pressure had been exerted on them to practice Islam.

Educational and social institutions contributed to the Islamic cultural reawakening during the 1970s. A number of nurseries and Islamic elementary and high schools were established, as well as Muslim associations for young men and women in Jerusalem and the Islamic Center in Gaza. And three Sharia colleges established in 1978 offered instruction in Islamic jurisprudence in Jerusalem, Hebron, and Gaza. Each year they produced many educated young Muslims, who replaced the more traditional imams in conducting prayers in the mosques of the West Bank and Gaza Strip.

The late 1970s also witnessed the formation of charity committees in several towns and villages to distribute money to the needy. Islamic bookstores opened in several towns, and eight magazines were regularly or occasionally published by various Islamic student blocs and institutions.[8] Further, a large number of Islamic magazines and books that were published outside the region were available in the occupied territories.

Followers of the Islamic movement began organizing politically to formulate positions on issues and problems confronting the Palestinian people. Their political attitudes were not original but corresponded with positions expressed by Islamic groups elsewhere. Indeed, West Bank Islamic groups considered themselves an integral part of the regional Islamic movement. Yet they did develop their own positions on issues such as relations with the nationalist forces in the occupied territories and with the PLO.

Islamic forces in the occupied territories did not have any open political apparatus to coordinate their activities or to mobilize mass followings. Thus, between 1979 and 1981, their most effective political activities were in the student movement, where they controlled eight of the ten university and junior college student councils within the region. At Bir Zeit University, where they represented 30–40 percent of the student body, as well as at Bethlehem University, the Muslim influence was limited by a considerable Christian presence.

The Islamic youth movement in the occupied territories consisted of the Muslim Brotherhood, Al-Tahrir, the pro-Khomeini group, the pro-Fatah Muslim group, and Al-Dawa wal-Tabligh. The mission of the last group was religious and educational rather than engaging in political activities and working for political power.

The Muslim Brotherhood aimed at reconstructing Islamic society and creating an Islamic state. It was convinced that reform of the individual was a prerequisite for the transformation of society and that the individual's emancipation from corruption, fear, ignorance, and materialism would lead to social reform. The Brotherhood believed that an Islamic reawakening could be brought about through peaceful change and by discouraging the individual from the use of violence or revolutionary means, and that the formation of a super-Islamic state would usher in a wave of Islamic conquests. In addition, the Muslim Brotherhood advocated ending Muslim dependency—economic, cultural, social, or political—on either Western or socialist countries.[9]

8. The magazines include *Al-Dawa, Al-Talia al-Islamiya, Filistin al-Muslima, Al-Nida, Al-Akhbar, Al-Sahwah, Al-Nur al-Ilahi,* and *Al-Muntalaq.*

9. Fathi Yakan, *Islamic Movement: Problems and Perspectives,* trans. Maneh al-

In the 1982 survey, 64 percent of the one hundred fifty respondents stated that they strongly supported the Muslim Brotherhood, and 32 percent that their support was moderate; only 4 percent expressed vehement opposition to the Brotherhood, considering it an agent of Israel and the United States.

In contrast to the Muslim Brotherhood, Al-Tahrir believed that the restoration of a proper Islamic way of life could be achieved only through an intellectual and political revolution and the dismantling of old ideas and current regimes. The transformation of society could be accelerated with assistance from the army. The aim of Al-Tahrir, according to the party's founder Ahmad Taqi al-Din al-Nabhani, was to rejuvenate Islamic life, culture, and civilization. In his Message of Party Formation, al-Nabhani urged a return to orthodox Islam and underlined the need to reconstitute the Islamic state.

Most support for Al-Tahrir came from university students in the Jerusalem, Hebron, and Gaza areas. Thirty percent of the one hundred fifty students in the survey expressed strong support for the party, 60 percent supported it moderately, and 10 percent expressed strong opposition. Older members continued to back the party. Nevertheless, its influence in the Islamic political movement in the West Bank and Gaza Strip was marginal.

A third political faction in the Islamic movement consisted of supporters of the Islamic revolution in Iran. They expressed great skepticism about the goals and techniques of the Muslim Brotherhood. And although most of them were Sunni Muslims, they were willing to overlook the differences between their own and the Shia sect and suggest that the caliphate be bestowed on Khomeini. For them, the Islamic revolution in Iran came to symbolize Islam's first modern victory against the West.

Although pro-Khomeini followers in the West Bank and Gaza were in the minority, their militancy and hostility toward Israel, the West, and various Arab regimes seemed likely to attract youth. Belief in the efficacy of revolutionary techniques as a means to an

---

Johani (Indianapolis, Indiana: American Trust Publications, 1984), pp. 117–19; Said Hawwa, *Introduction to the Mission of the Muslim Brotherhood: On the Occasion of Its Fiftieth Anniversary* (in Arabic), 2d ed. (n.p., 1979), pp. 92, 127–35; Muhammad Ali Dinnawi, *The Largest Islamic Movements in Contemporary Times* (in Arabic), Voice of Truth Series, 8 (Cairo: Cairo University Islamic Group, 1978), pp. 134–48.

end enhanced the attraction. Indeed, 30 percent of the respondents in the 1982 survey expressed strong support for the Islamic revolution in Iran; 48 percent declared moderate support, and 22 percent strong opposition.

Practicing Muslims who supported Fatah were another political faction whose influence was difficult to assess. Among its members were traditional Islamic leaders (including members of the Islamic Supreme Council in Jerusalem) and some members of the academic and professional communities. Fatah's support among Islamic youth was limited. Indeed, only 14 percent of the students in the 1982 survey strongly supported Fatah and 28 percent moderately; a majority—58 percent—expressed their opposition to Fatah.

The pro-Fatah faction argued that the PLO was reluctant to define its attitude toward the Islamic movement because the PLO's emphasis was on national liberation. Fatah followers among the Islamists believed that in the future the PLO would alter its posture and adopt Islam. Consequently, in the power struggle between nationalists and leftists on the one hand, and the Muslim Brotherhood on the other, the pro-Fatah faction was allied with the nationalists, which weakened their political influence in the Islamic movement.

Traditionally, the Islamic movement was concentrated in towns in the north and south of the West Bank and among refugees. It also appealed to landowners, merchants, shopkeepers, and workers. In a change from the 1950s and 1960s, the movement in the 1980s became popular among the intelligentsia, including university students and faculty. Indeed, many of its advocates were well-educated, upwardly mobile Palestinians hoping to improve the quality of their lives but also to avoid "Western moral corruption."

Followers of Islam maintained clubs in a number of major towns in the West Bank and Gaza Strip, including the Young Men's Muslim Association in Jerusalem and the Islamic Center in Gaza. They also sponsored lectures and formed study groups in mosques to disseminate Islamic values. Moreover, they celebrated Islamic holy days, circulated magazines and books, and distributed leaflets and statements expressing their political stands on a wide range of issues. Frequently the mosques were used as rallying sites for the followers of Islam to protest Israeli settler attacks on Muslim holy shrines.

Political Positions of the Islamists

With the unfolding political developments in the West Bank and Gaza Strip, proponents of an Islamic reawakening developed their own ideas on how to deal with Israel, the Arab countries, the PLO, and nationalist forces in the occupied territories. They believed that both Arab and Palestinian nationalism had been proven incapable of resolving the Palestinian question. This was not surprising to them because the concept of nationalism— borrowed from the West by a small group of intellectuals, mostly Christian, at the turn of the century—was alien to the Arab and Islamic cultural tradition. They contended that the Arab Muslim masses had not contributed to the development of the idea of nationalism. And during the rebellion against the Ottoman Empire they had remained committed to the preservation of Islamic unity under the banner of the empire.[10] Followers of the Islamic movement attributed splits in the Muslim world to the pervasiveness of secular nationalism, which they saw as divisive in nature. They believed that the prevailing secularist ideas of Palestinian and Arab nationalists were unsuited to cope with the religious struggle with Israel. Arab nationalism confined its conflict with Israel to the Arabs, and Palestinian nationalism narrowed that conflict to the Palestinian people. Marxism-Leninism viewed the struggle from a class perspective, thus limiting it to the Palestinian, Arab, and Israeli workers against the capitalist class in these three societies.

Because the concept of nationalism had geographic limitations, Islamists argued that a sense of commitment to the Palestinian question should be neither territorial nor national. A sole attachment to the land was dangerous since substitute lands could be found. From an Islamic perspective, the Palestinian question was first and foremost a religious one. Failure to make it an integral part of the larger Islamic movement was not only tantamount to treason but also excluded millions of Muslims from the dispute with Israel.

Those who professed this view claimed that Islam was capable of putting an end to the plight of the Palestinians, checking Israeli expansionism, and liberating all of Palestine. They recalled that

10. *Al-Nur al-Ilahi,* July 27 and October 19, 1982.

under Islam's banner the West had been defeated and Palestine liberated from the Crusaders. Thus they demanded that secular ideas be pushed aside to allow the Islamic movement to put its teachings into practice. They argued that the tenets of Islam had a broad perspective that did not contradict the ideas of nationalism.[11]

From an Islamic point of view, certain Arab regimes were unqualified to lead the struggle against Israel. Indeed, Islamists believed that Arabs had sustained repeated military defeats because wars against Israel had not been fought in the name of Islam. Because of their secular orientation, these regimes had failed not only to check Israel's expansion but to mobilize the Muslim masses and ensure Palestinian rights.[12] The pro-Western orientation of these Arab regimes meant that they had no support from the masses. It was naive to expect such countries to work "sincerely" and sacrifice to liberate Palestine. Proponents of the Islamic movement even asserted that none of the wars waged by Arab governments had been intended to free the occupied territories from Israel's control. Arab regimes had simply been trying to broaden their political legitimacy through identification and association with the Palestinian question.[13]

Adherents of Islam charged that over the years, radical and conservative Arab regimes had worked together to "liquidate" the Palestinian problem. Acceptance of the American-sponsored peace proposal known as the Rogers Plan in 1969, the Camp David Accords of 1978, the adoption of a peace plan at the Arab Summit Conference in Fez in 1982, and the initiation of a Jordanian-PLO dialogue following the 1982 Lebanon war were all clear examples of Arab unwillingness to deal squarely with the Palestinian question. The Islamic movement even traced what it perceived as an Arab betrayal of the Palestinians to the time when Arab regimes had assisted Britain and France in dividing the Ottoman Empire between them, and later when they had allowed Israel to occupy

11. Dinnawi, *Largest Islamic Movements*, pp. 152–53.

12. Muhammad Abd al-Halim, *The Islamic Call: Events That Made History* (in Arabic) (Alexandria, Egypt: Dar al-Dawa, 1979), vol. 1; *Al-Nida*, no. 2.

13. On the importance of Islam rejuvenating the Arab world after the 1948 and 1967 wars, see Tawfiq al-Tayyib, *The Islamic Solution after the Two Debacles* (in Arabic), 2d ed. (Cairo: Al-Mukhtar al-Islami, 1979).

considerable portions of Arab lands. These same regimes, Islamists asserted, had worked to limit the PLO's military operations against the Jewish state and had suppressed the Islamic movement in their own countries.[14]

Under the Likud government Israel has cast its claims to Palestine in religious and ideological arguments, thus increasing the reasons for conducting the struggle with Israel on religious grounds. The Islamic movement holds that the establishment of Israel in 1948 symbolized the triumph of evil over justice. And it perceives Israel as an integral part of the "Western offensive" against the domain of Islam. Advocates of Islam have argued that the West created Israel to advance Western interests in the region, preserve pro-Western Arab regimes, perpetuate division among Arabs, erode Islamic cultural identity, and keep the Muslims away from their religion. They assert that Israel is the nucleus for a larger Jewish state between the Euphrates and the Nile that Jews dream of.[15]

From an Islamic religious view, the Arab-Israeli conflict allows no room for compromise. The followers of the Islamic movement are adamant about not recognizing Israel or dealing with it, even if the PLO should authorize such a move. They believe that there is no room for reconciliation with the Jewish state. Those who share this view consider themselves at war with any country or organization that would accept recognition or territorial compromise with Israel. Confrontation with Israel should be total and comprehensive and fought with all available means. Above all, the preeminence and unity of Islam must be reestablished through an Islamic state, since it was the decline of Islam and the collapse of the Ottoman Empire that made possible the creation of Israel.

Until the mid-1980s these extremist arguments were not translated into tangible policies and actions against the Jewish state. Throughout the 1970s and early 1980s the followers of Islam avoided any confrontation with the Israeli military authorities, presumably in order not to provide the Israelis with a pretext for

14. "The Islamic Movement and the Palestinian Problem" (in Arabic), *Al-Nida*, no. 4. See also *Al-Nida*, no. 6; *Al-Risala* (occasional publication by Hebron College for Islamic Jurisprudence) (1982).

15. Islamic University in Gaza, "The Future of the Palestinian Problem and the Expected Role of the Islamic Movement" (in Arabic), *Al-Nida*, no. 6. See also *Al-Nida*, no. 2.

cracking down on the movement. Their immediate task was to disseminate their views and broaden their power base in the occupied territories.

In the second half of the 1980s, the followers of the Islamic movement launched several attacks on Israeli targets, including an assault on a group of soldiers at the Wailing Wall in October 1986. A considerable number of demonstrations and strikes in the occupied territories, especially in Gaza, were initiated by the proponents of Islam. The movement played an active role in the uprising that began in the Gaza Strip in December 1987.

Islam and the PLO

Islam's exclusion from the politics and deliberations of the PLO, proponents of the Islamic movement believe, has kept millions of Muslims from participating in the jihad to liberate Palestine.[16] The casting of the Palestinian question as essentially an Islamic issue and the call for the replacement of Palestinian nationalism by Islamic ideology conflict sharply with the PLO's secular orientation and its focus on Palestinian nationalism. This should not be surprising, since the PLO leadership has little claim on Islam and religious authority.

The Islamic movement has been critical of the PLO's search for a diplomatic solution to the Palestinian question. It considered the PLO's quest for a political solution "a liquidation of the Palestinian question" and a departure from military struggle. Islamic advocates have stated that they would oppose the initiation of any dialogue between the Israelis and the Palestinians. The PLO's endorsement of the Fez plan, its initiation of a dialogue with Jordan, and favorable reactions by some of its leaders to the Reagan initiative were denounced by Islamic activists in the West Bank and Gaza Strip as a deviation from the goal of liberating all of Palestine.

Islamic groups have expressed their opposition to the PLO's strategic goal of establishing a secular democratic state in Palestine and the narrower goal of forming a nationalist independent state in the West Bank and the Gaza Strip. Followers of Islam insist on

16. "The PLO and the Islamic Trend" (in Arabic), *Al-Mujtama al-Islami*, April 1981.

the elimination of any Israeli presence in Palestine and unequiv-
ocally demand an Islamic state governed by Islamic tradition. The
duties and obligations of the citizens of an Islamic state, whether
Muslims, Christians, or Jews, would be determined by Islamic law.
Many Islamists have stated their resolve to bring about such an
Islamic state even if violence were necessary. Two-thirds of those
interviewed in the 1982 survey contended that they would work
first through democratic means to bring about an Islamic state but
would not hesitate to resort to violence to realize their goal.

FAILURE TO RECOGNIZE THE PLO.   Although Islamic leaders in
the occupied territories have repeatedly asserted that they harbor
no hostile feelings toward the PLO and do not offer themselves
as an alternative to it, there is no doubt that the Islamic movement
aspires to become the true and only inspiration for the Palestinian
people in their struggle against Israel. Islamic groups prefer not
to address the thorny question of recognizing the PLO as the sole
legitimate representative of Palestinian national interests. They
have avoided outright rejection of the PLO, but neither have they
recognized its absolute mandate. Their ambivalence is intentional,
for clear denunciation of the organization would diminish Islam's
chances of widening its base of popular support and disseminating
its ideas in the Palestinian community.

Islamists have rejected PLO demands that they explicitly recognize the organization, complaining that the Islamic movement
alone has been singled out to do so. They contend that the 1974
Arab Summit resolution in Rabat, designating the PLO as the
exclusive spokesman for Palestinians, was meant to constrain
Jordan's ambitions to recover the occupied territories, not to extract
recognition of the PLO from Palestinians. They argue that repeated
demands to renew their allegiance to the PLO are not only
unacceptable but undemocratic, reflecting the PLO's intolerance
of differing views within the Palestinian community. The demands
portray weakness and political incompetence. The PLO's engagement in armed struggle and military operations gave it political
legitimacy, but as its leaders began to depart from the military
option, doubts and questions about its right to represent Palestinians
surfaced.

Followers of Islam have thus granted only a qualified mandate to the PLO. One exception is Al-Tahrir, whose followers have always been intensely hostile to the Palestinian organization. In a controversy at Hebron College in 1980 between nationalists and Islamic adherents, Al-Tahrir members accused the PLO of being atheistic and heretical; they regarded the formation of a Palestinian entity as a "great crime" serving only the interests of the West and Israel. The party reluctantly supports the PLO so long as the jihad against Israel and a commitment to the liberation of all of Palestine continue. Should the PLO accept a political settlement or agree to territorial concessions favoring Israel, the mandate would be revoked.

HOSTILITY TO MARXISTS.   Islamic groups also strongly resent the presence of Marxist elements in the PLO's ranks. The hostility of Islam to Marxist doctrine is unwavering and unequivocal. Marxism is perceived as a rival world view, similar in its comprehensiveness but antithetical to the precepts of Islam.

Islamic groups viewed the Soviet invasion of Afghanistan as an assault on Islam and the Afghan resistance as an Islamic struggle that should be backed by the Muslim world. They found the PLO's neutrality toward the resistance perplexing and in conflict with its commitment to struggles of national liberation movements.

AMBIVALENCE TOWARD FATAH.   The Islamic movement's reluctance to sever all ties with the PLO probably is as much due to the popularity of the mainstream Fatah among Palestinians as to the PLO's position of power. Fatah's relations with the Islamic movement have sometimes been cooperative and sometimes adversarial. At the time of its inception, leading Fatah figures, including Arafat himself, proclaimed their Islamic ties. The influence of Islam, however, began to recede as secular nationalism came to be the official ideology of Fatah. Islamists have repeatedly contended that Fatah's leaders have resisted all attempts to have Islam incorporated in the PLO's political program.[17] Thus the majority of the Islamic groups has remained independent of the PLO, willing to work with Fatah on occasion but not the PLO's more leftist factions.

17. Ibid. See also "Islam and the Palestinian Question" (in Arabic), *Al-Talia al-Islamiya,* January 1983.

Fatah's nationalist orientation has made possible temporary alliances with Islamic groups—particularly the Muslim Brotherhood—aimed at containment of Marxist forces in the West Bank and Gaza Strip. Only a small minority of the Islamic followers is willing to work from within Fatah's organization.

This limited rapprochement has often been disturbed by the insistence of Fatah's leaders on excluding Islam from the PLO's doctrine. For their part, proponents of Islam have accused Fatah of directing a public campaign against their movement and trying to arrest the growth of its support. They were critical of pro-Fatah groups' joining anti-Islamic forces in January 1982 in signing a political statement condemning the Muslim Brotherhood. Fatah has also been part of a national bloc formed to check the advancement of the Islamic movement in student council elections, labor unions, and other institutions and professional associations.

Political developments within the PLO in the spring of 1983 reduced the tension between Fatah and the Islamic groups in the occupied territories. The Syrian regime's hostility to both Arafat and the Muslim Brotherhood created a commonality of interests between them that helped to ease the tension in their relations.

SUPPORT OF ARAFAT. Despite its wavering relationship with Fatah, almost every group in the Islamic movement joined in condemnation of the mutiny against Arafat inside Fatah in the spring of 1983. Proponents of the Islamic movement called the mutiny "a criminal act" and the mutineers "puppets moved by Syria." They attributed the rebellion to the presence of "alien ideologies" in the PLO, envisaging a "conspiracy" of Palestinian leftist forces, Arab Marxists, and the Soviet Union as well as both Syria and Libya.[18] Islamic followers contended that the objective of these forces was to break up Fatah from within, liquidate the Palestinian question, and eliminate the military option.

Arafat was blamed for tolerating leftist forces, cooperating with the Soviet Union, and forming alliances with Syria and Libya. The mutiny was seen as a first step in the process of a final crackdown on the followers of Islam in the occupied territories and an attempt to foil any effort by Fatah's leaders to move closer to the Islamic

18. *Al-Muntalaq* (published by the Islamic bloc at Al-Najah University), September 1983.

movement. Leaders of the Islamic movement appealed to Fatah to purge its ranks of Marxist elements, to see the futility of secularism, and to cooperate more closely with the Muslim groups.

The Islamic movement bitterly attacked the Syrian regime for supporting the rebels. Supporters of the Islamic youth movement issued a number of statements contending that the government of Hafiz Asad had always conspired against the PLO.[19] Even before his coming to power in November 1970 Asad, they asserted, had been hostile toward Palestinians, as manifested in his refusal to commit the Syrian army to the Palestinians' cause during the 1970 civil war in Jordan. Likewise, during the Lebanese civil war in the mid-1970s Asad had ordered his troops in Lebanon to attack the PLO forces, and during the Israeli seige of Beirut in the summer of 1982 he did not order Syrian troops stationed in Lebanon to fight alongside the PLO. An Islamic publication bluntly stated that "the Syrian military presence in Lebanon was not meant to repel the Israelis but to attack the Palestinians."[20]

Asad's hostility toward Arafat culminated in the support that Damascus lent to the rebels against the PLO chairman and the eviction of the remainder of Fatah's troops from northern Lebanon in December 1983. And Syria encouraged the Amal Shia seizure of Palestinian refugee camps around Beirut between 1985 and 1987. Islamists maintained that the underlying motives behind these actions were to strip the PLO of its military capability, isolate it from the confrontation with Israel, and facilitate the process of accommodation with both Israel and the United States.[21]

The expulsion of Arafat from Damascus on June 24, 1983, drew a sharp reaction from leading Islamists in the occupied territories. In a public rally at Al-Aqsa Mosque in Jerusalem the day after Arafat's deportation, Saad al-Din al-Alami, the head of the Islamic Supreme Council in Jerusalem, sharply denounced the Syrian regime and proclaimed that the assassination of the Syrian president was the duty of every Muslim.[22]

The Islamic movement's attitude toward the PLO continued to

19. Statements signed by various Islamic blocs in the West Bank and the Gaza Strip, November 17 and December 20, 1983, and by the Islamic bloc at Bir Zeit University, January 1984.

20. "The Resistance and Asad" (in Arabic), *Al-Nida*, no. 3.

21. *Al-Muntalaq*, December 1983; *Al-Dawa* (published by the Islamic Endowment Council in Jerusalem), August 1983.

22. *Al-Nida*, no. 4.

be governed by Arafat's diplomatic maneuvering. The pro-Khomeini group severely attacked the Arafat policy of rapprochement with Jordan and the attempt to resolve the Palestinian question through American mediation. While attacking the ideology of pro-PLO hard-line groups, it nevertheless aligned itself with them against the mainstream PLO. The Syrian-Jordanian rapprochement in the first half of 1986 and the breakdown of the Arafat-Hussein dialogue in February of that year lessened the tension between the Islamic movement and the PLO. The tension faded during the rebellion that took place in the occupied territories in late 1987 and 1988.

Opposition to the Islamic Youth Movement

The consolidation of the Islamic youth movement by 1980 brought a temporary halt to the struggle between Fatah supporters and the followers of the PLO's rejectionist factions for control of West Bank institutions and mass organizations. Encouraged by the PLO, representatives of the student movement, labor unions, and professional organizations joined to promote unity among their followers and to contain the rising Islamic tide. Agreement on nationalist candidates for student council elections in 1982–83 succeeded in preventing followers of the Islamic movement from controlling the councils of Al-Najah University and Hebron College.

In a public campaign against the followers of Islam, nationalist forces accused the proponents of the Islamic movement of being "nonrevolutionaries" and "reactionaries" and "agents" of the United States, Israel, and moderate Arab countries. They charged that West Bank Islamic groups were primarily concerned with "fighting" the PLO and Palestinian nationalism rather than Israel. In a rally at Bir Zeit University on February 12, 1982, representatives of various student councils in the West Bank and Gaza denounced the Islamic movement. They alleged that the Islamic movement, like the village leagues, was encouraged, if not sponsored, by the Israeli government to serve Israeli interests, contain Palestinian nationalism, and create an alternative leadership to the PLO in the occupied territories. They concluded that advocates were using Islam and the mosques to spread hatred and divide Palestinians, and they ruled out any reconciliation with the proponents of Islam.

Supporters of the Islamic youth movement argued that nationalist leaders and pro-PLO institutions were working to suppress their movement. Their cause had been distorted by the local press and they had been wrongly portrayed as being in direct confrontation with the PLO rather than with Israel. They further asserted that their groups were discriminated against in the universities and other institutions and that they had been denied freedom of expression and the right to celebrate religious festivals.[23] They denied any intention of taking from the PLO the role of representing Palestinian interests and demanded that the PLO respect their rights and beliefs and not coerce them into abandoning their views.

Islamists also complained about the way that steadfastness money was being distributed.[24] They charged that the Joint Jordanian-Palestinian Economic Committee was using the money to buy political influence among West Bank politicians and leaders instead of channeling it to the needy and investing it in social, economic, and cultural projects.

They also challenged the legitimacy of the nationalist leadership and institutions in the West Bank and Gaza Strip. The pro-PLO forces were unqualified to provide guidance and leadership, they contended, because they did not represent the true feelings and beliefs of Palestinians. From an Islamic perspective, those leaders were unable to present a unified and harmonious stance because their allegiance was split among rival PLO factions and they were concerned with advancing their own vested interests.

This incompatibility in political objectives of Islamic followers and pro-PLO forces severely limited the prospects for reconciliation between them before 1987. Violence was a natural outcome of attempts of the opposing camps to assert themselves on the local political scene. University campuses in particular were the scene of bloody conflict and bitter fighting—for instance, at Al-Najah University in early 1981, at Bir Zeit University in late spring 1983,

23. These grievances were mentioned in statements signed by representatives of various Islamic student councils and Islamic blocs, January 10, 1982, and by the Islamic bloc at Bir Zeit University, January 9, 1983.

24. The 1978 Arab summit conference in Baghdad allocated an annual sum of $150 million to buttress the steadfastness of the Palestinians in the West Bank and the Gaza Strip.

repeatedly at the Islamic University in Gaza, and at Hebron College between 1983 and 1985. Islamists singled out communist targets, like the Palestinian Red Crescent premises in Gaza which were set on fire in January 1980. Islamic militants also occasionally attacked movie theaters in their determination to purify their society of corrupting Western influence.

Prospects of the Islamic Movement

Despite its recent origin, the Islamic movement has become one of the major political forces in the West Bank and Gaza Strip. Whether Islamism will be more successful in addressing Palestinian national grievances than either pan-Arabism or Palestinian nationalism is an open question. Yet opportunities for the further dissemination of the Islamic movement will depend on developments inside and outside the occupied territories. On the domestic side, the concept of national unity among pro-PLO forces has helped to contain the influence of the Islamic youth movement in the universities. Bitter internecine rivalries in the PLO, however, have undermined the nationalists' "containment policy." The mutiny within Fatah, Arafat's rift with Syria and his reconciliation with Egypt, the emergence and subsequent failure of a joint diplomatic approach between the PLO and Jordan have pitted supporters and opponents of PLO Chairman Arafat against each other. Their conflicts have shattered the national front that they had erected to counter the rising Islamic challenge. As long as the strength and vigor of secular ideologies are sapped by the competition among their adherents, Islam will be in an advantageous position.

Palestinian nationalism, which has remained popular among a majority of Palestinians despite the conservative nature of the society, will continue to be an obstacle to a complete Islamic takeover in the West Bank. Many of the urban political groups in the West Bank continue to be essentially secular in their orientation, and the presence of a Christian minority in West Bank Palestinian society may forestall impressive Islamic political gains in the West Bank central towns of Jerusalem, Bethlehem, and Ramallah. This, however, is not the case in the Gaza Strip, where Islam has for many years effectively challenged Palestinian nationalism.

The Islamic movement's viability depends also on whether its followers can preserve a degree of unity among themselves. The political gains of the movement can be undermined if rivalries break out between the Muslim Brotherhood and the more militant followers of Al-Tahrir and the pro-Khomeini group (these subgroupings for some time have been competing at the Islamic University of Gaza). Though the hostility of outside forces has muted the differences among the four political groupings in the Islamic movement, rivalry among them may break out over political and religious issues. Which group truly represents the interests and aspirations of the Muslims? Their rivalry might be exacerbated as each of the groups tries to win the Palestinian audience.

The absence of strong leadership and a well-structured political organization also obstructs the growth of the Islamic movement and prevents its followers from competing effectively with pro-PLO and communist groups. Moreover, the several groups within the Islamic movement without central leadership may eventually go their separate ways.

The Islamic movement must devise a set of political strategies and tactics to guide its activities and put its theories into practice that will give credibility to its claim of leadership in the Palestinian struggle. Until the mid-1980s the movement avoided any campaign of sustained resistance to Israel's military occupation and advised caution and restraint in student demonstrations and strikes. Such a cautious approach appears to have been abandoned in the second half of the 1980s. Since then, the followers of the Islamic movement have not hesitated to attack Israeli targets and have actively participated in the wave of unrest that erupted in December 1987. The Islamic political activism is intended to increase the credibility and popularity of Islam's followers in the occupied territories.

The success or suppression of Islamic revivalist groups through-out the region will affect the Islamic movement in the occupied territories. Thus, the continued inability of the Iranian Islamic revolution to realize its dreams of establishing a strong and viable Islamic state and of exporting the Islamic revolution to neighboring countries, coupled with Iran's involvement in a prolonged and inconclusive war with Iraq, has slowed the momentum and enthusiasm for a generalized Islamic resurgence. Those setbacks dampen the morale of Islam's followers in the West Bank and Gaza Strip.

Other developments can work in Islam's favor. Diplomatic efforts to resolve the Palestinian question have been so ineffective that disillusionment with secular approaches to fulfilling Palestinian national aspirations may become widespread. Many more Palestinians may come to believe that Islam, coupled with the concept of jihad, alone will liberate Palestine.

Yet the tolerance of Israel's military government has been vital to the Islamic movement in the occupied territories. Israel's acquiescence is likely to continue as long as the Islamic movement opposes the PLO's secular orientation and Palestinian nationalism. From an Israeli perspective, the long-range Islamic goal of an Islamic state in all of Palestine does not constitute an immediate threat to Israel's desire to control the West Bank and Gaza Strip. Yet the frequent participation of the followers of the Islamic movement in violent strikes and demonstrations and their engagement in military operations against the Israeli army and civilians compelled the Israeli government to revise its policy toward the Islamists in the second half of the 1980s. Thus the Israeli government imprisoned several of the Islamic activists, and it deported some Islamic leaders to Lebanon in January and April 1988.

While tactical considerations have encouraged a policy of tolerance toward the Islamic movement, there is little doubt that the increasing power of religious groups in Israel will lessen the tolerance. In response, more West Bank Palestinians are likely to invoke Islam. Indeed, Islam could serve not only as a rallying point and center of attraction for Palestinians in the occupied territories but for Palestinians in the diaspora as well. The Islamic religion would offer Palestinians in the occupied territories an indisputable title to the land and a way of reaffirming their historic claim to Palestine and reasserting their ethnic national identity and cultural purity in the face of mounting Israeli challenges and threats.

Other aspects of Israel's policy in the West Bank and Gaza Strip also may compel an increasing number of Palestinians to embrace Islam. For example, local political activists may be driven to embrace religion because of Israel's restrictive measures against proponents of secular ideologies and because of its policy of denying the local populace the right to form political groups. Thus, as has happened in other countries, the manipulation of religious symbols might provide followers of the Islamic movement with relative immunity from the Israeli government. As a consequence, mosques would serve as sites for political activity and protest movements.

Support from Jordan is another factor that will determine the ability of the Islamic movement to expand its power base in the occupied territories. Jordan's interest in the growth of the Islamic movement in the West Bank and Gaza Strip has been based on Islamic political gains that come at the expense of Jordan's long-time rival, the PLO. Moreover, Jordan's tolerance of the Muslim Brotherhood's activities has been based in part on the Brotherhood's reciprocal support of the Jordanian government and in part on traditional hostilities between Jordan and Syria. However, with the improvement of relations between Jordan and Syria, this may change. In November 1985, as a political gesture to the Syrian president, King Hussein instructed his government to put an end to the anti-Syrian political activities of the Islamic movement. But Jordanian support for the West Bank Islamic movement may not be affected by the regime's stand against the Brotherhood.

Political developments in the PLO are also likely to have some bearing on the prospects of the Islamic movement in the West Bank. Reconciliation within the PLO may enable its followers in the occupied territories to work jointly to check the growth and influence of the Islamic movement. Conversely, the persistence of division in the PLO will make it difficult for pro-PLO groups to contain the growing popularity of Islam.

With the PLO weakened politically and militarily, Islam most likely will continue to offer itself as a point of reference that provides ready-made solutions without the obscurity and diplomatic flexibility that secular ideologies entail. Islam may present itself as a more powerful and legitimizing instrument for mass mobilization and recruitment than the PLO, for it furnishes its followers with a mystical and universal rationalization for the correctness of the people's cause and their indisputable right to the land. Thus the absence of a solution to the Palestinian question, the continuing diplomatic setbacks for the PLO, and mounting Jewish threats indicate that a return to religion will have an increasing appeal among the West Bank population. The fusion of religion and politics in Arab political culture and prevailing socioeconomic conditions most likely will facilitate the trend toward replacing secular ideologies with religion.

In such a situation, the choice facing West Bank Palestinians will perhaps no longer be between secular nationalism and religion but between the conservative side of Islam represented by the Muslim Brotherhood (the group that so far has been dominant and has maintained close links with Jordan and West Bank religious establishments) and the more activist, interventionist, revolutionary type of Islam modeled after the Iranian Islamic revolution and Lebanon's militant Islamic groups. The latter, radical Islamic movement undoubtedly would affect the modes and patterns of action and protest against Israel's occupation.

It would be wrong to conclude from the analysis here that a complete Islamic displacement of secular nationalism is imminent in the occupied territories. The Islamic movement will inevitably have a Palestinian nationalist tone because of the struggle with Israel over Palestine. The movement has stressed the need for political and economic independence, Arab ethnic identity and cultural purity, and strong anticolonial and anti-Western sentiments.

Even as the Islamic movement has deepened its influence among youth, a parallel trend toward pragmatism and political realism among the urban elite has become discernible in the 1980s. The two trends serve as tangible signs of the West Bank's growing dissatisfaction with the prevailing ideologies and approaches in the region. While followers of the Islamic movement have invoked religion to replace secular ideologies, proponents of political pragmatism have lowered their expectations. They have begun to advocate both an association of the West Bank and Gaza with Jordan and the formation of a joint Jordanian-Palestinian delegation to take part in negotiations to find a solution to the Palestinian problem.

CHAPTER EIGHT

The Crisis of Leadership in the West Bank

🔄 🔄 🔄

WITH THE outlawing of the National Guidance Committee, the latest of three attempts by the West Bank urban elite to create a framework for the articulation of their interests against Israel's occupation (the Islamic Supreme Council, the Palestine National Front, and the National Guidance Committee) was brought to an end. The ousting of several West Bank mayors from office was particularly detrimental to the political influence of the nationalist and leftist politicians. Despite their weakened position, however, these politicians continued to seek a more assertive Palestine Liberation Organization—a PLO that would look toward Syria rather than to Jordan and that would cultivate the support of the Soviet Union rather than seek collaboration with the West, and with the United States in particular. In addition, they continued to hope for a PLO that would establish a West Bank–Gaza Palestinian state rather than a confederation with Jordan.

The Ascendancy of the Moderates and Pragmatists, 1982–86

Political developments after the 1982 Lebanon war caused the balance of power to shift in favor of both the pro-Jordanian traditional elite and the pro-PLO pragmatic politicians.[1] Over time, these politicians had developed an appreciation for a system of Jordanian-PLO diplomatic coordination and some had shown unusual flexibility in dealing with the Israeli military authorities.

---

1. Among them were Elias Freij, mayor of Bethlehem, and Rashad al-Shawwa, former mayor of Gaza, who were pro-Jordanian. Hanna Siniora, editor of *Al-Fajr;* Fayiz Abu Rahmah, a lawyer from Gaza; Faisal Husaini, director of the Arab Studies Center in Jerusalem; Zafer al-Masri, the appointed mayor of Nablus; and Sari Nusseibeh, professor of philosophy at Bir Zeit University, were pro-PLO.

Further, they had established a dialogue with the Israeli peace camp and political parties. Analysis of the factors that led to the revival of this group may offer clues about the likelihood of its long-term stability and survival.

Although Israel's effort to create a rural-based Palestinian leadership had failed, it had nevertheless undermined the political power of the West Bank nationalist elite. A residue of the pro-Jordanians' political power, however, remained intact. The pro-Jordanian conservative elite had been spared such restrictive measures as town arrests and removal from office, but that was no indication that Israel wished to protect them. Simply, their restraint and pragmatic style had made them relatively immune from Defense Minister Ariel Sharon's crippling blows.

Indeed, it was this pragmatic style of politics that accounted for the survival of the pro-Jordanian elite over the years. Their approach enabled them both to cope with an unfavorable political environment and to adjust to changing political conditions. During their period of high political vulnerability and insecurity in the mid- to late 1970s, pro-Jordanian politicians did not choose to challenge the prevailing political norms but decided to acquiesce to them. Instead of confronting the PLO, these politicians viewed the organization as the sole legitimate representative of the Palestinian people and supported its goal of forming an independent Palestinian state in the occupied territories.

After their defeat in the 1976 municipal elections these adaptable politicians looked for new channels to build up their power centers. The need to extend the educational system to absorb the rising number of students seeking higher education in the West Bank and Gaza Strip gave pro-Jordanian leaders an opportunity to broaden their political influence. With financial assistance from the Jordanian government, they established new universities and colleges and expanded existing ones. Thus pro-Jordanian figures have occupied key positions in the administration of all of the universities and colleges except Bir Zeit University.

Traditional leaders also benefited from Jordan's financial assistance and political support over the years. Pro-Jordanian figures gained too from the various political shake-ups that took place in the second half of the 1970s and early 1980s. For instance, the outbreak of the civil war in Lebanon in the mid-1970s and the

resulting Syrian-PLO rift, as well as the signing of the Camp David
Accords, forced the PLO to forge a limited reconciliation with the
Jordanian government. With such rapprochement, much of the
criticism launched by leftist politicians against the pro-Jordanian
elite for dealing with Amman lost momentum and strength.

The PLO leaders, seeking to widen the base of support for their
organization, made conciliatory gestures to the pro-Jordanian
politicians. The traditional politicians' close ties with Egypt and
Jordan made them ideal middlemen in managing the PLO's
relations with these two countries. And the accommodation of the
pro-Jordanian politicians was a sign to King Hussein of the PLO's
desire for reconciliation.

The struggle within the PLO for control of the occupied
territories also served the interests of the pro-Jordanian elite.
Indeed, Fatah leaders made diplomatic overtures to key pro-
Jordanian figures—Arafat even met with some of them—and from
time to time issued statements of support for these politicians.
Fatah used its access to the $150 million allocated annually by the
Arab countries to the occupied territories to offer economic rewards
to its supporters and to gain the political backing of pro-Jordanian
politicians.

Political events after the 1982 Lebanon war also gave impetus
to the reemergence of pro-Jordanian leaders and allowed for the
crystallization of a class of pro-PLO pragmatic elite. The launching
of the Reagan initiative and the commencement of the Jordanian-
PLO dialogue improved Jordan's influence and stature. As a result,
Jordan's role in the resolution of the Palestinian question could no
longer be ignored.

THE PRIMACY OF THE OCCUPIED TERRITORIES.   With the dismantling of the PLO's political headquarters in Beirut and its
military infrastructure in southern Lebanon—and the accompanying dispersal of its troops to several Arab countries—the West
Bank and Gaza became the PLO's primary constituency and
resource for political survival and legitimacy. Leaders of the PLO
therefore had to be attentive to the interests and concerns of the
Palestinians in the occupied territories and were compelled to
assign more weight to diplomacy as a means of resolving the
Palestinian question. To make the diplomatic option more viable,

PLO leaders made efforts to temper their traditional enmity with the Hashemite regime and forge a diplomatic alliance with their former adversary. Similarly, the split within the ranks of the Palestinian organization in the spring of 1983 meant that Arafat was no longer paralyzed by his concern that Palestinian unity be preserved at all costs. From then on, the PLO exhibited a greater degree of political flexibility and moderation.

The interest of PLO leaders in finding a political solution to the Palestinian problem gave the pro-Jordanian politicians and the pragmatic elite added encouragement and energy. In particular, the signing of an agreement for joint diplomatic coordination between King Hussein and Yasir Arafat in February 1985 significantly enhanced the stature of the pragmatic politicians. The Arafat-Hussein accord advocating an exchange of land for peace, the confederation of a Palestinian state in the occupied territories with Jordan, and the formation of a joint Jordanian-Palestinian delegation were, after all, in line with the long-held position of the pro-Jordanian politicians.

Dissension within the PLO's ranks after the Lebanon war opened new political opportunities on the West Bank. The mutiny in Fatah and the rift between the PLO's mainstream and rejectionist factions, culminating in the boycott by the latter groups of the seventeenth session of the Palestine National Council in Amman in November 1984, shattered the unity of the pro-PLO forces in the occupied territories. As a consequence the political status of the members of the pragmatic camp was advanced. Those politicians felt that they had to seek a more active role in any future political game.

When the Labor party joined Israel's National Unity government in the fall of 1984, members of the pragmatic camp had their hopes raised that a political solution of the occupied territories' status was possible. In contrast to the uncompromising attitude of the Likud bloc over the future of the occupied territories, Israel's Labor party favored some territorial compromise with Jordan. The leaders of the party seemed also willing to begin negotiations with a joint Jordanian-Palestinian delegation, but excluding the PLO, under international auspices.

The net effect of all these political developments was the political reactivation of the pro-Jordanian elite and the advent of a different class of pro-PLO pragmatic politician. Leaders of both groups supported the PLO's efforts to forge closer ties with Egypt and Jordan. They wanted the PLO to concentrate on diplomacy and abandon the recourse to violence. And they also displayed a willingness to deal simultaneously with Israel, Jordan, and the PLO and balance their competing interests.

In the face of formidable challenges between 1983 and 1986, Arafat needed the support of both groups for his political survival and the survival of his brand of PLO. Arafat's pro-Jordan–pro-Egypt policies as well as his anti-Syria posture received full political backing from the pro-Jordanian and the pro-PLO pragmatic camp. Several political rallies were convened and frequent statements issued to denounce the Syrian regime for its expulsion of Arafat in June 1983 and its deepening of the split in the ranks of the PLO. Both camps also strongly condemned the mutiny that broke out in Fatah against Arafat's leadership.

THE URGENCY OF ENDING ISRAEL'S OCCUPATION. The pro-Jordanian and pro-PLO groups, despite their support for the PLO and the Jordanian-PLO joint diplomatic initiative, differed over the price and concessions to be made for the sake of ending Israel's military occupation. The pro-PLO politicians insisted on advance American recognition of the Palestinian national right of self-determination in return for the PLO's acceptance of United Nations Security Council Resolutions 242 and 338 calling for peace in the region. The pro-Jordanian elite did not attach the same significance to the right of self-determination. Their foremost priority was to salvage the land and to end Israel's military control. They viewed Jordan's participation in the peace process and the PLO's political concessions as indispensable steps toward rescuing the land. The mayors of Bethlehem and Gaza, Elias Freij and Rashad al-Shawwa, repeatedly warned that time was not working on the side of the Palestinians and that any delay in the search for a solution to the Palestinian question would allow Israel to swallow up more land. Under the slogan of salvaging whatever could be salvaged, Mayor Freij asserted: "We in the West Bank and the Gaza Strip welcome any solution that will liberate us from occupation. Our primary aim is to get rid of occupation and to salvage the land. Our foremost source of suffering has been the continuous loss of land."[2]

2. Interview in *Al-Quds*, May 2, 1983.

Several pro-Jordanian politicians signed a Peace Document in November 1982 that asserted the inseparable unity between the Palestinians and both banks of the Jordan River.[3] It urged the PLO to publicly recognize Israel's right to exist, to accept UN Resolutions 242 and 338, and to renounce the use of violence. In addition, the document underlined the centrality of Jordan's role in any political settlement and asserted that Arab sovereignty over the occupied territories could be attained only through a Jordanian-PLO joint diplomatic initiative.

Despite the different weights pro-Jordanian and pro-PLO pragmatic politicians placed on the attainment of Palestinian political rights, they had similar views on many issues. Both believed that the PLO's military defeat in southern Lebanon in the summer of 1982 pointed to the irrelevance and illusive character of the strategy of military struggle as a medium to end Israel's military occupation. As Hanna Siniora, editor-in-chief of *Al-Fajr* and a member of the proposed Jordanian-Palestinian joint delegation, argued: "We—the Palestinians—have tried the military option; we relied on Arab states in 1948 and in 1967 and we lost every inch of Palestine." Israel's military occupation could, he believed, be ended "by political means and not through the use of force. Force has failed in the past to achieve a solution to the Palestinian-Israeli problem."[4]

Another key figure in the pro-PLO pragmatic camp who expressed dissatisfaction with the military option was Fayiz Abu Rahmah, a Gaza lawyer designated by the PLO to serve as a representative in the Jordanian-Palestinian joint delegation. "I would like to see a peaceful solution to our problem," he stated. "Any means that puts an end to this tragedy without bloodshed and violence should be adopted. It is time we seek peaceful channels to end the conflict."[5]

Followers of the pragmatic camp appealed to both Israel and the PLO to adopt the doctrine of peaceful coexistence and to

3. They included the mayors of Bethlehem and Gaza; Anwar al-Khatib, former governor of Jerusalem; Mahmoud Abu al-Zuluf, editor of *Al-Quds*; Saad al-Din al-Alami, chief of the Islamic Supreme Council; and Hikmat al-Masri, a prominent Nablus politician.

4. Interview, "Hanna Siniora and Fayez Abu Rahmeh: The Palestinian-Jordanian Joint Delegation," *Journal of Palestine Studies*, vol. 15 (Autumn 1985), p. 4.

5. Ibid., p. 13.

recognize each other's right to self-determination. In particular, they asked their fellow Palestinians in the hard-line camp to be realistic and to desist from pursuing maximalist demands. Abu Rahmah pointed out, "The Palestinians should understand that peace requires moderation, and in a settlement no one gets all he wants."[6]

RESOLUTION OF THE PALESTINIAN QUESTION. The pro-PLO pragmatic politicians did not insist on the formation of a completely independent Palestinian state but instead accepted the concept of confederating the Palestinian state in the occupied territories with the East Bank of Jordan. Similarly, they welcomed the idea of forming a joint Jordanian-Palestinian delegation to represent Palestinian interests in the negotiations. The pro-PLO and pro-Jordanian politicians welcomed an agreement signed by King Hussein and Arafat on February 11, 1985, that called for joint diplomatic action. Politicians from both groups endorsed the agreement on pan-Arab grounds, arguing that confederation between the West Bank–Gaza Palestinian state and the East Bank of Jordan would be a prelude to Arab unity. No one was interested in a return to the situation that had prevailed before the 1967 June war. In their opinion, the relationship between the occupied territories and East Jordan should be based on the principle of equality and mutual respect.

In response to leftist groups inside and outside the occupied territories who opposed a diplomatic approach, leaders of the pragmatic camp asserted that the opinion of the majority should prevail in the PLO's deliberations and policymaking. They urged the leftist camp to operate as a "constructive" and "loyal" opposition and support the views of the majority that wanted to give diplomacy a chance.

Realism also characterized the pro-Jordanian and pro-PLO pragmatists' position toward Israel. They harbored no illusions about the National Unity government's inability to make territorial concessions because of the Likud's opposition. But they made distinctions between the Likud and the Labor party. Labor, under the leadership of Shimon Peres, appeared to them flexible and

6. Ibid., p. 16.

willing to make territorial compromises, the Likud to be unyielding and uncompromising. For this reason, they were anxious to have talks with Israel commence while Shimon Peres was still prime minister.

Several of the pragmatic politicians attempted to translate their political stands into action. The mayors of Bethlehem and Gaza expressed their willingness to be included at any time in a Jordanian-Palestinian delegation, should the PLO ask them to do so. Hanna Siniora and Fayiz Abu Rahmah in the summer of 1985 accepted the PLO's nomination to represent the interests of West Bank and Gaza Palestinians in the joint Jordanian-Palestinian delegation.[7] In addition, a number of members of the pragmatic camp served as go-betweens for Jordan and the PLO, and Jordan and Israel. In December 1985, twelve politicians unsuccessfully applied to the Israeli government to travel to Amman to urge a reconciliation between Arafat and Hussein and to convince the PLO chairman to accept UN Resolutions 242 and 338. After the Jordanian-PLO talks broke down in February 1986, several West Bank politicians who had been mediating between the two sides expressed their disappointment over the collapse of the talks and their hope that Arafat and Hussein would clear their misunderstandings in the interests of both peoples. They held the Reagan administration responsible for the failure of the talks because of its reluctance to recognize the Palestinian national right of self-determination. With the prolongation of the Jordanian-PLO rift, the pro-PLO pragmatic politicians stopped calling for the confederation of the occupied territories with Jordan. Instead they insisted on the formation of an independent state in the West Bank and Gaza Strip and the representation of Palestinian interests through a separate Palestinian delegation rather than a joint Palestinian-Jordanian negotiating team.

Several members of the pragmatic camp in their efforts to find a peaceful solution of the Palestinian question even took personal risks and accepted appointment by the military government to act as mayors in their towns. In late November 1985, Zafer al-Masri was appointed mayor of Nablus, replacing an Israeli military officer

7. Before 1982 these politicians had repeatedly asserted that the PLO was the only political body qualified to represent Palestinian interests.

who had been in charge of the municipal affairs since the ousting of Bassam al-Shaka, the elected mayor, in March 1982.

The moderation and flexibility of the pragmatists were anathema to Palestinian radicals, who viewed their behavior as a departure from the "true course of the revolution." The deadly wrath of the extremists was unleashed in March 1986 when Zafer al-Masri was assassinated by a follower of the Popular Front for the Liberation of Palestine. The Palestinian extremists branded al-Masri a "collaborator" and "traitor."

Public debate in Israel, particularly concerning the Labor party leaders' intention to introduce unilateral autonomy and reduce Israel's military control over West Bank civilian affairs, began to politicize the appointment process. With the Arafat-Hussein talks breaking down, many pragmatic politicians saw little reason to assume mayoral appointments and they were unwilling to associate themselves with the introduction of autonomy (an unpopular political solution to the Palestinian question). After the assassination of al-Masri, candidates for mayor in the towns of Ramallah, Al-Birah, and Hebron withdrew, and the Palestinians who accepted appointment as mayors for these towns six months later stressed that their role was purely administrative and not political.[8]

DIALOGUE WITH ISRAELIS.   Pragmatic politicians also initiated talks with Israeli political leaders and private citizens. On several occasions after the 1982 Lebanon war, pro-Jordanian politicians met with Labor party leaders, members of the Likud bloc, members of the Mapam party, and other Israeli leftist groups and parties. Their meetings often served as a channel of communication between Israeli politicians and Jordan.[9]

Functioning as liaisons for the PLO, some of the pragmatic politicians initiated contacts with individual Israeli politicians. In

8. The appointees were Khalil Musa Khalil, a Ramallah businessman, Hassan al-Tawil from Al-Birah, and Abd al-Majid al-Zir, head of the Health Department in Hebron, all known for their pro-Jordanian tendencies.

9. In January 1984, there was a meeting of a Gaza delegation led by Rashad al-Shawwa with Mapam party leaders in Tel Aviv. In March 1984, a meeting took place between West Bank Palestinians and Israelis. Among the participants were Said Kanan, Hanna Siniora, Sari Nusseibeh, and Faisal Husaini. See Hillel Schenker, "Dialogue: Israelis and Palestinians in Jerusalem," *New Outlook*, vol. 27 (May 1984), pp. 30–33.

the summer of 1987 Sari Nusseibeh, professor of philosophy at Bir Zeit University, and Faisal Husaini, director of the Arab Studies Center in Jerusalem, explored with Moshe Amirav, a young Likud politician, the details of a plan to resolve the Palestinian-Israeli conflict. The two sides agreed that West Bank–Gaza Palestinians should have a semiautonomous status, control over the land and water resources, and their own passports and flag. The PLO, for its part, would be expected to renounce the use of violence and accept Israel's right to exist. The Israeli government, in its turn, would recognize the PLO and stop settlement activities in the occupied territories.

Some of the talks between West Bank academicians and journalists and their Israeli counterparts were aimed at promoting mutual understanding and peaceful coexistence between Israelis and Palestinians. These dialogues arose partly as an expression of West Bank Palestinians' growing disillusionment with armed struggle but they were also a sign of West Bankers' appreciation for the political attitudes and peace initiatives of Israel's peace groups. From a Palestinian perspective, the long-term goal of such contacts would be to encourage Israel's peace camp and so advance its popularity and political weight that it would become a crucial factor in the formation and composition of any Israeli government.

These Palestinian-Israeli contacts have been confined to a small number of groups. The overwhelming majority of West Bank Palestinians continue to look toward external actors, particularly the PLO and to a lesser extent Jordan, to promote their cause and bring about a solution to their predicament. The PLO's leaders have allowed a controlled dialogue, filtered through PLO followers in the occupied territories. They fear that uncontrolled contacts might be exploited by potential collaborators to promote "defeatist" solutions. Moreover, an open dialogue could so increase the political credibility of those involved that they might act independently of the PLO. A move of this sort could undermine the PLO's status as the exclusive representative of Palestinian interests. The PLO's rejectionist camps and their followers in the West Bank have bitterly attacked proponents of a Palestinian-Israeli dialogue. They argue that such contacts strike at the core of the PLO's political legitimacy and at its representation of Palestinian interests.

BREAKING AWAY FROM CONVENTIONAL THINKING. Despite their support for the PLO, West Bank pragmatic politicians were critical of some of the PLO's radical factions and terrorist activities. They specifically deplored the PLO-inspired attacks on Israeli civilians in December 1983 and the hijacking of the *Achille Lauro* (a luxurious Italian cruise ship) and killing of innocent passengers at airports in Rome and Vienna in late 1985. They also criticized the failure of the PLO's representatives in the Jordanian-Palestinian delegation to meet with the British foreign minister in October 1985. Such attitudes indicated that the West Bank pragmatic elite no longer gave automatic and unconditional approval to what they perceived to be wrong actions on the part of the PLO.

With the prolongation of Israel's military occupation and the diplomatic deadlock, some West Bank pragmatic elite began to advocate new ideas and approaches for the resolution of the Palestinian question that departed sharply from the conventional wisdom. Sari Nusseibeh proposed that his fellow Palestinians demand equal political rights within the Jewish state. His proposal was prompted by Israel's refusal to withdraw from the occupied territories, its policy of creeping annexation, and its opposition to the establishment of an independent Palestinian state. Nusseibeh believed that the incorporation of the Palestinians into Israel would be preferable to the continuation of the military occupation under which Palestinians were denied their political rights. In his opinion, the Palestinians, with their high birth rate, would constitute a majority of Israel's population within two decades, thus leading to the establishment of a binational state. Such a demographic threat had already caused some of Israel's politicians, especially the Labor party, to advocate some territorial compromise in any future deal over the West Bank and Gaza Strip.

As a practical translation of Nusseibeh's ideas, Hanna Siniora in early June of 1987 announced his intention to enter the November 1988 municipal elections in Jerusalem. Siniora's decision was partly prompted by the diplomatic deadlock in the peace process and partly conceived to press the Israeli government to come up with a definitive solution to the future of the occupied territories. Siniora also believed that his running for a municipal seat would reconfirm Arab political rights in Jerusalem and help to expand municipal services to the Arab inhabitants of the city.

The introduction of nonviolence as a technique to resist Israel's military occupation was another manifestation of the new thinking among West Bank intellectuals. In 1986 Mubarak Awad, an American citizen of Palestinian origin, opened the Center for Nonviolence in East Jerusalem and tried to educate West Bank Palestinians in the utility and effectiveness of passive resistance. In January 1988, for instance, advocates of nonviolence called on the local populace to boycott Israeli cigarettes and soft drinks and to abstain from paying Israeli taxes.

The ideas of nonviolence and the quest for political equality inside Israel circulated primarily among a few West Bank intellectuals. The high degree of emotionalism and the deep-seated hostility associated with the Palestinian-Israeli conflict limit the appeal of these ideas among the mass public. In addition, such ideas did not generate official Arab and Palestinian support outside the occupied territories. Certainly, nonviolent tactics clash sharply with the PLO's advocacy of armed struggle as an avenue to end Israel's occupation. Nonetheless, civil disobedience has gained wide support as the main means of carrying out the current uprising.

The Future of the Pragmatic Elite

After 1985 many of the elements that had brought strength to the pro-Jordanian and pro-PLO pragmatic camps had disappeared and the long-term survival and longevity of this class of politicians were seriously in doubt. The Labor party's participation in Israel's National Unity government and the party's willingness to make some territorial concessions in return for peace with the Arabs had encouraged many pragmatic politicians to hope for a political settlement of the Palestinian question. But the inflexible stands of the Likud over the future of the occupied territories, the inability of Foreign Minister Shimon Peres to enlist the support of the Israeli government in convening an international peace conference, and the iron-fisted policy pursued by Yitzhak Rabin, the Israeli defense minister, undermined the political standing and credibility of West Bank pragmatic politicians.

The Jordanian-PLO joint diplomatic initiative, the linchpin of the pragmatic elite, completely collapsed. In February of 1986, King Hussein suspended his dialogue with the chairman of the

PLO, supposedly because of Arafat's reluctance to accept uncon-
ditionally UN Resolution 242. The relationship was further strained
when Arafat canceled his accord with King Hussein in April 1987
to pave the way for reconciliation between the PLO's moderate
and rejectionist factions. Such a reconciliation was achieved during
the eighteenth session of the Palestine National Council that
convened in Algiers in that month.

Given the complex problems blocking the path of an Israeli-
Palestinian peace and the rigid stance of the primary actors, West
Bank moderate leaders can perform a number of functions that
are significant to the peace process. The long-term survival of
moderate leaders would give them the legitimacy and recognition
needed to constitute an effective pressure group on Jordan and
the PLO. In view of the centrality of the West Bank and Gaza to
the PLO's political survival, pragmatic politicians would then be
expected to help Palestinian leaders overcome ideological and
organizational constraints by focusing their attention on the concerns of the Palestinian people in the occupied territories. Likewise,
they would strengthen Jordan's bargaining position vis-à-vis rival
Arab regimes for the custodianship of Palestinian rights. Finally,
in view of the conflicting priorities between Jordan and the PLO,
West Bank pragmatic leaders would operate as a go-between to
reconcile the opposing views of the two.

Though the final political settlement for the Palestinian problem
cannot be carved out by West Bank politicians, they could step
into the peace process in behalf of the PLO. In view of the
opposition of the vast majority of the Israelis to the PLO and the
refusal of the United States to deal with that organization, West
Bank–Gaza leaders are better suited than the PLO to deal with
Israel. The pragmatists could also help to bring about change in
Israeli society by broadening their contacts in Israel and informing
their Israeli counterparts of their peaceful intentions and desire
to find a political solution to their problem. Such contacts would
lend credibility to the political stands of the moderate camp within
Israel and elicit additional support for Palestinian interests and
rights.

The West Bank elite need a solid domestic constituency and
recognition, an accumulation of accomplishments and achievements, and economic independence and political office. The

presence of such assets would enable West Bank–Gaza moderate politicians to consolidate their authority and broaden their legitimacy. In the absence of such assets those leaders would be unable to take political initiatives or make decisions on critical issues without outside authorization and clearance.

Two decades of Israeli occupation have brought the Palestinian question no closer to resolution than it has ever been. The political paralysis inside Israel, the Jordanian-PLO rift, the PLO's reluctance to recognize Israel, and Jordan's inability to negotiate with Israel without collective Arab support are serious impediments to progress toward solution of the Palestinian-Israeli dispute. In such an unfavorable environment would West Bank Palestinians be likely to take the initiative and attempt to solve their own problem? Their land and their future are at stake. West Bank politicians are aware of the dangers in the political stalemate and are thus anxious to see an immediate Israeli withdrawal from their territory. The local politicians will continue to make demands and issue calls to find a quick solution to their predicament. The 1987–88 uprising reflected the collective desire of West Bank–Gaza Palestinians to end Israel's military occupation. In light of the uprising, local politicians may become more assertive. Yet this does not mean that they will try to separate themselves from the rest of the Palestinian community and the Arab world.

The history of West Bank politics since the 1967 June war indicates that neither moderate nor hard-line politicians were likely or able to develop an indigenous leadership that could address the narrow interests of their Palestinian community. Their political weakness, long-term isolation, and exclusion from the political game have deterred West Bank Palestinians from embarking on the hazardous course of separating themselves from the rest of the Palestinian people.

Determinants of the Elite's Political Behavior

The combination of four factors will ensure that the West Bank urban elite will not promote a separate solution to the Palestinian question and will not develop their own autonomous leadership independent from the PLO. The four factors include the geopolitical insecurities of West Bank politicians, the lack of an independent viable economic base, the pressure and intervention of outside forces in West Bank local politics, and the emergence of the phenomenon of mass politics.

GEOPOLITICAL INSECURITIES. The long-held expectation of Palestinians in the occupied territories for an externally devised political solution to their problem has compelled them to shy away from launching initiatives. The West Bank Palestinians' perception of themselves as an integral part of the Palestinian and Arab community has sustained their reliance on outside forces. In fact, the presence of strong religious, cultural, and linguistic ties with the rest of the Arab world has reinforced their sense of belonging to the Arab fold. The Palestinian question has been at the core of all Arab concerns for so long that it would be almost impossible to devolve its leadership exclusively to local politicians.

West Bankers, sensitive to charges that they are trying to pursue a separate solution to the problem of the occupied territories, habitually assert that the Palestinian question is indivisible, that Palestinians inside and outside the occupied territories are one. Many of the West Bank urban elite argue that they have neither the authority nor the political strength to speak for all Palestinians; others maintain that they cannot effectively negotiate so long as they remain under Israel's military occupation. Indeed, the psychological, political, and physical vulnerability of Palestinians to a formidable adversary and the mounting threat posed by Jewish settlers push West Bank Palestinians to find an external force that will ensure their cultural continuity, national identity, and political rights. Some West Bankers, intimidated by the violence of PLO extremists, refuse to act independently.

West Bank–Gaza Palestinians' habitual reliance on outside players may wane in the wake of the 1987–88 popular uprising. The rebellion increased the Palestinians' self-confidence and provided them with a sense of victory and achievement. The youth seized the initiative for the promotion of the Palestinian cause from the PLO and the exiled Palestinians. It remains uncertain whether the youth's determination to draw world attention to their grievances and political aspirations can be converted into a capacity to negotiate a deal with Israel independent from the PLO.

ECONOMIC DEPENDENCY. Without a sound independent economic base, West Bank elite groups will continue to depend for
their influence on external sources. More to the point, the shortage
of indigenous economic resources will sustain the West Bank elite's
economic dependency and vulnerability to outside pressures and
manipulation. Aid is seldom free of political strings and expectations. Uncooperative groups are frequently subjected to punitive
measures—independent political thinking and initiative can prompt
a patron to halt the flow of economic rewards and benefits. This
selective allocation of economic assistance by rival external powers
increases the elite's fragmentation, sensitivities, and mutual hostilities and suspicions.

Improvement of the West Bank economy and an increase in
the standard of living would create a sound economic base of
support and a source of legitimacy for the local elite and save the
area from political instability and extremist ideologies and movements. The allocation of economic aid to the occupied territories
by the Arab oil-producing states and other members of the
international community would reduce the vulnerability of local
politicians to outside pressure, penetration, and manipulation.

Since its occupation of the West Bank in 1967 the Israeli
government has avoided any substantial investment in the occupied
territories' economic infrastructure. The persistence of such a
situation would reinforce the local elite's dependency on outside
actors for survival and would not help in building up confidence
and generating a domestic source of legitimacy for West Bank
moderate leaders.

THE IMPACT OF THE OUTSIDE ENVIRONMENT. The fortunes of
the West Bank urban elite also turn on the quality of relations
between Jordan, the PLO, and Israel. The degree of tolerance or
restrictiveness of each of these players to the political activities of
West Bank Palestinians will affect political trends and the orientation of the local populace. Indeed, as a consequence of the
pressures and counterpressures of these rival external forces, the
signs for the elite's consolidation and professional sophistication
will remain confusing and tentative. Individual politicians will find

it difficult to sustain their interest in political activities, to develop long-term strategies, and to act assertively and cohesively.

The policies of Israel seem to have the most serious implications for future Palestinian leaders. Continuation of Israel's military occupation of the West Bank and Gaza Strip will reinforce the position of extremist groups and proponents of radical ideologies. West Bank leaders can hardly maintain a moderate and a pragmatic stance without concrete evidence of Israel's flexibility and political liberalization. The periods of Israel's relatively liberal rule have been too short and sporadic for any stratification and professional sophistication to occur or political accomplishments to accumulate among elite groups.

The frequent harassment of West Bank citizens will impede local politicians' efforts to develop a constituency. In particular, Israel's harsh measures, including the frequent killing of Palestinian youths, the wounding and beating of young demonstrators, the deportation and administrative detention of local leaders, and the demolishing of houses, cannot be expected to encourage political moderation within the occupied territories. Similarly, Israel's refusal to allow Palestinians in the occupied territories to form their own political associations, exercise their basic political rights and freedoms, and have free access to mass media would not enable the local politicians to consolidate their authority. Equally important, Israel's refusal to sanction municipal elections will deprive the local elite of the opportunity to consolidate their ties with their local constituents. The holding of elections is long overdue, the Israeli government having refused to allow them to take place since 1976. It is difficult to imagine how West Bank leaders can establish their authority without the presence of such supportive institutions.

The policy of banning West Bank Palestinians from participating in the PLO's political councils is harmful to the interest of the local politicians. This policy limits the influence of the Palestinian inhabitants of the occupied territories on the larger Palestinian nationalist movement. The direct participation of West Bank Palestinians in the PLO's policymaking institutions would ensure that the flow of influence would be a two-way process rather than being heavily one-sided. It would also reduce the ability of the

PLO's leaders to force their wishes and policies on West Bank politicians and instead compel them to be more responsive to West Bank needs and concerns.

Whether the relationship between Jordan and the PLO is conflictual or cooperative will also affect political trends on the West Bank. Reconciliation between the two would provide opportunities for elite consensus and a medium for the flourishing of moderate leadership. And it would narrow the gap between the political perceptions of pro-Jordanian politicians and supporters of the PLO. A Jordanian-PLO diplomatic alliance would enable West Bank politicians to press their demands for a negotiated solution of the Palestinian question. Conversely, intense competition and heightened conflict between the two will work in the opposite direction, impeding consensus and sharpening the differences between the followers of the two camps. Undoubtedly, the Jordanian government and its supporters in the occupied territories stand to lose more than the PLO camp in a prolonged conflict.

The Jordanian government could employ many of the economic and political resources at its disposal to influence political development in the occupied territories. As the PLO's economic capabilities and political clout have diminished, Jordan has enhanced the manipulation of its financial resources in its dealings with the West Bank–Gaza politicians. In September 1986, the Jordanian government announced a five-year plan for the development of the West Bank's economy. The plan proposed an investment of roughly $1.2 billion in the West Bank's industrial, agricultural, health, and educational sectors. The drop in oil prices in the Middle East made it impossible for Jordan to come up with such a substantial amount. Indeed, two years after the announcement of the plan, the Jordanian government was only able to come up with $50 million, a token of the total sum.

In another power move, the Jordanian parliament in March 1986 passed legislation increasing the size of the parliament from sixty to one hundred forty-two, with seventy-one seats allocated to inhabitants of the East Bank, sixty to West Bank Palestinians, and eleven to inhabitants of the refugee camps. Coming after the failure of the Jordanian-PLO dialogue, Hussein's move was intended to apply additional pressure on the PLO to be more flexible.

It is unlikely, however, that increasing Palestinian representation in the Jordanian parliament would give Jordan a substitute for the PLO in negotiations with Israel. It is doubtful if such pro-Jordanian politicians would acquire legitimacy and recognition among West Bank Palestinians.

Jordan would hold a trump card in the event that it could carry out negotiations with Israel. Unlike the PLO, the Hashemite regime is an acceptable negotiating partner to the majority of Israelis. The combination of Jordan's economic inducements and political expediency may entice West Bank leaders to seek a modus vivendi with the regime of King Hussein despite their misgivings about that government. But can Hussein's assets outweigh those of the PLO? The dilemma of the Hashemite regime is that it does not embody a value system and a reference point for the vast majority of Palestinians in the occupied territories. The PLO remains the institutional embodiment of West Bank Palestinians' collective political will and the locus for their allegiance and ideological identification.

Despite its utilitarian resources, Jordan will not be able to restore the traditional political leaders to the position of power and influence they held before 1967. Though the supporters of the pro-Jordanian camp possess a number of resources, including wealth, family preeminence, and political links with the Jordanian government, their scope of power and numerical weight remain limited. It is true that the pro-Jordanian politicians seem to have become more willing to take political risks, accepting mayoral appointments and welcoming the Jordanian economic development plan. But that is no indication that they could act independently and in defiance of the PLO, challenging its role of representing Palestinian interests.

The traditional elite can be expected to remain ambivalent in their political stance and avoid making a choice between the PLO and the government of King Hussein. The saliency of Palestinian nationalism and the PLO's command of legitimacy and mass support would make it very difficult for the elite to break away from the PLO. The traditional leaders have not been able to produce a political formula that could capture the imagination of the West Bank mass public. They have no serious constituency among the youth, who constitute a large majority of the Palestinian population in the occupied territories. Their weakness is compounded by the refusal of the Israeli government to make any attractive offer to Jordan over the future of the occupied territories.

NEW SOCIAL FORCES.   The emergence of new social forces and the primacy of ideological issues and considerations in local politics will continue to complicate the process of forming a political elite and contribute to the fragmentation and disunity among potential leaders. New social forces have already widened the political arena and the circle of participatory politics, questioned the authority and legitimacy of the local elite, constrained their ability to engage in diplomatic maneuvering, and narrowed their political choices. In contemporary West Bank life, politics is no longer the province primarily of the older politicians and members of key families.

The political activism of the youth in the second half of the 1980s significantly enhanced the influence of West Bank new social forces. After 1985, the middle and high school youth became actively engaged on the local political scene. In contrast to the 1970s, there was a sixfold increase (from 500) in the number of violent demonstrations and strikes by the Palestinian youth. Most of these activities were spontaneous, not the result of the PLO's incitement. The youth's political activism reached a climax in the 1987–88 popular uprising. By this time the urban areas were no longer the primary scene for opposition to Israeli occupation. The inhabitants of refugee camps and villages in the West Bank and Gaza began to play an increasingly active role. The late 1980s were also marked by the participation of different age groups, including children, men, women, and the elderly, in the political protest. This was contrasted with the waves of demonstrations and strikes in the 1970s and early 1980s, which were waged by college students.

The reality of mass politics and the politicization of the youth suggest that the roles of many of the traditional players (West Bank politicians, Jordan, the PLO, the Arab countries) have been seriously challenged. With regard to West Bank politicians, the increasing politicization of the youth further eclipsed the local elite. The new generation was dissatisfied with the tactics the local politicians used to find a solution to the Palestinian problem. Unlike their parents, the youth do not fear the Israeli army and seem to be determined to influence the political future of the occupied territories. Past formulas and traditional patterns and modes of dealing primarily with the older politicians and members of key families are therefore concepts of diminishing utility.

The lack of any progress toward a political solution is bound to erode further the legitimacy of the pragmatic politicians. The political stalemate has already paved the way for the rise of the more militant leadership inside the occupied territories. The nucleus for such a leadership surfaced in January and February of 1988 when an underground committee for the perpetuation of the uprising (the United National Command for the Uprising) was formed. This leadership was drawn from former political prisoners and the representatives of Fatah, the Popular Front, the Popular Front–General Command, the Democratic Front, the local communists, and the Islamic movement. Unlike the National Guidance Committee, the leaders of the National Command operated in a clandestine manner, away from foreign media exposure and political visibility. Their style of leadership was managerial and organizational as they preoccupied themselves with the task of perpetuating the uprising and expanding its scope. Their access to mass organizations, including workers' unions, women's organizations, and youth groups and committees, facilitated their task. These leaders managed to transform the spontaneous demonstrations and strikes into organized ones and to introduce different forms of protest, including collective resignation by Palestinians working in the Israeli civil administration and the police force in the West Bank and Gaza Strip. In their repeated public appeals, or calls, the leaders of the *intifadah* urged the local population to refuse to pay taxes to the Israeli authorities and to boycott Israeli products. Self-sufficiency and the deliberate avoidance of using lethal weapons were also central in the tactics of the leaders of the uprising.

Despite the immediate adverse effects it had on the existing elite, the uprising increased the political weight of the Palestinian inhabitants of the West Bank and Gaza Strip and legitimized the local Palestinians' political role within the larger Palestinian nationalist movement. The rebellion shifted the locus of struggle and leadership for the promotion of the Palestinian cause from the exiled PLO to the inhabitants of the occupied territories. The firmness of the leaders of the uprising and the diplomatic gains

to the Palestinian cause can be contrasted with the political vacil-
lation, inconclusiveness, and increasing bureaucratization of the
PLO. The PLO leaders who received badly needed political support
from the uprising will be more responsive and attentive to the
demands and interests of the West Bank–Gaza Palestinians. Political
passivity on the part of West Bank Palestinians can no longer be
assumed. They would insist on having a more influential voice in
the determination of their political destiny. The consolidation of
such an attitude would conflict with the PLO's conception of itself
as the only organ that can speak in the name of the entire Palestinian
people.

This observation, however, should not be taken to mean that
the Palestinians in the occupied territories are about to abandon
the PLO. On the contrary, the vast majority of these Palestinians
envisage the PLO as a symbol of Palestinian national unity. Many
West Bank youths strongly identify with the ideology of Palestinian
nationalism, are firmly committed to finding a solution to the
problem of the Palestinians in and outside the occupied territories,
and consider the PLO their sole legitimate representative. Such
attitudes lend more support to the PLO and give it an edge in the
competition with Jordan for control of the occupied territories.

The 1987–88 uprising was particularly detrimental to Jordan's
interests. Despite the Jordanian government's instrumental role in
the effort to end Israel's military occupation, the uprising made
King Hussein less relevant to the aspirations of Palestinians in the
occupied territories. The pervasiveness of the ideology of Palestinian nationalism coupled with strong PLO sentiments casts serious
doubt on the emergence of a pro-Jordanian leadership that could
demand legitimacy and respect from the majority of West Bank
inhabitants. About 70 percent of the population in the occupied
territories is below the age of twenty-five. A whole generation has
grown up under conditions of military occupation, nourished on
the slogans of Palestinian nationalism and identification with the
PLO. Members of this generation have no interest in seeing Jordan's
sovereignty over the West Bank restored. They see the Jordanian
government's economic inducements as nothing but tools to facilitate a Hashemite comeback, shattering their dream of an independent Palestinian state.

The reality of mass politics suggests that West Bank Palestinians cannot be depoliticized. Likewise, the advent of a pro-Israeli surrogate leadership that would enjoy credibility and legitimacy in the eyes of the local population can simply be ruled out as a possibility.

The politicization of the youth also has serious repercussions on Israel itself. The intensity and the widespread nature of the 1987-88 demonstrations and strikes clearly indicated that time was not working in Israel's favor. The uprising negated Israel's assumption that its occupation of the West Bank and Gaza could continue indefinitely with minimum cost. More important, the intensity and the long duration of the uprising undermined Israel's consideration of the occupied territories as a security zone. In time of crisis, West Bank–Gaza Palestinians alongside their compatriots inside Israel could pose a serious security risk to the Jewish state. The unrest also suggested that the youth were determined to make Israel's military occupation of the West Bank and Gaza morally and politically costly. Additionally, the West Bank–Gaza youth began to seriously challenge the deterrent capability of the Israeli army and its control over the locally organized riots. In its previous encounters with the Arab conventional armies, the Israeli government was able to establish the prerogative of its military superiority. Yet such a military outcome cannot be attained in a conflict with unarmed civilians. The deployment of the army against West Bank–Gaza Palestinians will only serve to demoralize the Israeli soldiers, heighten public indignation around the world (and especially in the United States), harden attitudes of both Israelis and Palestinians, and strengthen the resolve of the youth to defy and mock the Israeli military machine.

The uprising transformed the interstate dispute between Arabs and Israelis into an intercommunal conflict between Israelis and Palestinians. Such a phenomenon was in the making since the mid-1980s. By seizing the initiative to promote the Palestinian cause, West Bank–Gaza Palestinians put an end to the so-called Jordan option. Henceforth, Israel will have to deal directly with Palestinians, both those within the occupied territories and those living elsewhere. In any case, the West Bank–Gaza Palestinians will increasingly shape the direction of the Palestinian national movement, but as a component of the PLO, not as an alternative to it.

The Future Struggle

While the opportunities for West Bank Palestinians' participation in any future political round may continue to be controlled by outside events and players, the new social forces in the occupied territories are still capable of complicating the diplomatic efforts of external powers and of vetoing those political solutions that are not congruent with local political preferences and interests. The social and political transformation of West Bank society since 1967 has introduced complexities that cannot be ignored in moving toward an Israeli-Palestinian peace. Diplomatic initiatives that do not envisage a direct and active role for the Palestinians within and outside the occupied territories and that will not satisfy their political expectations cannot be imposed on the local populace against their wishes.

The 1987–88 uprising reinforced the resolve of the Palestinians. It gave them new self-confidence and a sense of victory and achievement that would strengthen their bargaining position in any negotiations. By seizing the initiative, the West Bank–Gaza Palestinians gave the Palestinian question greater visibility on the international scene. Before the uprising the future of the West Bank and Gaza was relegated to the sidelines. In addition to refocusing Arab attention, the rebellion compelled the Reagan administration in its last few months in office to reactivate the search for a diplomatic solution to the Palestinian question after a long period of neglect. The uprising also exposed the Israeli army's excessive use of military force against an unarmed civilian population.

Though the youth's rebellion revealed the diminishing confidence of the West Bank–Gaza population in the ability of Arab and PLO leaders to end Israel's military occupation, the predicament of the new social forces is that they lack a united and an institutionalized local leadership. Notwithstanding the unity and coordination among rival political groups in the West Bank and Gaza during the 1987-88 uprising, sharp ideological cleavages normally pervade their ranks. Their value systems and ideological orientations range from Palestinian nationalism to Marxism and Islamic fundamentalism. Despite their ideological cleavages, West Bank–Gaza youth are united in their opposition to Israel, determined to end the military occupation, and committed to the establishment of a Palestinian state. The future generation of West Bank–Gaza leaders will come from the ranks of these militant youth who are the backbone of the new social forces.

The youth are optimistic about their future and resolute in their struggle to realize Palestinian rights for self-determination. They firmly believe that history is on their side and that their cause is just. To many, such political considerations surpass in their significance the imperatives of economic concern and development. Over the last few years, West Bank youth have become even more nationalistic in their attitudes and daring in their opposition to Israel's military presence. The youth's tendency to wage violent strikes and demonstrations and to take matters into their own hands is likely to continue in the wake of the self-confidence generated by the uprising. Such militant stands would give additional credentials to the PLO's rejectionist factions and compel the moderates within the organization to follow in the footsteps of the new generation.

The prolongation of Israel's military occupation, the increase in power of Israeli hard-line groups, the political and military weakness of the PLO, and the inconclusiveness of diplomatic efforts to solve the Israeli-Palestinian conflict provide fertile ground for extremist and fundamentalist ideologies and movements. Under such gloomy conditions it is hard to imagine how the West Bank and Gaza Strip can be a breeding ground for moderation and pragmatism.

The political frustration among West Bank youth is compounded by mounting unemployment in the occupied territories and a lack of jobs in Jordan and the Arab Persian Gulf region for educated Palestinians. It is a recipe for political instability, militancy, and turmoil. Further consolidation of the power of such militant youth would leave little room for compromise and flexibility. Not only does the absence of any tangible and immediate progress toward settlement of the Israeli-Palestinian dispute threaten the influence of the pragmatic elite and the pro-Jordanian politicians, but it promises to turn ideological fervor in the West Bank away from Palestinian nationalism and secularism toward Islamic fundamentalism.

For a growing number of Palestinians, the PLO and Palestinian nationalism no longer seem to offer a panacea for Palestinian wounds and injuries. The placement of the youth's faith in the PLO is turning out to be as illusive as their parents' trust in the Arab regimes and the ideology of pan-Arabism before 1967. For an increasing number of the new generation there is another hope of a different quality. For young Palestinians who are becoming increasingly desperate both economically and politically, religion offers the invaluable assets of hope, refuge, and guidance. It also offers ready-made answers to their problems and provides them with a sense of mission, a source of identity, and a mechanism for discipline and self-preservation.

Just as Palestinians have turned increasingly to Islam, there has been a rise of Jewish fundamentalism and of militancy in Israel's social fabric and among Jewish settlers in the West Bank and the Gaza Strip. With religious extremism on both sides of the Palestinian-Israeli conflict, there would certainly be no room for reconciliation. Indeed, in such a situation, one side would always be correct and the opponent always wrong. The crucial question is whether the future leadership of both the Palestinians and the Israelis will be drawn from such rising religious camps. If so, it will be the religious zealots who carry on the struggle for the exclusive control of Palestine.

Bibliography

⊡ ⊡ ⊡

Abd al-Hadi, Mahdi. *The Palestinian Question and Proposals for Political Solutions, 1934–1974* (in Arabic). Beirut: Al-Maktabah al-Asriyah, 1975.

Abid, Ibrahim. *Israel and Human Rights.* Palestine Books 24. Beirut: Palestine Liberation Organization Research Center, 1969.

———, ed. *Human Rights in the Occupied Territories, 1971.* Palestine Books 49. Beirut: Palestine Liberation Organization Research Center, 1973.

———. *Selected Essays on the Palestinian Question.* Palestine Books 20. Beirut: Palestine Liberation Organization Research Center, 1969.

Abu Kishk, Dais. *The National Reawakening of the Palestinian Trade Union Movement in the Occupied Territories* (in Arabic). Beirut: Manshurat al-Wihdah, 1981.

Adams, Michael. "Israel's Treatment of the Arabs in the Occupied Territories." *Journal of Palestine Studies,* vol. 6 (Winter 1977), pp. 19–40.

Allon, Yigal. "Israel: The Case for Defensible Borders." *Foreign Affairs,* vol. 55 (October 1976), pp. 38–53.

Anabtawi, Munther. "On the Occasion of the Municipal Elections in the West Bank: Israel's Ping-Pong Game" (in Arabic). *Shuun Filistiniya,* April 1972, pp. 15–27.

Arab Areas Occupied by Israel in June, 1967. Information Papers 2. Chicago, Illinois: Association of Arab-American University Graduates, September 1970.

The Arabs under Israeli Occupation, 1979. Beirut: Institute for Palestine Studies, 1980.

Aruri, Naseer H. *Jordan: A Study in Political Development (1921–1965).* The Hague: Nijhoff, 1972.

Awad, Munir Ahmad. *Higher Education in the West Bank and the Gaza Strip: Its Development and Foundation* (in Arabic). Nablus, West Bank (Israel): Al-Najah University, Markaz al-Dirasat al-Rifiyah, 1983.

Badran, Nabil A. "The Means of Survival: Education and the Palestinian Community, 1948–1967." *Journal of Palestine Studies,* vol. 9 (Summer 1980), pp. 44–74.

Bailey, Clinton. "Changing Attitudes toward Jordan in the West Bank." *Middle East Journal,* vol. 32 (Spring 1978), pp. 155–66.

Benvenisti, Meron. *U.S. Government Funded Projects in the West Bank and*

Gaza (1977–1983). Working Paper 13. Jerusalem: West Bank Data Base Project, 1984.

———. *The West Bank Data Project : A Survey of Israel's Policies*. Washington, D.C.: American Enterprise Institute, 1984.

Bregman, Arie. *Economic Growth in the Administered Areas, 1968–1973*. Jerusalem: Bank of Israel, Research Department, 1975.

Budeiri, Dr. Musa. "The Universities of the West Bank." *Middle East International*, no. 111 (October 26, 1979), pp. 9–10.

Bull, Vivian A. *The West Bank—Is It Viable?* Lexington, Mass.: Lexington Books, 1975.

Cohen, Amnon. "The Changing Patterns of West Bank Politics." *Jerusalem Quarterly*, no. 5 (Fall 1977), pp. 105–13.

———. "Does a 'Jordanian Option' Still Exist?" *Jerusalem Quarterly*, no. 16 (Summer 1980), pp. 111–20.

———. *Political Parties in the West Bank under the Jordanian Regime, 1949– 1967*. Ithaca, N.Y.: Cornell University Press, 1982.

Cohen, Shalom. "Khomeinism in Gaza." *New Outlook*, vol. 23 (March 1980), pp. 6–9.

Coordinator of Government Operations in Judaea and Samaria, Gaza District, Sinai, Golan Heights. "A Thirteen Year Survey, 1967–80." Israel: Ministry of Defence, 1981.

Davies, Philip E. "The Educated West Bank Palestinians." *Journal of Palestine Studies*, vol. 8 (Spring 1979), pp. 65–80.

Davis, Uri, Antonia E. L. Maks, and John Richardson. "Israel's Water Policies." *Journal of Palestine Studies*, vol. 9 (Winter 1980), pp. 3–31.

Dayan, Moshe. *Moshe Dayan: Story of My Life*. New York: William Morrow, 1976.

Declaration of the Mayors and Leaders of the West Bank and Gaza. *MERIP Reports*, no. 72 (November 1978), p. 15.

Dinnawi, Muhammad Ali. *The Largest Islamic Movements in Contemporary Times* (in Arabic). Voice of Truth Series 8. Cairo: Cairo University Islamic Group, 1978.

Elazar, Daniel J., ed. *Governing Peoples and Territories*. Philadelphia: Institute for the Study of Human Issues, 1982.

———. *Judea, Samaria, and Gaza: Views on the Present and Future*. Washington, D.C.: American Enterprise Institute, 1982.

———. *Self Rule/Shared Rule: Federal Solutions to the Middle East Conflict*. Ramat Gan, Israel: Turtledove Publishing, 1979.

Garfinkle, Adam M. "Negotiating by Proxy: Jordanian Foreign Policy and U.S. Options in the Middle East." *Orbis*, vol. 24 (Winter 1981), pp. 847–80.

Gazit, Shlomo. "Early Attempts at Establishing West Bank Autonomy (The 1968 Case Study)." *Harvard Journal of Law and Public Policy*, vol. 3 (1980), pp. 129–53.

Gharaibeh, Fawzi A. *The Economies of the West Bank and Gaza Strip*. Boulder, Colo.: Westview Press, 1985.

Gubser, Peter. *Jordan: Crossroads of Middle Eastern Events.* Boulder, Colo.: Westview Press, 1983.

Halabi, Rafik. *The West Bank Story.* Translated by Ina Friedman. New York: Harcourt Brace Jovanovich, 1982.

Hamid, Rashid. "What Is the PLO?" *Journal of Palestine Studies,* vol. 4 (Summer 1975), pp. 90–109.

Hammud, Said. "The Municipal Elections in the Occupied West Bank" (in Arabic). *Shuun Filistiniya,* April 1972, pp. 8–14.

Harris, William Wilson. *Taking Root: Israeli Settlement in the West Bank, the Golan, and Gaza-Sinai, 1967–1980.* New York: Research Studies Press, 1980.

Hassan bin Talal, Crown Prince of Jordan. *Palestinian Self-Determination: A Study of the West Bank and Gaza Strip.* New York: Quartet Books, 1981.

Heller, Mark A. *A Palestinian State: The Implications for Israel.* Cambridge: Harvard University Press, 1983.

Hilal, Jamil. *The West Bank: Social and Economic Structure, 1948–1974* (in Arabic). Palestine Books 60. Beirut: Palestine Liberation Organization Research Center, 1975.

Hurewitz, J. C. *The Struggle for Palestine.* New York: Greenwood Press, 1968.

Isaac, Rael Jean. *Israel Divided: Ideological Politics in the Jewish State.* Baltimore: Johns Hopkins University Press, 1976.

Jaffal, Mustafa. *The Palestinian Working Class and the Labor Union Movements in the West Bank and the Gaza Strip.* Beirut: Dar al-Jamahir, 1980.

Kapeliuk, Amnon. "Communism in the West Bank." *New Outlook,* vol. 23 (May 1980), pp. 18–21.

Klieman, Aaron S. "Israel, Jordan, Palestine: The Search for a Durable Peace." *Washington Papers,* vol. 9, no. 83 (1981).

Kreczko, Alan J. "Support Reagan's Initiative." *Foreign Policy,* no. 49 (Winter 1982–83), pp. 140–53.

Kuttab, Jonathan, and Raja Shehadeh. *Civilian Administration in the Occupied West Bank: Analysis of Israeli Military Government Order No. 947.* Ramallah, West Bank (Israel): Law in the Service of Man, 1982.

Laipson, Ellen. "Israeli Settlements in the Occupied Territories: Israeli, Arab, and American Perspectives." Congressional Research Report 83-189F. Washington, D.C.: Library of Congress, September 30, 1983.

Lerner, Abba, and Haim Ben-Shahar. *The Economics of Efficiency and Growth: Lessons from Israel and the West Bank.* Cambridge, Mass.: Ballinger, 1975.

Lesch, Ann Mosely. *Arab Politics in Palestine, 1917–1939: The Frustration of a Nationalist Movement.* Ithaca, N.Y.: Cornell University Press, 1979.

———. "Israeli Deportation of Palestinians from the West Bank and the Gaza Strip, 1967–1978." *Journal of Palestine Studies,* vol. 8 (Winter 1979), pp. 101–31, and (Spring 1979), pp. 81–112.

———. "Israeli Settlements in the Occupied Territories." *Journal of Palestine Studies,* vol. 8 (Autumn 1978), pp. 100–19.

————. "Israeli Settlements in the Occupied Territories, 1967–1977." *Journal of Palestine Studies*, vol. 7 (Autumn 1977), pp. 26–47.

————. *Israel's Occupation of the West Bank: The First Two Years*. Report RM-6296-ARPA. Santa Monica, Calif.: Rand Corporation, August 1970.

————. *Political Perceptions of the Palestinians on the West Bank and the Gaza Strip*. Special Study 3. Washington, D.C.: Middle East Institute, 1980.

Litani, Yehuda. "Leadership in the West Bank and Gaza." *Jerusalem Quarterly*, no. 14 (Winter 1980), pp. 99–109.

Mallison, Sally V., and W. Thomas Mallison. *Settlements and the Law: A Juridical Analysis of the Israeli Settlements in the Occupied Territories*. Washington, D.C.: American Educational Trust, 1982.

Maoz, Moshe. *Palestinian Leadership on the West Bank: The Changing Role of the Arab Mayors under Jordan and Israel*. London: Frank Cass and Co., 1984.

Mazur, Michael P. *Economic Growth and Development in Jordan*. Boulder, Colo: Westview Press, 1979.

Meron, Raphael. *The Economy of the Administered Areas, 1977–1978*. Jerusalem: Bank of Israel, Research Department, 1980.

Metzger, Jan, Martin Orth, and Christian Sterzing. *This Land Is Our Land: The West Bank under Israeli Occupation*. Translated by Dan and Judy Bryant, Janet Goodwin, and Stefan Schaaf. London: Zed Press, 1983.

Migdal, Joel S., ed. *Palestinian Society and Politics*. Princeton, N.J.: Princeton University Press, 1980.

Milson, Menahem. "How to Make Peace with the Palestinians." *Commentary*, May 1981, pp. 25–35.

————, ed. *Society and Political Structure in the Arab World*. New York: Humanities Press, 1973.

Mishal, Shaul. *West Bank/East Bank: The Palestinians in Jordan, 1949–1967*. New Haven, Conn.: Yale University Press, 1978.

Monroe, Elizabeth. "The West Bank: Palestinian or Israeli?" *Middle East Journal*, vol. 31 (Autumn 1977), pp. 397–412.

Nakhleh, Emile A. *The West Bank and Gaza: Toward the Making of a Palestinian State*. Washington, D.C.: American Enterprise Institute, 1979.

————, ed. *A Palestinian Agenda for the West Bank and Gaza*. Washington, D.C.: American Enterprise Institute, 1980.

Nakhleh, Khalil. *Palestinian Dilemma: Nationalist Consciousness and University Education in Israel*. Detroit: Association of Arab-American University Graduates, 1979.

Nakhleh, Khalil, and Elia Zureik, eds. *The Sociology of the Palestinians*. London: Croom Helm, 1980.

Nevo, Joseph. "Is There a Jordanian Entity?" *Jerusalem Quarterly*, no. 16 (Summer 1980), pp. 98–110.

Nisan, Mordechai. "Gush Emunim: A Rational Perspective." *Forum on the Jewish People, Zionism, and Israel*, no. 36 (Fall–Winter 1979), pp. 15–23.

————. *Israel and the Territories: A Study in Control, 1967–1977*. Ramat Gan, Israel: Turtledove Publishing, 1978.

Nyrop, Richard F., and others. *Area Handbook for the Hashemite Kingdom of Jordan.* 2d ed. Washington, D.C.: U.S. Government Printing Office, 1974.

Oden, David H. "Education and Politics in the Gaza Strip." *New Outlook,* vol. 18 (February 1975), pp. 53–57.

Peretz, Don. *The West Bank: History, Politics, Society, and Economy.* Boulder, Colo.: Westview Press, 1986.

Peretz, Don, Evan M. Wilson, and Richard J. Ward. *A Palestine Entity?* Special Study 1. Washington, D.C.: Middle East Institute, 1970.

Pirolić, Zoran. "The West Bank and Gaza—The First Palestinian State?" *Review of International Affairs* (Belgrade), vol. 33 (November 5, 1982), pp. 12–14.

Plascov, Avi. *The Palestinian Refugees in Jordan, 1948–1957.* London: Frank Cass and Co., 1981.

Quandt, William B., Fuad Jabber, and Ann Mosely Lesch. *The Politics of Palestinian Nationalism.* Berkeley: University of California Press, 1973.

Reich, Walter. *A Stranger in My House: Jews and Arabs in the West Bank.* New York: Holt, Rinehart, and Winston, 1984.

Rejwan, Nissim. "The Palestinian Press under Israeli Administration." *Midstream,* vol. 19 (November 1973), pp. 15–23.

Richardson, John P. *The West Bank: A Portrait.* Special Study 5. Washington, D.C.: Middle East Institute, 1984.

Rifkin, Lena. "Peace Treaty Sharpens Struggle on West Bank." *MERIP Reports,* no. 83 (December 1979), pp. 3–11.

Sahliyeh, Emile F. *The PLO after the Lebanon War.* Boulder, Colo.: Westview Press, 1986.

———. "The West Bank Pragmatic Elite: The Uncertain Future." *Journal of Palestine Studies,* vol. 15 (Summer 1986), pp. 34–45.

Sandler, Shmuel, and Hillel Frisch. *Israel, the Palestinians, and the West Bank: A Study in Intercommunal Conflict.* Lexington, Mass.: Lexington Books, 1984.

Schiff, Gary S. *Tradition and Politics: The Religious Parties of Israel.* Detroit: Wayne State University Press, 1977.

Schölch, Alexander, ed. *Palestinians over the Green Line: Studies on the Relations between Palestinians on Both Sides of the 1949 Armistice Line since 1967.* London: Ithaca Press, 1983.

Seale, Patrick, ed. *The Shaping of an Arab Statesman: Sharif Abd al-Hamid Sharaf and the Modern Arab World.* New York: Quartet Books, 1983.

Sela, Abraham. "The PLO, the West Bank and Gaza Strip." *Jerusalem Quarterly,* no. 8 (Summer 1978), pp. 66–77.

Shaath, Nabil. "The Palestine of Tomorrow" (in Arabic). *Shuun Filistiniya,* May 1971, pp. 5–23.

Shafiq, Munir. "Why Do the Palestinians Reject the Proposal of a Palestinian State in the West Bank and Gaza Strip? (in Arabic). *Shuun Filistiniya,* March 1972, pp. 65–73.

Sharif, Maher al-. *Communism and the Arab National Question in Palestine,*

1919–1948: The Nationalist and the Classist in the Resistance Liberation Revolution against Imperialism and Zionism (in Arabic). Beirut: Palestine Liberation Organization Research Center, 1981.

Shehadeh, Raja. *The Third Way: A Journal of Life in the West Bank: Between Mute Submission and Blind Hate.* New York: Quartet Books, 1982.

Shehadeh, Raja, assisted by Jonathan Kuttab. *The West Bank and the Rule of Law: A Study.* Geneva: International Commission of Jurists and Law in the Service of Man, 1980.

Shemesh, Moshe. "The West Bank: Rise and Decline of Traditional Leadership, June 1967 to October 1973." *Middle Eastern Studies,* vol. 20 (July 1984), pp. 290–323.

Shihadeh, Aziz. "Freedom from Outside Influences." *New Outlook,* vol. 12 (November–December 1969), pp. 41–43.

Shwadran, Benjamin. *Jordan: A State of Tension.* New York: Council for Middle Eastern Affairs Press, 1959.

Sinai, Anne, and Allen Pollack, eds. *The Hashemite Kingdom of Jordan and the West Bank: A Handbook.* New York: American Academic Association for Peace in the Middle East, 1977.

Singer, Joel. *The Establishment of a Civil Administration in the Areas Administered by Israel.* Tel Aviv: Faculty of Law, Tel Aviv University, 1982.

Sofer, Naim. "The Political Status of Jerusalem in the Hashemite Kingdom of Jordan, 1948–1967." *Middle Eastern Studies,* vol. 12 (January 1976), pp. 73–94.

Susser, Asher. "Jordanian Influence in the West Bank." *Jerusalem Quarterly,* no. 8 (Summer 1978), pp. 53–65.

Tamari, Salim. "In League with Zion: Israel's Search for a Native Pillar." *Journal of Palestine Studies,* vol. 12. (Summer 1983), pp. 41–56.

Tayyib, Tawfiq al-. *The Islamic Solution after the Two Debacles* (in Arabic). 2d ed. Cairo: Al-Mukhtar al-Islami, 1979.

Tessler, Mark A. "Israel's Arabs and the Palestinian Problem." *Middle East Journal,* vol. 31 (Summer 1977), pp. 313–29.

Thorpe, Merle, Jr. *Prescription for Conflict: Israel's West Bank Settlement Policy.* Washington, D.C.: Foundation for Middle East Peace, 1984.

Tsimhoni, Daphna. "The Christian Communities in Jerusalem and the West Bank, 1948–1967." *Middle East Review,* vol. 9 (Fall 1976), pp. 41–46.

Van Arkadie, Brian. *Benefits and Burdens: A Report on the West Bank and Gaza Strip Economies since 1967.* New York: Carnegie Endowment for International Peace, 1977.

Ward, Richard J., Don Peretz, and Evan M. Wilson. *The Palestine State: A Rational Approach.* Port Washington, N.Y.: Kennikat Press, 1977.

Yaari, Arieh. "The Jordanian Option: A Persistent Illusion." *New Outlook,* vol. 23 (June–July 1980), pp. 32–35.

Yakan, Fathi. *Islamic Movement: Problems and Perspectives.* Translated by Maneh al-Johani. Indianapolis, Ind.: American Trust Publications, 1984.

Index

Abasi, Esam, 62n
Abd al-Fattah, Mahmoud, 104n
Abd al-Hadi, Mahdi, 23n, 27n, 28n
Abd al-Halim, Muhammad, 149n
Abd al-Nasser, Gamal. *See* Nasser,
    Gamal Abd al-
Abd al-Shafi, Haidar, 73n
Abdullah, 10
Abu al-Zuluf, Mahmoud, 168n
Abu Kishk, Dais, 104n
Abu Maizer, Abd al-Muhsin, 24
Abu Rahmah, Fayiz, 163n, 168, 169,
    170
Abu Sharar, Majid, 81n
Abu Shilbaya, Muhammad, 28, 30
Achille Lauro hijacking, 173
Adams, Michael, 33n, 47n
Aden-Algiers Agreement, 112
Afghanistan, 153
Alami, Musa al-, 28
Alami, Saad al-Din al-, 24, 155, 168n
Amin, Sadiq, 138n
Amirav, Moshe, 172
Anabtawi, Munther, 38n
Arab Liberation Front, 65
Arab Palestine, 17–18. *See also* West
    Bank–Gaza Palestinian state
Arafat, Yasir, 73, 78, 153; communist
    students' criticism, 129–31; coordi-
    nation with Jordan, 2, 98–99, 111–
    12, 166, 170, 171, 174–75; Fatah re-
    bellion, 154–55; Islamics' support,
    154–56; PNF's endorsement, 58;
    pragmatic politicians and, 165, 167;
    as student, 116
Armouti, Muhammad Nazzal al-, 63n
Aruri, Naseer H., 11n, 45n, 122n,
    127n, 135n
Asad, Hafiz, 155
Ashhab, Naim al-, 94n, 95n, 110
Autonomy issue, 2, 74–75. *See also*

Leadership, autonomous West Bank;
    West Bank–Gaza Palestinian state
Awad, Mubarak, 174
Awad, Munir Ahmad, 122n
Awwad, Arabi Musa, 91, 97

Baath party, 16, 17, 21, 34, 77, 139
Baghdad Pact, 17
Bailey, Clinton, 26n, 27n, 31n, 35n,
    36n
Barghuthi, Bashir al-, 73n, 84n, 88n,
    89n, 90n, 91, 107, 109n
Barghuthi, Iyad al-, 123n
Begin, Menachem, 71, 75, 83, 84, 141
Benziman, Uzi, 23n
Bethlehem University, 107, 128, 145
Bir Zeit University, 106, 107, 124, 126,
    128, 133, 142, 145, 156, 157
Budeiri, Musa, 88n
Bull, Vivian A., 13n, 45n

Camp David Accords: autonomy plan,
    2, 74–75; communist opposition,
    109; Islamic opposition, 149; NGC
    opposition, 71–72, 74–75, 82; PNF
    opposition, 78; student opposition,
    120, 122, 127–28
Carter, Jimmy, 70
Civil Administration Plan, 55
Civil disobedience movement, 33
Cobban, Helena, 65n, 82n
Cohen, Amnon, 16n, 17n, 89n, 90n,
    138n
Cohen, Shalom, 143n
Communists, 5; Al-Ansar, 91; on
    armed struggle, 26–27, 110–11; au-
    tonomous organization in Palestine,
    94–98; on Camp David Accords,
    109; Fatah and, 59–61, 96, 99, 100,
    101, 102, 113; internal divisions, 90–
    91; Islamic movement and, 114,

153; Israeli Communist party, 88, 93, 99; Israeli tolerance, 93; on Israel's right to exist, 108–09; Jordanian Communist party, 21, 87, 89–92, 94–95, 96–97, 112, 116; on Jordanian rule of West Bank, 90, 91–92; labor unions and, 101–02, 103–06; in Lebanon, 97; municipal elections and, 38–39, 100, 103; National Liberation League, 88–89, 90; NGC and, 73, 75–76; Palestine Communist Organization, 95; Palestine Communist Organization of Lebanon, 97; Palestine Communist party, 88, 97–98; PLO and, 87–88, 92–94, 96, 98–102, 108–12, 113; PNF and, 57, 59–60, 77, 78, 93, 100, 103; political base, 87–88; political mobilization of Palestinians, 102–07; political stance, 108–12; pro-PLO elite and, 49; prospects, 112–14; publications, 107; refugees and, 103; social barriers, 113; student movement and, 106–07, 118, 119, 121, 125–26, 129–32; in urban areas, 102–03; voluntary work program, 106; on West Bank–Gaza Palestinian state, 89, 92, 93–94, 98, 108–09
Confino, Michael, 89n

Dajani, Amin al-, 73n
Dajani, Kamal al-, 24
Dakkak, Ibrahim, 22n, 23n, 24n, 27n, 44n, 52n, 53n, 54n, 56n, 58n, 59n, 60n, 61n, 71n, 73n, 77n, 84n
Dann, Uriel, 17n
Dayan, Moshe, 8, 83
Deportation of Palestinians, 8, 24, 33, 46, 62, 69
Din, Said Ala al-, 73n
Din, Salah al-, 94n
Dinnawi, Muhammad Ali, 146n, 149n
Dudin, Mustafa, 36

Economy, West Bank, 12–13, 44–46, 178, 180
Egypt, 2, 16, 34, 44, 57, 138, 139
Eitan, Raphael, 83
Elite, pro-PLO, 5, 7–9; anti-Jordanian sentiments, 48; communists and, 49; deportation, 46, 69; diplomacy, 68; election victories, 66–67; intelligent-sia and professionals, 47; Israeli legal system and, 49; Israeli policies, 51, 62, 81–86; local government and, 49; as municipal leaders, 67–69; national and political issues, 47–48; nationalism, 48; newspapers, 42, 49, 69; PLO's domination, 49–51; political organization, 48–49; political weakness, 48; pragmatists and hard-liners, 70–71, 75–77; rise, 44; students and, 121; traditional elite and, 47; on United States, 70–71, 76; on West Bank–Gaza Palestinian state, 42–43, 66. See also National Guidance Committee; Palestine National Front; Pragmatic politicians
Elite, traditional, 4–5, 7–9; deportation, 33; Israeli occupation, 22–26; in Jerusalem, 11; under Jordanian rule, 13–15, 16, 18; on Jordanian rule, 24–26, 32, 35–36; leaders, 22; municipal elections of 1972, 38, 39–40; organizations, 23–24, 26; PLO and, 38, 67; political influence, 41, 43–47, 49; political paralysis, 33–35, 38, 40–41; student campaigns, 121–22; United Arab Kingdom plan, 35–36; on West Bank–Gaza Palestinian state, 24, 27–30. See also Pragmatic politicians

Farouqi, Hamdi al-Taji al-, 28, 29, 44n
Fasheh, Munir, 122n
Fatah, 118; communists and, 60–61, 96, 99, 100, 101, 102, 113; Islamics and, 147, 153–54; labor unions and, 102; NGC and, 75, 76–77; PNF and, 60–61, 80–81; pragmatic politicians and, 165; rebellion against Arafat, 154–55; Saudi Arabia and, 71; student bloc and, 128, 132–33, 136; Syria and, 112; youth committees, 102
Fayiz, Isam Ahmad al-, 53n
Fez peace plan, 149, 151
Freij, Elias, 66, 70, 73, 163n, 167
Friedman, Ina, 23n, 69n
Front of Steadfastness and Confrontation States, 108

Gazit, Shlomo, 27n, 28n, 30n

General Federation of High School
Students, 130
General Federation of the Students of
Palestine, 116–18, 119
Geneva Peace Conference, 56, 61
Ghanim, Adil, 73n, 102n
Graham-Brown, Sarah, 11n, 14n, 45n,
122n
Great Britain, 4
Gush Emunim, 83, 141

Habash, George, 116
Halabi, Rafik, 22n, 24n, 25n, 28n, 69n,
70n, 75n, 77n
Hallaj, Muhammad, 14n, 122n
Hamad, Jamil al-, 28
Hamdallah, Wahid al-, 66, 73n, 84n
Hammud, Said, 37n
Haniyah, Akram, 73n, 84n
Hanoun, Hilmi, 40, 42, 55, 70, 73n
Harb, Ghassan, 105n
Hassan, Bilal al-, 60
Hawwa, Said, 146n
Hebron College, 128, 129, 153, 156,
158
Hebron province, 12
Heller, Mark, 43n, 45n
Higher Committee for National Guid-
ance, 23, 24, 26, 46, 52, 92
Hikmat, Salim, 101n
Hilal, Jamil, 45n
Hourani, Faisal, 53n
Husaini, Faisal, 163n, 171n, 172
Hussein, 25, 38, 91, 161, 180; coordi-
nation with PLO, 2, 98–99, 111,
166, 170, 171, 174–75; influence in
West Bank, 44; United Arab King-
dom plan, 29, 35–36

Intifadah. See Uprising of 1987–88
Iran, 126, 140, 146, 159
Iraq, 79, 159
Islamic movement, 4, 86; on Arab regimes, 149–50; on Arafat, 154–56;
on Camp David Accords, 149; communists and, 114, 153; conservative
constituency, 141–42; education and,
143–44; factions, 145–47, 159; Fatah
and, 147, 153–54; in Gaza, 158; intelligentsia and, 147; Islamic reawakening, 144–47; on Israel, 150–51,
152, 159; Israeli actions and, 140–
41; Israeli policy, 137, 143, 160–61;
Jordanian policy, 137, 142–43, 161;
under Jordanian rule, 138–39; in
Lebanon, 140, 141; on nationalism,
148–49, 158, 162; in 1930s and
1940s, 137–38; Palestinians and,
139–44, 161–62; PLO and, 126–29,
139–40, 143, 151–56; political positions, 145; pro-Khomeini bloc, 146–
47, 156; prospects, 158–62; religious
extremism, 150–51, 152, 187–88; religious perspective on Palestinian
question, 148–49; student bloc, 123,
126–29, 145, 156–58; Al-Tahrir,
138, 139, 146, 153; weaknesses, 159;
youth and, 187–88. See also Muslim
Brotherhood
Islamic Supreme Council, 23–24, 26,
34, 42, 44, 46, 51–52
Islamic University, 158, 159
Israel: autonomous West Bank leadership and, 8–9, 81–83, 85, 179; biblical claim, 1, 85–86, 141; Civil
Administration Plan, 55; on communists, 93; deportation policy, 9, 24,
33, 46, 62, 69; economic policy, 44–
46; incorporation of Palestinians,
173, 174; Islamic movement and,
137, 143, 150–51, 152, 159; 160–61;
Labor party, 25, 46–47, 64, 81–82;
on labor unions, 104–05; Lebanon
invasion, 86, 110–11, 140, 141;
Likud party, 1, 51, 71, 82–86, 140–
41; on municipal elections, 36–37,
40, 63–64; National Unity government, 166, 169–70; Palestinians'
sense of vulnerability, 19; on PLO,
2, 64; on PNF, 61–62; pragmatic
politicians and, 164, 169–70, 171–
72, 174; pro-PLO elite and, 51, 62,
81–86; religious extremism, 1, 51,
85–86, 141, 188; settlements in occupied territories, 51, 83, 85–86,
141; student movement and, 135;
uprising of 1987–88, 185, 186; on
West Bank–Gaza Palestinian state,
30–31; West Bank workers, 45
Israeli Communist party, 88, 93, 99
Israeli-Palestinian dialogue, 171–72

Jabari, Burhan al-, 70

Jabari, Muhammad Ali al-, 28–29, 32, 41

Jaffal, Mustafa, 102n, 104n

Janho, Abd al-Nur, 50

JCP. *See* Jordanian Communist party

Jerusalem, 11, 22–23, 33, 173

Johani, Maneh al-, 145–46n

Jordan, 68; on autonomous West Bank leadership, 8, 180–82; civil war with PLO, 34, 35, 43; claim to West Bank, 1, 2; coordination with PLO, 2, 98–99, 111–12, 166, 169, 170, 171, 174–75; economic aid, 180; Islamic movement and, 137, 142–43, 161; labor law of *1960*, 104; on municipal elections, 37–38, 65; NGC and, 73; Palestinian representation in parliament, 180; PNF attitude, 79–80; political influence in West Bank, 8, 43–44, 72, 180–81; pragmatic politicians and, 164–65; United Arab Kingdom plan, 35–36; on West Bank–Gaza Palestinian state, 31

Jordanian-British defense treaty, 17

Jordanian Communist party (JCP), 21, 87, 89–92, 94–95, 96–97, 112, 116

Jordanian-Palestinian Economic Committee, Joint, 76, 77, 80, 157

Jordanian rule of West Bank (*1948–67*), 4; administrative provinces, 11–12; annexation, 10; Arab nationalism and, 16–17; co-optation of Palestinian interests, 13–15, 16, 18; economic situation, 12–13; educational programs, 14; elite, role of, 13–15, 16, 18; fragmentation of West Bank power, 15–16, 19; integration policies, 13–18; Islamic movement, 138–39; opposition parties, 16–18, 19–20; population figures, 10; as transitional arrangement, 13, 19–20; West Bankers' reasons for maintaining, 18–20

Jordanian rule of West Bank, resumption of: alternative to Israel, 24–26, 32, 35–36; communists and, 90, 91–92; confederation plan, 2, 98–99, 111–12, 166, 169

Jordanian Student Union (JSU), 116–17, 118, 119

Kahane, Meir, 141

Kanafani, Ghassan, 32n

Kanan, Hamdi, 24–25, 26, 36, 39, 44n

Kanan, Said, 171n

Kapeliouk, Olga, 135n

Khalaf, Karim, 40, 42, 67n, 70, 73n, 77, 80

Khalil, Musa Khalil, 171n

Khalil, Samiha, 73n, 84n

Khatib, Amin al-, 44n

Khatib, Anwar al-, 73, 168n

Khatib, Rouhi al-, 22, 24, 37

Khatib, Yusif al-, 50

Khomeini, Ruhollah, 146

Khouri, Jiryis, 73n

Khury, Ilya, 51

Khuzandar, Hashim, 50

Labor unions, 46, 101–06

Langer, Felicia, 62n

Leadership, autonomous West Bank: economic dependency, 178; geopolitical insecurities, 177; Israeli encouragement, 81–83, 85; Israeli policies, 8–9, 179; Jordan's influence, 7, 180–82; new social forces, 182–85, 186–87; obstacles, 6–7, 176; PLO as representative of Palestinians, 7–8, 50; PLO-Jordan relationship, 180–82

Lebanon: civil war, 62, 63–64, 68; communists, 97; Israeli invasion, 86, 110–11, 140, 141; PLO, 34

Lesch, Ann Mosely, 22n, 26n, 27n, 30n, 32, 33n, 36n, 48n, 52n, 53n, 54n, 55n, 56n, 62n, 64n, 68n, 69n, 70n, 71n, 75n, 119n

Libya, 154

Lijan al-Shabibah, 102

Linowitz, Sol, 74n

Litani, Yehuda, 67n

Madi, Muhammad, 23n

Mahshi, Khalil, 14n

Manasrah, Muhammad Musa, 98n, 104n

Maoz, Moshe, 17n, 28n, 36n, 37n, 40n, 48n, 63n, 64n, 66n, 67n, 69n, 75n, 82n, 83n, 84n, 85n

Marxists. *See* Communists

Masri, Hikmat al-, 73, 168n

Masri, Zafer al-, 163n, 170, 171
Mayors. *See* Municipal leaders
Migdal, Joel S., 11n, 13n, 14n, 43n, 47n
Milhim, Muhammad, 51, 73n
Milson, Menahem, 17n, 82–83, 84, 85
Minawi, Shahadeh, 102n
Mishal, Shaul, 10n, 16n, 17n, 19n, 89n
Muhtasib, Hilmi al-, 22, 23, 24
Municipal elections of *1972*, 35, 36–40
Municipal elections of *1976*, 63–67, 100, 103
Municipal leaders, 63, 67–69, 170–71
Murad, Ahmed, 123n
Muslim Brotherhood, 19, 21, 154; as conservative organization, 162; establishment in Palestine, 138; goals, 145–46; in Jordan, 143, 161; student criticism, 126–27; suppression, 138–39

Nabhani, Ahmad Taqi al-Din al-, 138, 146
Nablus province, 11–12
Najah University, Al-, 128, 129, 142, 156, 157
Najjab, Sulaiman Rashid al-, 91
Nakhleh, Emile A., 14n, 63n
Naser, Hanna, 51
Nassar, Fuad, 88, 90, 91
Nasser, Gamal Abd al-, 6, 16, 25, 34, 43, 139
National Guidance Committee (NGC), 49; on Camp David Accords, 71–72, 74–75, 82; communist influence, 73, 75–76; establishment, 71, 72; Fatah's influence, 75, 76–77; inner committee, 73–74; internal dissension, 75–77; Israeli policy, 51, 82, 83, 84, 163; Jordan's influence, 73; members, 72–73; PNF and, 78; students and, 121
National Liberation League, 88–89, 90
National Union party, 35–36
New social forces, 3–6, 182–85, 186–87. *See also* Islamic movement; Student movement; Youth
NGC. *See* National Guidance Committee
1967 June war, 1, 6, 21, 139

1973 October war, 44, 54, 56, 93, 119, 121, 139
Nusseibeh, Anwar, 22, 77
Nusseibeh, Sari, 163n, 171n, 172, 173

Ottoman Empire, 4

Palestine Communist Organization (PCO), 95
Palestine Communist Organization of Lebanon (PCOL), 97
Palestine Communist party (PCP), 88, 97–98
Palestine Liberation Organization (PLO): armed struggle strategy, 33–34; autonomous West Bank leadership and, 7–8, 50, 179–81; civil war with Jordan, 34, 35, 43; communists and, 87–88, 92–94, 96, 98–102, 108–12, 113; communist students' criticism, 129–31; coordination with Jordan, 2, 98–99, 111–12, 166, 169, 170, 171, 174–75; disorganization in West Bank, 25, 34; flexibility in policies, 166; intimidation, 50; Islamic movement and, 126–29, 139–40, 143, 151–56; on Israeli-Palestinian dialogue, 172; Israeli policy on, 2, 64; labor unions and, 101–02; in Lebanon, 34; on municipal elections, 38, 65; Palestinians' preference, 49–50, 183–84; PNF and, 49, 55–61, 79–80; political solutions, 165–66; pragmatic politicians and, 164–65, 167; as representative of Palestinians, 2, 55–56; Soviet recognition, 93; student movement and, 101, 115, 119, 121–22, 126–29, 133, 134, 135–36; terrorist tactics, 173; traditional elite and, 38, 67; United Arab Kingdom plan, 38; West Bankers' participation, 50–51, 179, 185; on West Bank–Gaza Palestinian state, 29, 31–32. *See also* Elite, pro-PLO; Fatah
Palestine National Council (PNC), 58, 94, 98, 99, 100, 166, 175; function, 59; occupied territories represented, 50–51; student involvement, 116; on West Bank–Gaza Palestinian state, 2, 68

Palestine National Front (PNF), 121; assessment, 62–63; on Camp David Accords, 78; collapse, 59–63; communist influence, 57, 59–60, 77, 78, 93, 100, 103; Fatah and, 60–61, 80–81; Israeli policy on, 61–62; on Israel's right to exist, 57; on Jordanian role in West Bank, 79–80; members, 53; NGC and, 78; origins, 52–53; passive resistance, 54–55; on peace negotiations, 56; PLO and, 49, 55–61, 79–80; policies, 56–58; political program, 53–55, 78–79; purposes, 51–52; reactivation, 77–81; self-determination, 55; on United States, 79; on West Bank–Gaza Palestinian state, 56, 57
Palestine Student Union (PSU), 107, 119
PCP. See Palestine Communist party
Peace conference, international, 109–10
Peres, Shimon, 55, 64, 82, 119, 169–70, 174
PLO. See Palestine Liberation Organization
PNC. See Palestine National Council
PNF. See Palestine National Front
Popular Front for the Liberation of Palestine (PFLP), 21, 27, 53, 65, 117
Popular Front–General Command, 65
Popular Resistance Front, 26
Popular Struggle Front, 65
Pragmatic politicians, 9, 162, 163–64; Arafat and, 165, 167; on armed struggle, 168; assessment, 176; diplomatic focus, 169–70; education policy, 164; Fatah and, 165; incorporation of Palestinians into Israel, 173, 174; Israeli policy on, 164; Israelis, policy for dealing with, 169–70, 171–72, 174; Jordanian support, 164–65; Jordan-Palestine confederation plan, 169, 170; mayoral appointments, 170–71; nonviolent approach, 173–74; peaceful coexistence policy, 167–69; in peace process, 175–76; PLO and, 164–65, 167; PLO participation denied, 179; on PLO terrorist tactics, 173; political influence, 166–67. See also Leadership, autonomous West Bank

Qassam, Iz al-Din al-, 137–38
Qawasmah, Fahd al-, 51, 70, 73n

Rabat conference, 2, 55, 62
Rabin, Yitzhak, 174
Raphaeli, Nimrod, 46n
Rayis, Zuhair al-, 73n
Reagan initiative, 111, 120, 127–28, 151
Reich, Walter, 141n
Religious extremism: in Islamic movement, 150–51, 152, 188; in Israel, 1, 51, 85–86, 141, 188
Richardson, John P., 36n
Rifai, Zaid al-, 35
Rihan, Ramzi, 14n
Rivalries among West Bank towns, 47

Sabri, Ikrima, 73n
Sadat, Anwar, 70, 71, 140
Sahliyeh, Emile F., 45n, 86n, 112n, 127n, 133n
Saiyih, Abd al-Hamid al-, 22, 23
Salem, Walid, 123n
Salfiti, Fahmi al-, 90, 91, 94
Salhi, Bassam al-, 123n
Salih, Abd al-Jawad, 40, 42, 51, 52
Samarah, Samih, 81n, 88n
Saudi Arabia, 71, 143
Sayid, Mamoun al-, 73n, 84n
Schenker, Hillel, 171n
Schölch, Alexander, 22n, 44n
Shaath, Nabil, 32n
Shafiq, Munir, 31n, 98n
Shahwan, Osama, 63n
Shaka, Bassam al-, 67n, 70, 73n, 77, 80, 171
Shamir, Shimon, 89n
Shamir, Yitzhak, 83
Sharif, Maher al-, 88n
Sharon, Ariel, 83, 84, 164
Shawwa, Rashad al-, 70, 73, 163n, 167, 171n
Shemesh, Moshe, 22n, 27n, 28n, 30n, 36n, 40n
Shihadah, Aziz, 28, 29–30, 30n
Shuaibi, Azmi al-, 73n
Siniora, Hanna, 163n, 168, 170, 171n, 173
Socialist party, 88
Soviet Union, 93, 108, 109, 113, 153, 154
Sprinzak, Ehud, 141n

Student Action Front, 127, 129, 131
Student movement, 4, 46, 86; assessment, 134–35; blocs, 126; on Camp David Accords, 120, 122, 127–28; collapse, 133; communist role, 106–07, 118, 119, 121, 125–26, 129–32; demographics, 142; foreigners and, 124; General Federation of High School Students, 130; General Federation of the Students of Palestine, 116–18, 119; Islamic bloc, 123, 126–29, 145, 156–58; on Israeli occupation, 117–18; Israeli policy on, 135; Jordanian Student Union, 116–17, 118, 119; leadership, 121, 123, 134; modernization goals, 124; nationalist orientation, 120–21; national unity blocs, 126–29; Palestine Student Union, 107, 119; PLO and, 101, 115, 119, 121–22, 126–29, 133, 134, 135–36; PLO and communist blocs, 129–33; PLO and Islamic blocs, 126–29, 156–58; PNC and, 116; pro-PLO elite and, 121; prospects, 134–36; on Reagan initiative, 120, 127–28; society's support, 135; strikes and demonstrations, 119, 120–21, 125; Student Action Front, 127, 129, 131; student congresses, 128; student councils, 128; student solidarity, 123–25; Student Union bloc, 128, 129–30; Student Unity bloc, 128, 131–32; Student Youth movement, 128, 132–33, 136; traditional elite, 121–22; Union of Palestinian Students, 116; university administration and, 124–25; university life, 122–23. See also Uprising of 1987–88; Youth
Sunni Muslims, 146
Syria, 16, 34, 44, 57, 61, 62, 68, 79, 112, 139; on Arafat, 154–55; student criticism, 131–33

Tahrir, Al-, 138, 139, 146, 153
Tamari, Salim, 85n
Tawil, Hassan al-, 171n
Tawil, Ibrahim al-, 67n, 73n, 84n
Tayyib, Tawfiq al-, 149n
Taziz, Ali al-, 73n

Union of Palestinian Students, 116

United Arab Kingdom plan, 29, 35–36, 38
United National Command for the Uprising, 183
United Nations General Assembly Resolution 181, 89
United Nations Security Council Resolution 242, 1, 25, 31, 91, 92
United Nations Security Council Resolution 338, 56
United States: on PLO, 2; PNF's attitude, 79; pro-PLO elite's attitude, 70–71, 76. See also Camp David Accords; Reagan initiative
Universities, 122–23
Uprising of 1987–88, 133, 134; as act of political autonomy, 3, 9, 177, 183–84; command committee, 183; Islamic role, 159; Israel, implications for, 185, 186; Jordanian interests, 184, 185; Palestinian self-confidence, 177, 186; as youth movement, 6, 125, 182

Van Arkadie, Brian, 13n, 45n
Vance, Cyrus, 68
Village leagues, 85
Voluntary work program, 106

Warrad, Faiq, 94, 96
Weizman, Ezer, 82, 83
West Bank–Gaza Palestinian state: communist position, 89, 92, 93–94, 98, 108–09; domestic opposition, 32; Israeli position, 30–31; Jordanian position, 31; PLO position, 29, 31–32; PNC position, 2, 68; PNF position, 56, 57; post-1967 initiative, 27–33; pro-PLO elite's position, 42–43, 66; traditional elite's position, 24, 27–30
West Bank General Federation of Labor Unions, 101, 103–05

Yakan, Fathi, 145n
Youth, 6; determination, 186–87; divisions, 186; Islam's appeal, 188; political frustration, 187; politicization, 182–85. See also Uprising of 1987–88

Zaiyaddien, Yaqoub, 94n
Zaru, Nadim al-, 37
Zir, Abd al-Majid al-, 171n